# Help Me! Guide to the Kindle Fire HD 6

## By Charles Hughes

I0439075

## Table of Contents

# Getting Started

---

## Table of Contents

---

## 1. Button Layout

The Kindle Fire HD 6 has three buttons, a headphone jack, and a micro-USB port. The touchscreen is used to control all functions on the Kindle Fire HD 6, with the exception of turning on the device and controlling the volume. The Kindle Fire HD 6 has the following buttons:

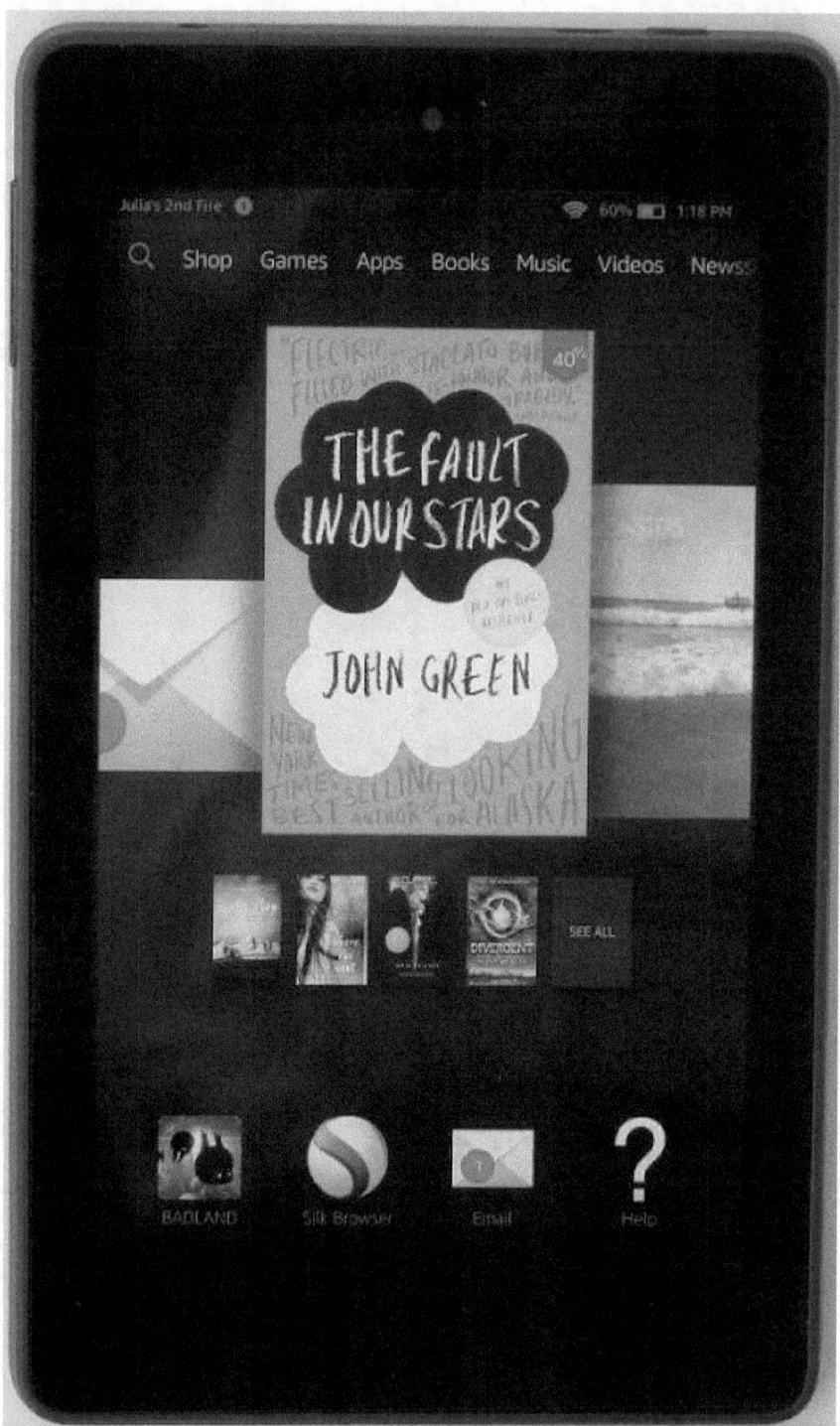

*Figure 1: Front View*

**Touchscreen -** Used to control all functions on the Kindle Fire HD 6.

# Power Button   Micro-USB Port   Headphone Jack

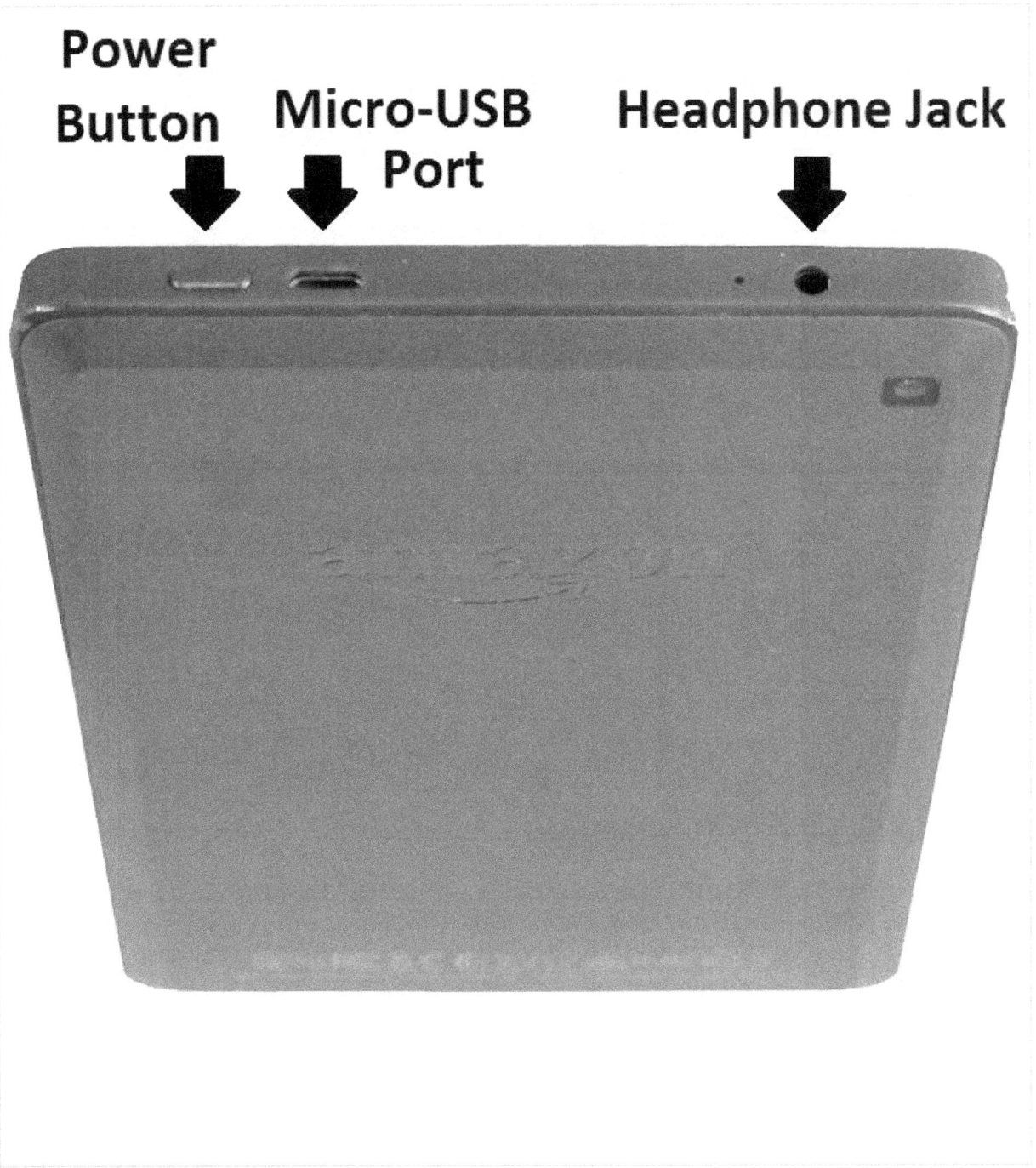

*Figure 2: Top View*

- **Power Button** - Turns the Kindle Fire HD 6 on and off, locks, and unlocks the device.
- **Micro-USB Port -** Connects the Kindle Fire HD 6 to a computer to transfer data.
- **Headphone Jack** - Allows headphones to be connected to the Kindle Fire HD 6 to listen to audio.

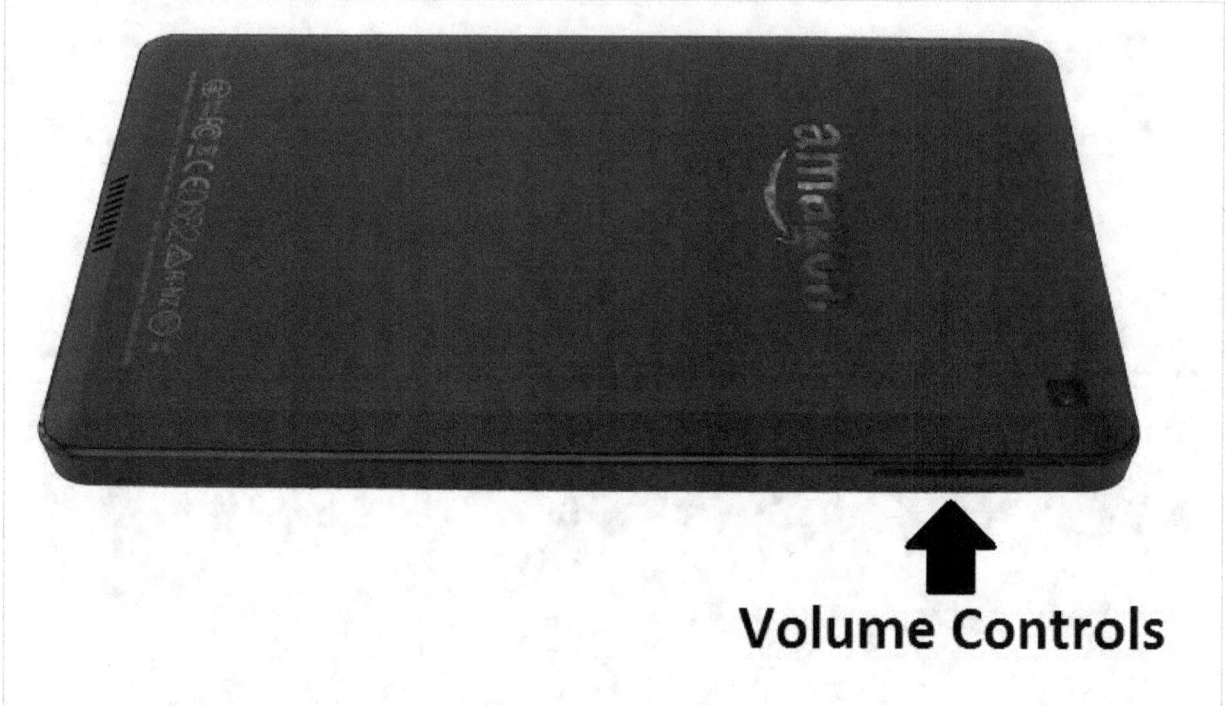

*Figure 3: Left Side View*

**Volume Controls** - Increases and decreases the media volume.

## 2. Charging the Kindle Fire HD 6

You can charge the Kindle Fire HD 6 in one of two ways: use the Micro-USB charger, such as the one that comes with the Kindle Fire HD 6 (recommended method), or use the USB to Micro-USB cable included with your device to plug the device into any USB port on a computer. Note that the device will charge much more slowly when connected to a computer. When the device is charged, 100% appears next to the battery icon in the upper right-hand corner of the screen.

## 3. Turning the Kindle Fire HD 6 On and Off

To turn the Kindle Fire HD 6 on, press the **Power** button on the top of the device, and immediately release it. The Kindle Fire HD 6 turns on. When the device is fully turned on, the Lock screen appears.
To turn the Kindle Fire HD 6 off, press and hold the **Power** button for two seconds. The Shut Down confirmation appears, as shown in **Figure 4**. Touch **Power off**. The Kindle Fire HD 6 turns off. Alternatively, touch **Cancel** if you wish to keep the device turned on.

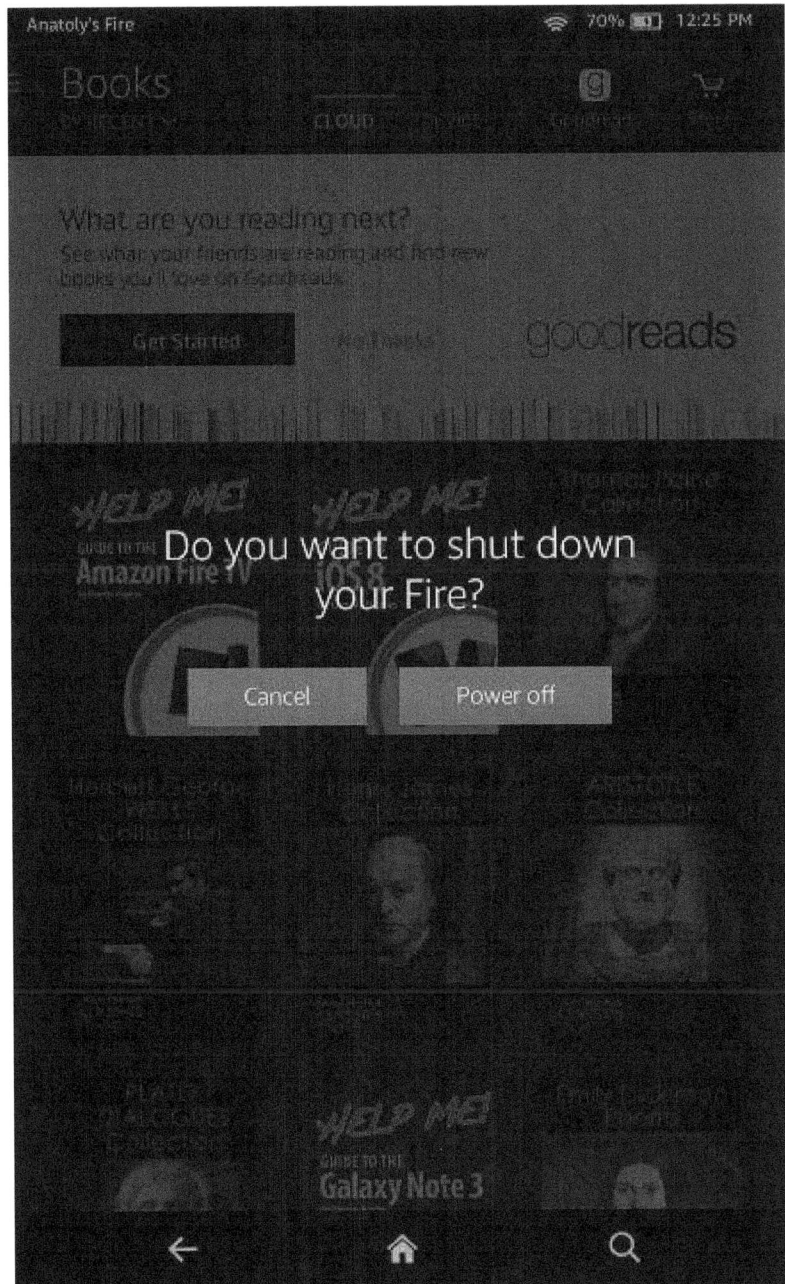

*Figure 4: Shut Down Confirmation*

# 4. Setting Up the Fire HD 6 for the First Time

The first time the Kindle Fire HD 6 is turned on, it must be set up. To perform first-time setup:
*Note: If your Kindle Fire HD 6 came registered to the account you used to purchase it, steps 6 and 7 below are not required.*

1. Press the **Power** button at the bottom of the screen and immediately release it. The Kindle Fire HD 6 turns on and the Language screen appears after a few moments, as shown in **Figure 5**.
2. Touch a language in the list, and then touch **Continue**. The Wi-Fi Networks screen appears, as shown in **Figure 6**.
3. Touch a network in the list. The Network Password prompt appears.
4. Enter the password for the Wi-Fi network that you selected, and touch **Connect**. The device connects to the selected network, provided that the password is correct. The Registration screen appears, as shown in **Figure 7**.
5. Enter your Amazon username and password, and touch **Continue**. The Kindle Fire HD 6 is registered to your account, and the Time Zone screen appears.
6. Select your time zone, and touch **Continue**. The Backup screen appears, as shown in **Figure 8**. Touch **Yes, enable backup for this Fire**, if you wish to back up your settings and content to the Amazon cloud. If you use another Fire, or plan on purchasing another model in the future, enable this feature.
7. Touch **Continue**. The Social Network screen appears, as shown in **Figure 9**.
8. Touch a social network in the list to connect to it. Enter your credentials on the following screen to connect to one of these networks. If you wish to proceed without connecting to a social network, just touch **Continue**. The Amazon Prime screen appears.
9. Touch **Get started** if you wish to sign up for the service. Otherwise, touch **Continue without FREE Two-Day Shipping**. The Kindle Fire HD 6 setup is complete, and your device is ready for use. Touch **Skip** to skip the tutorial.

*Note: The device may need to download additional software before you can use it.*

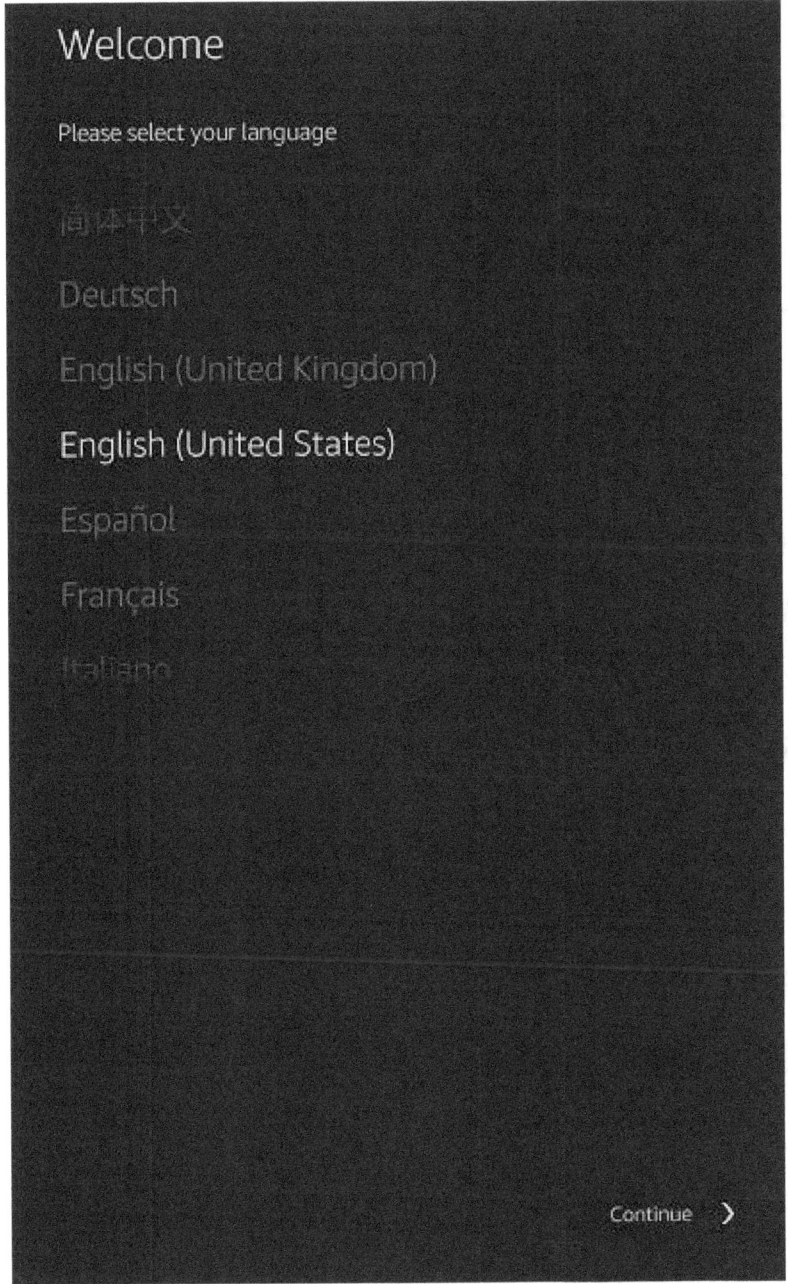

*Figure 5: Language Screen*

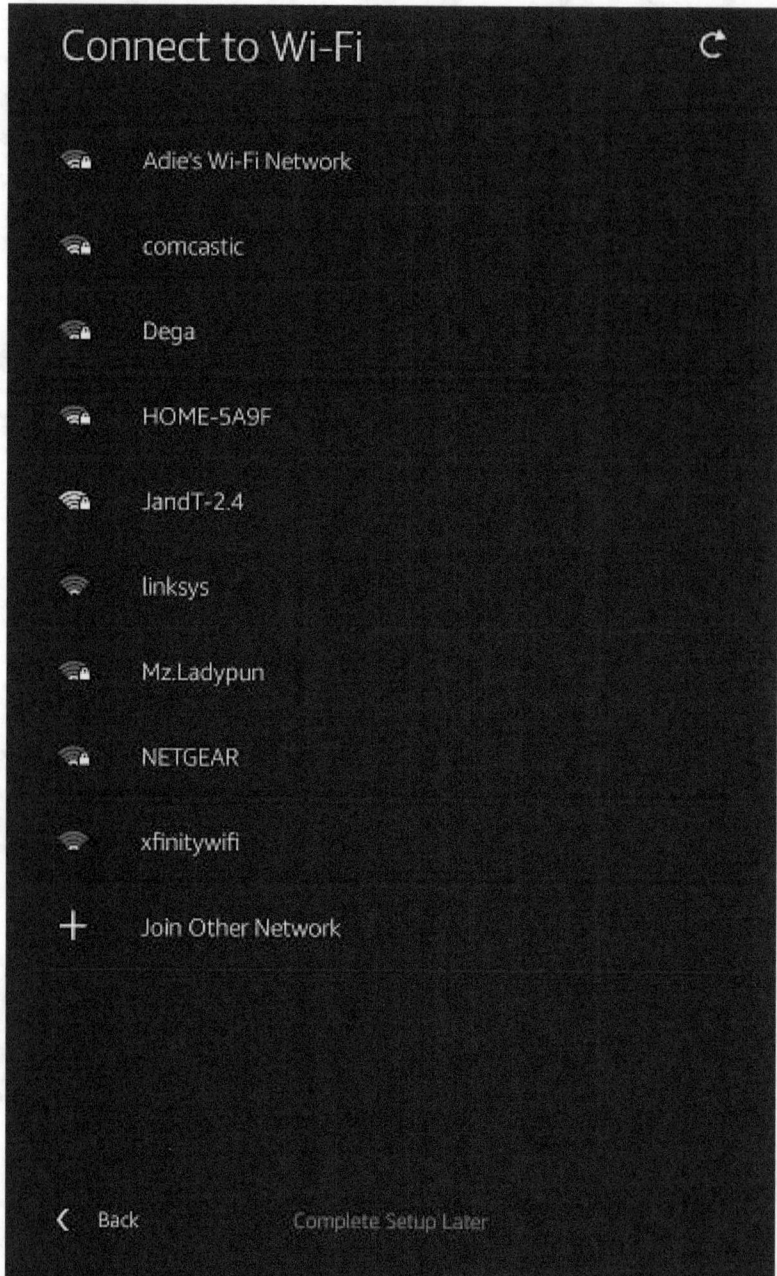

*Figure 6: Wi-Fi Networks Screen*

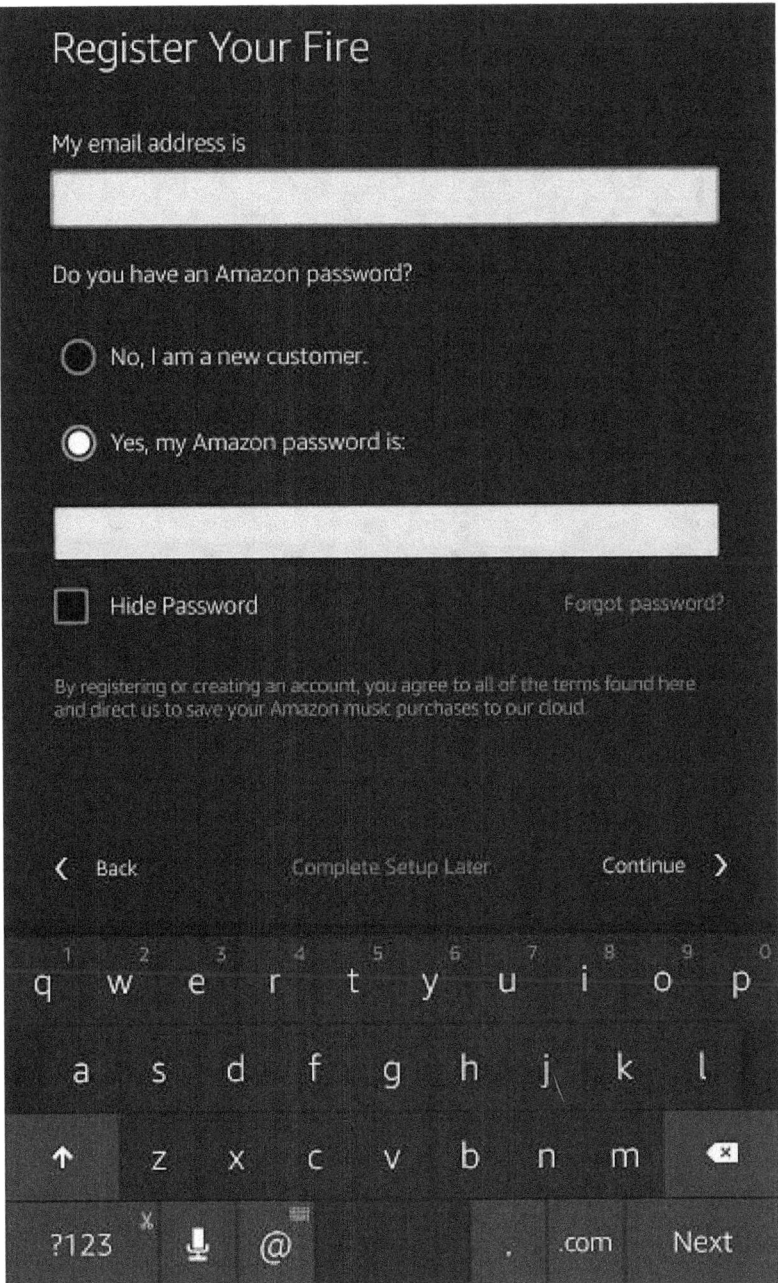

*Figure 7: Registration Screen*

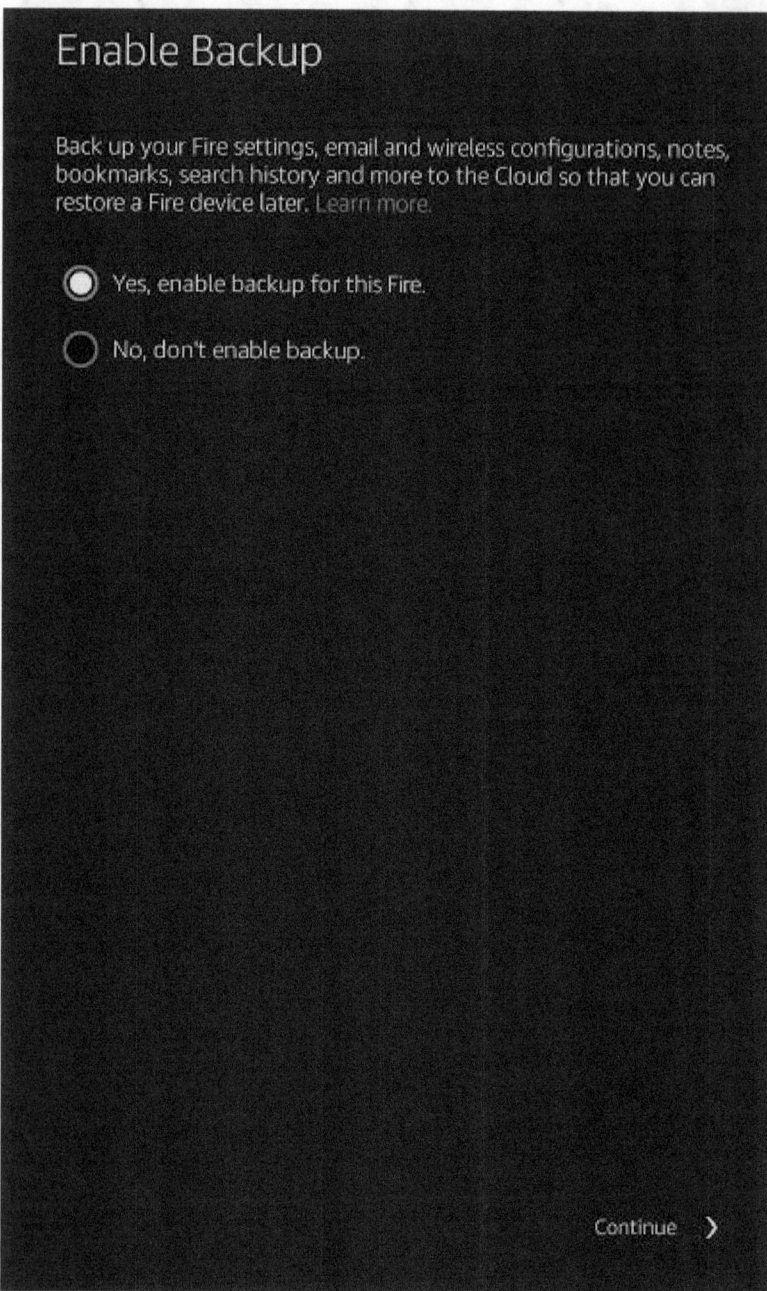

*Figure 8: Backup Screen*

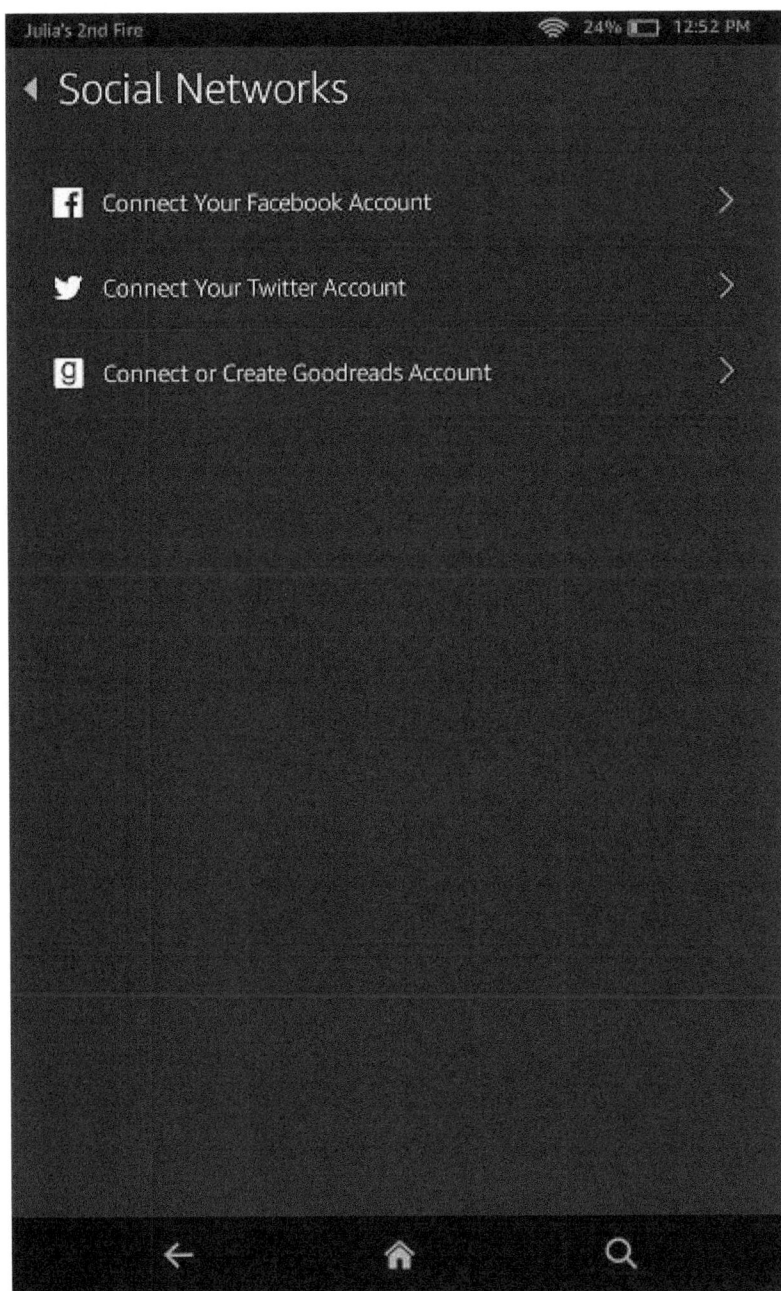

*Figure 9: Social Network Screen*

# 5. Deregistering and Re-registering the Kindle Fire HD 6

If you want to use the Kindle Fire HD 6 with an Amazon account other than your own, you need to re-register it. To deregister and re-register the Kindle Fire HD 6:

1. Touch the time at the top of the screen and slide your finger down. The Notification Center appears, as shown in **Figure 10**.

2. Touch the ⚙ icon in the upper right-hand corner of the screen, as outlined in **Figure 10**. The Settings screen appears, as shown in **Figure 11**.

3. Touch **My Account**. The My Account screen appears, as shown in **Figure 12**.

4. Touch **Deregister**. A confirmation dialog appears.

5. Touch **Deregister** again. The Kindle Fire HD 6 is deregistered and the Deregistered My Account screen appears.

6. Touch **Register**. The Register Your Fire screen appears, as shown in **Figure 13**.

7. Enter the email address and password associated with your Amazon account and touch the **Register** button. The Kindle Fire HD 6 is registered to your Amazon account.

*Figure 10: Notification Center*

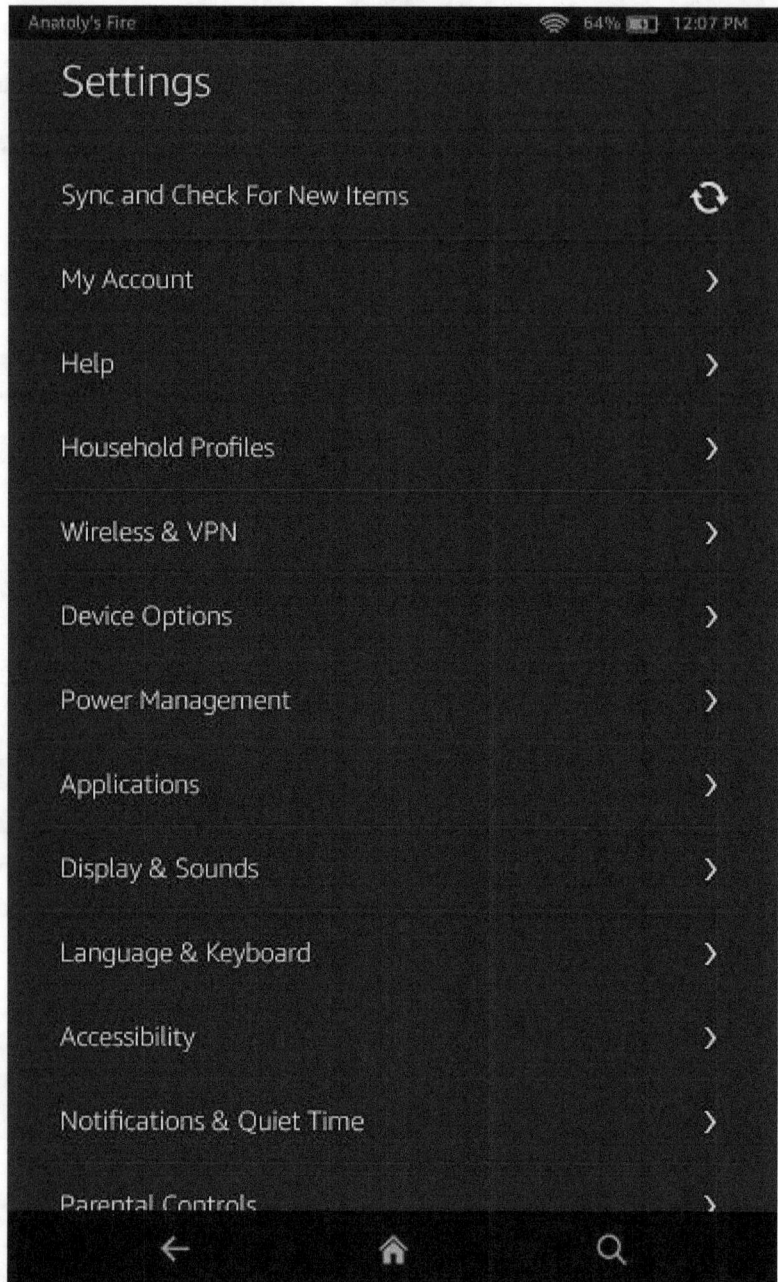

*Figure 11: Settings Screen*

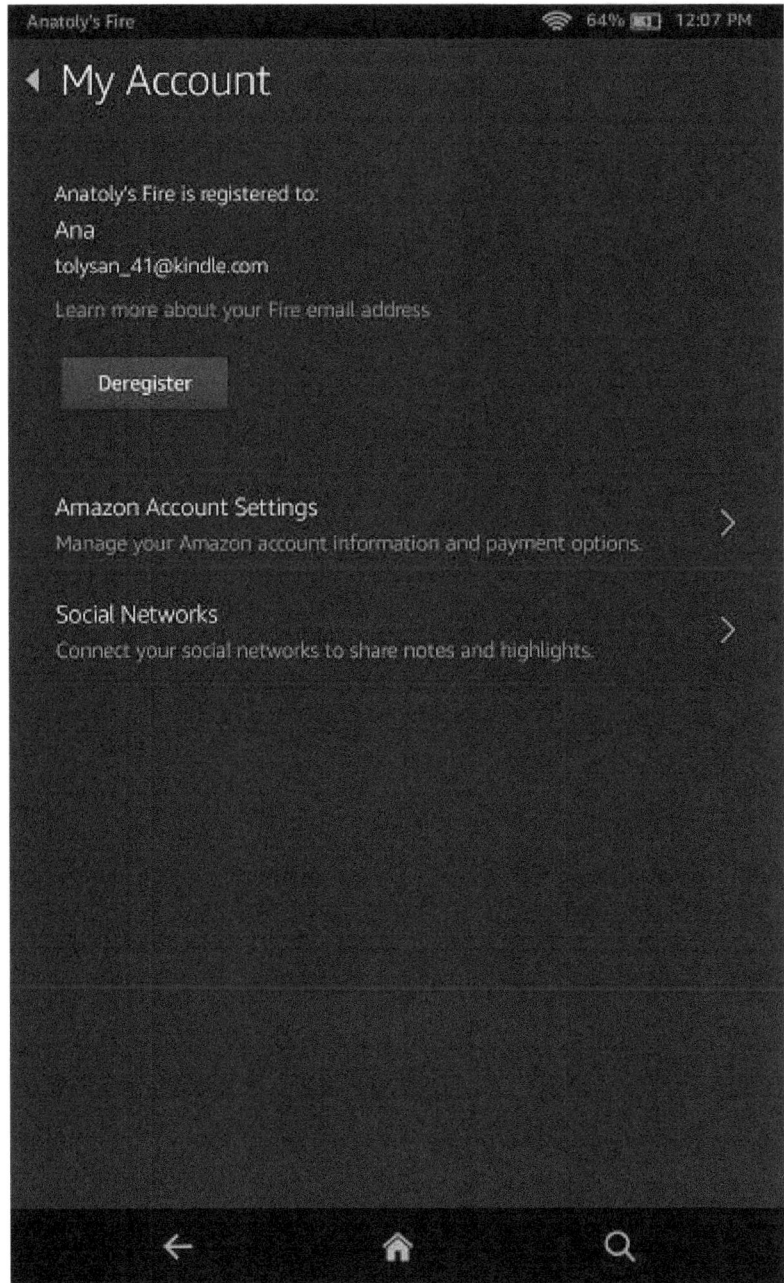

*Figure 12: My Account Screen*

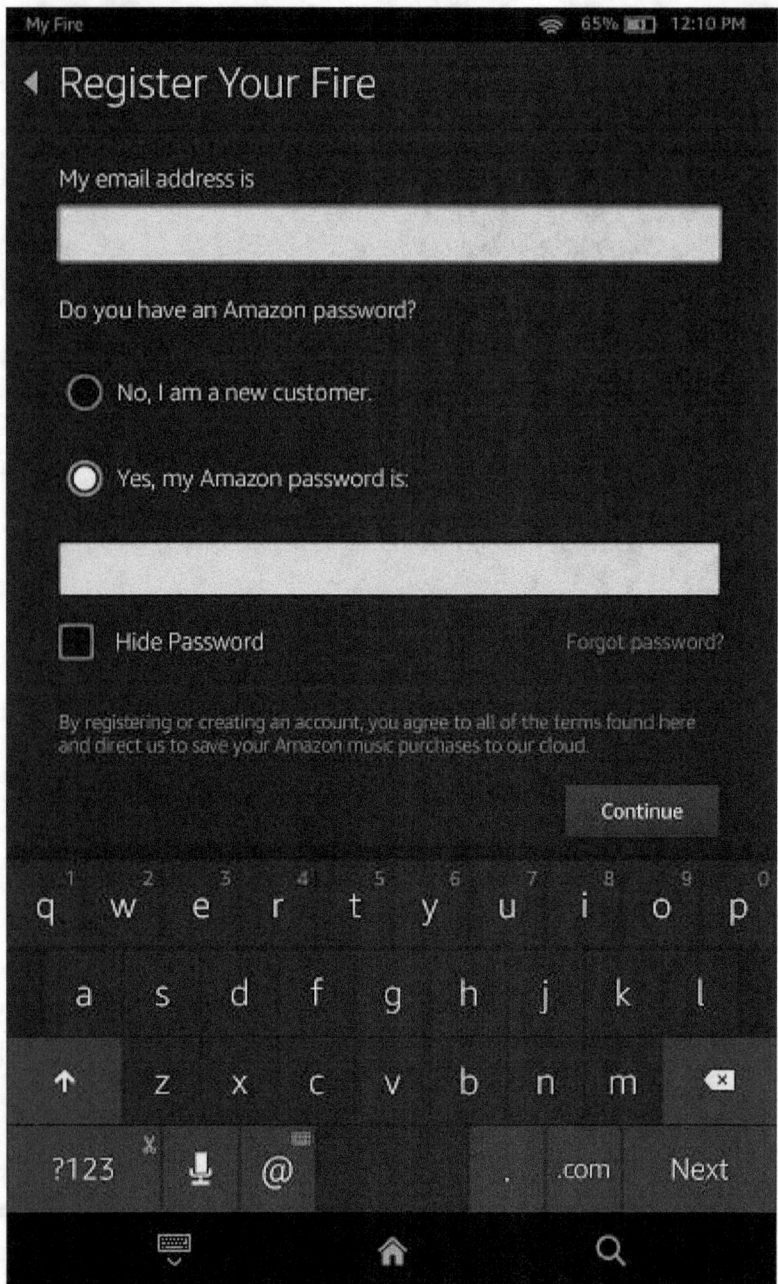

*Figure 13: Register Your Fire Screen*

# 6. Navigating the Screens

There are many ways to navigate the Kindle Fire HD 6. These are just three of the methods:

- Touch the [home button] button to return to the Library at any time. Any application or eBook will be in the same state when it is re-opened.
- Touch the [back button] button to return to the previous screen or menu, or to hide the keyboard.
- Touch the left edge of the screen and slide your finger to the right to open the navigation menu at any time.

# 7. Connecting the Kindle Fire HD 6 to a PC or Mac

eBooks, photos, and other media can be imported to the Kindle Fire HD 6. To import media:

1. Connect the Kindle Fire HD 6 to your computer using the provided USB cable. Your computer will make a sound or a notification will appear in the lower right-hand corner of the monitor to notify you that the device is connected.
2. Open **My Computer** on a PC and double-click the 'KINDLE Portable Media' removable drive. On a Mac, you will need to download the Android File Transfer utility, which can be found at **https://www.android.com/filetransfer/**. The Kindle Fire HD 6 folder opens.
3. Double-click **Internal Storage**. The Kindle Folders open on a PC, as shown in **Figure 14**, or on a Mac, as shown in **Figure 15**.
4. Double-click a folder. The folder opens.
5. Drag and drop a file into the open folder. The file is copied and will appear in the corresponding library.

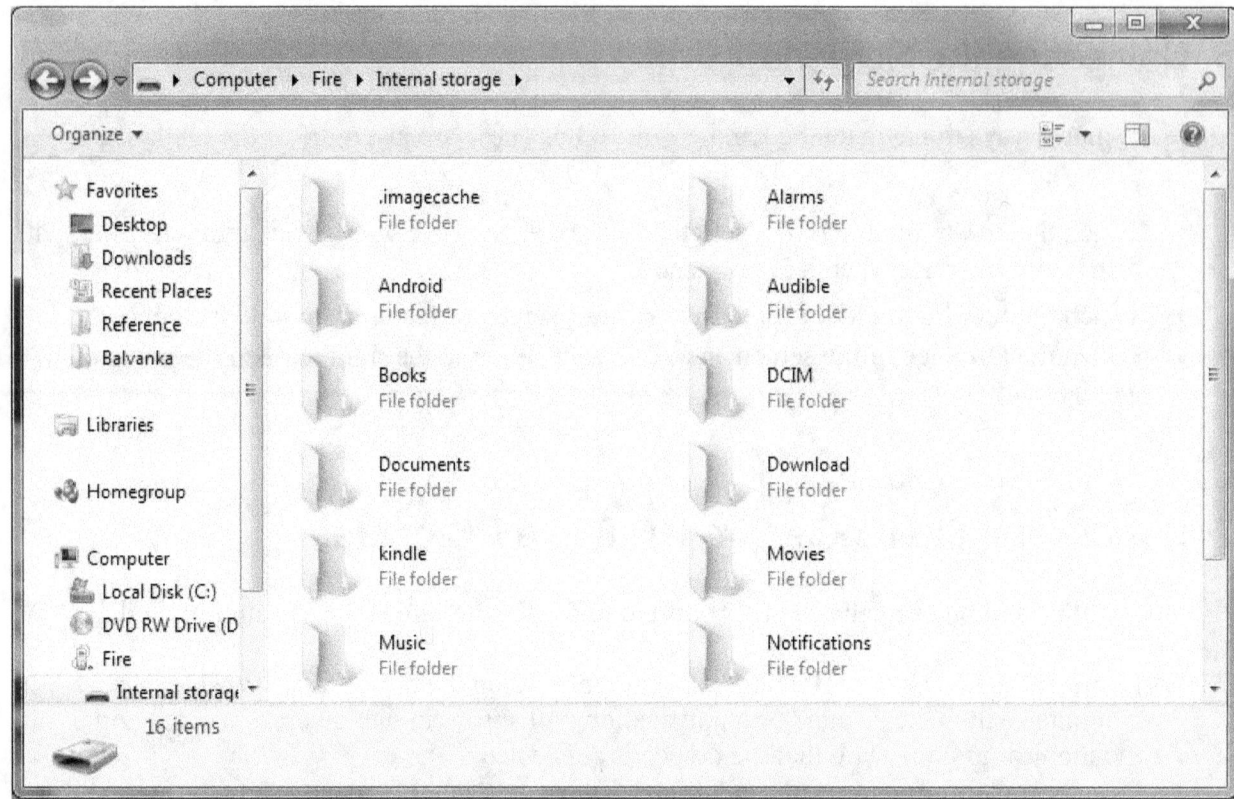

*Figure 14: Kindle Folders on a PC*

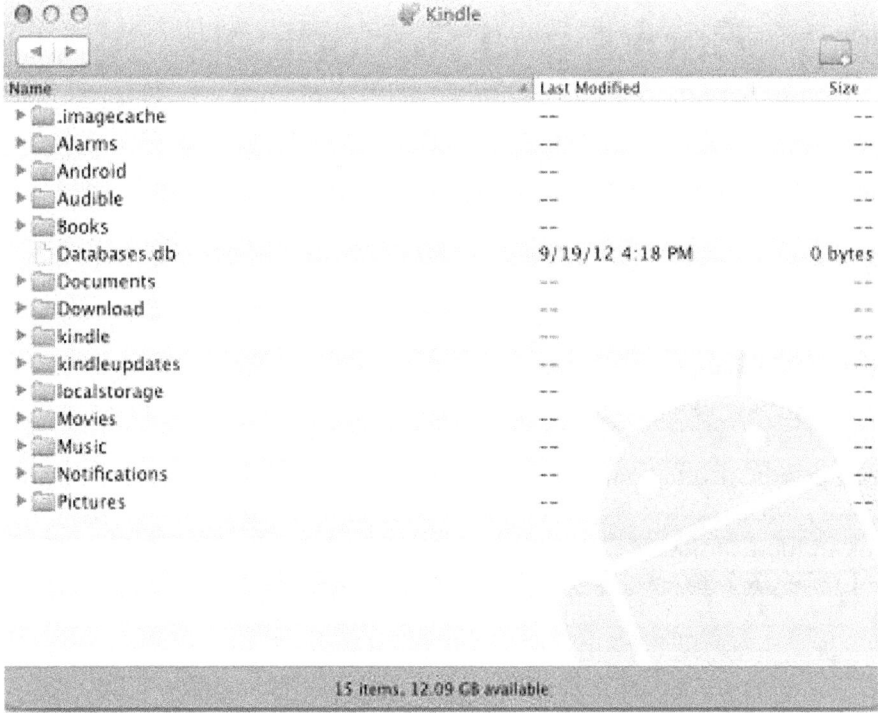

*Figure 15: Kindle Folders on a Mac*

# Managing eBooks and Periodicals

## Table of Contents

## 1. Buying an eBook on the Kindle Fire HD 6

You can buy an eBook from the Amazon Kindle Store using your Kindle Fire HD 6. To buy an eBook:

*Warning: Before touching BUY, make sure that you want the eBook. The Kindle Store uses one-click purchasing. Once you leave the Confirmation screen, you cannot cancel the order.*

1. Touch **Shop** at the top of the Home screen. The Kindle Store opens, as shown in **Figure 1**.
2. Touch **Search** in the upper right-hand corner of the screen. The virtual keyboard appears at the bottom of the screen.
3. Enter the name of an author or eBook. The most popular results appear as you type.
4. Touch **Go**. A list of matching eBook results appears, as shown in **Figure 2**. Touch **See all** under 'SHOP AMAZON' to view all results.
5. Touch the title of an eBook. The eBook description appears, as shown in **Figure 3**.
6. Touch **Buy for $##.##** where the ##.## represents the price of the eBook. The eBook is purchased and downloaded to your Kindle Fire HD 6 Library.
7. Touch **Read Now** to read the eBook immediately. The eBook opens.

*Note: Touch **Cancel Order** below 'Read Now' on the Confirmation screen if you did not mean to purchase the eBook. You may only cancel the order until you leave the Amazon Kindle store.*

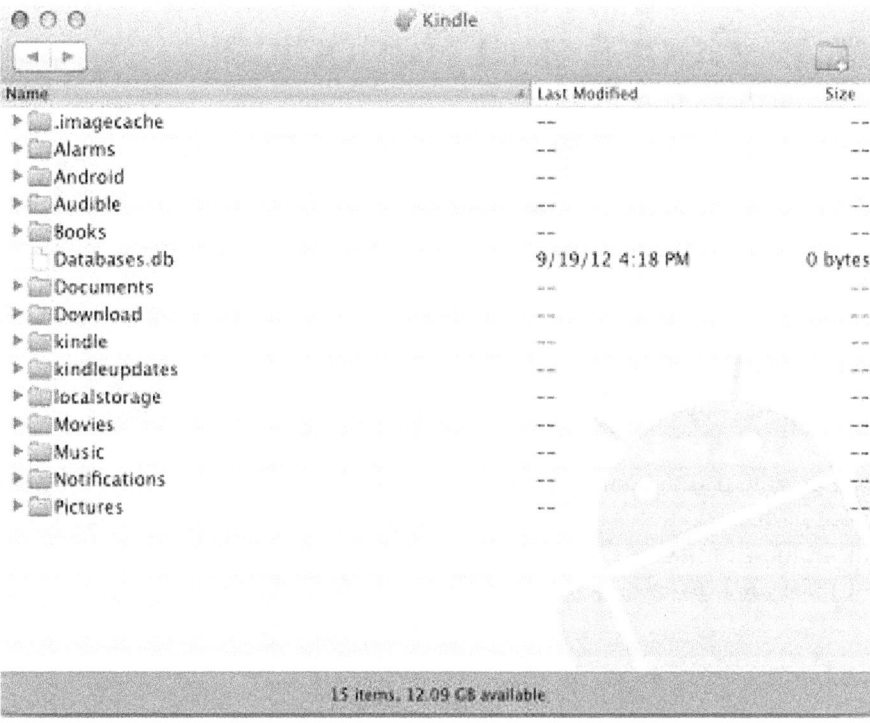

*Figure 15: Kindle Folders on a Mac*

# Managing eBooks and Periodicals

## Table of Contents

## 1. Buying an eBook on the Kindle Fire HD 6

You can buy an eBook from the Amazon Kindle Store using your Kindle Fire HD 6. To buy an eBook:

*Warning: Before touching BUY, make sure that you want the eBook. The Kindle Store uses one-click purchasing. Once you leave the Confirmation screen, you cannot cancel the order.*

1. Touch **Shop** at the top of the Home screen. The Kindle Store opens, as shown in **Figure 1**.
2. Touch **Search** in the upper right-hand corner of the screen. The virtual keyboard appears at the bottom of the screen.
3. Enter the name of an author or eBook. The most popular results appear as you type.
4. Touch **Go**. A list of matching eBook results appears, as shown in **Figure 2**. Touch **See all** under 'SHOP AMAZON' to view all results.
5. Touch the title of an eBook. The eBook description appears, as shown in **Figure 3**.
6. Touch **Buy for $##.##** where the ##.## represents the price of the eBook. The eBook is purchased and downloaded to your Kindle Fire HD 6 Library.
7. Touch **Read Now** to read the eBook immediately. The eBook opens.

*Note: Touch **Cancel Order** below 'Read Now' on the Confirmation screen if you did not mean to purchase the eBook. You may only cancel the order until you leave the Amazon Kindle store.*

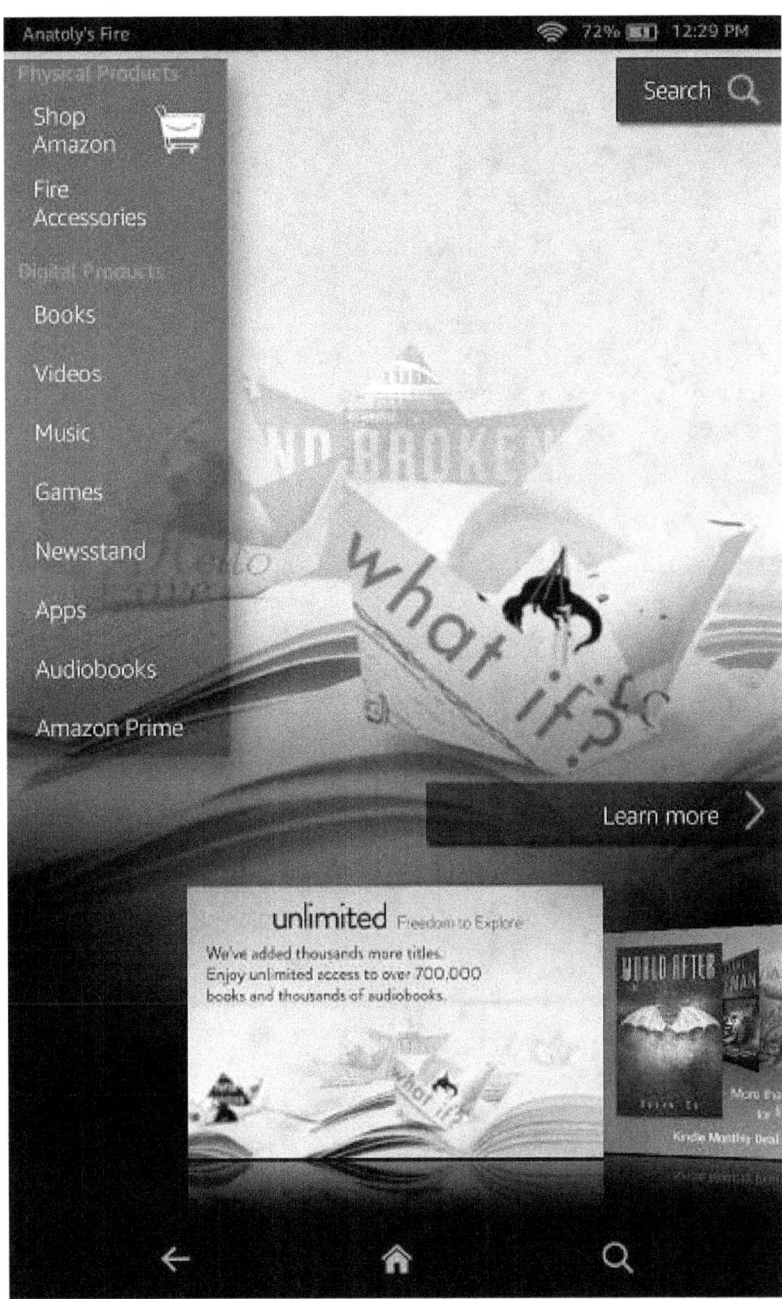

*Figure 1: Kindle Store*

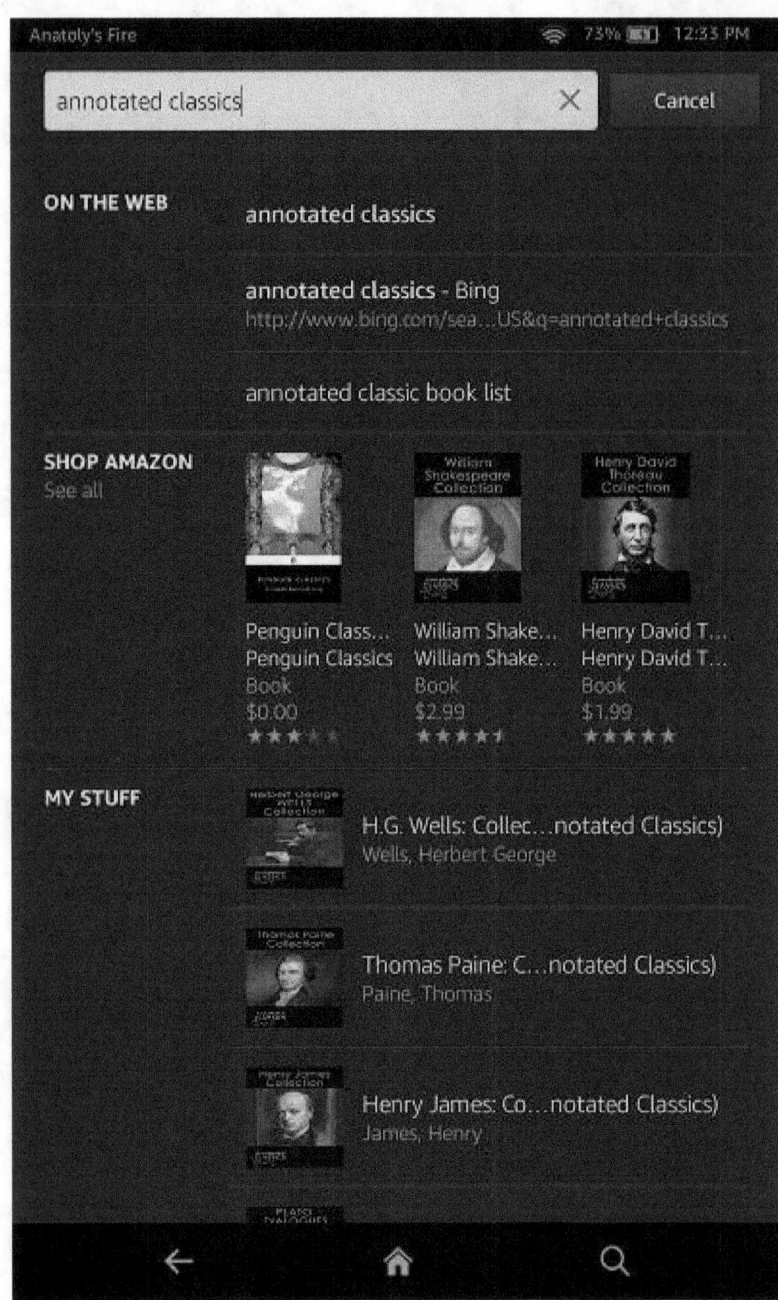

*Figure 2: List of Available eBook Results*

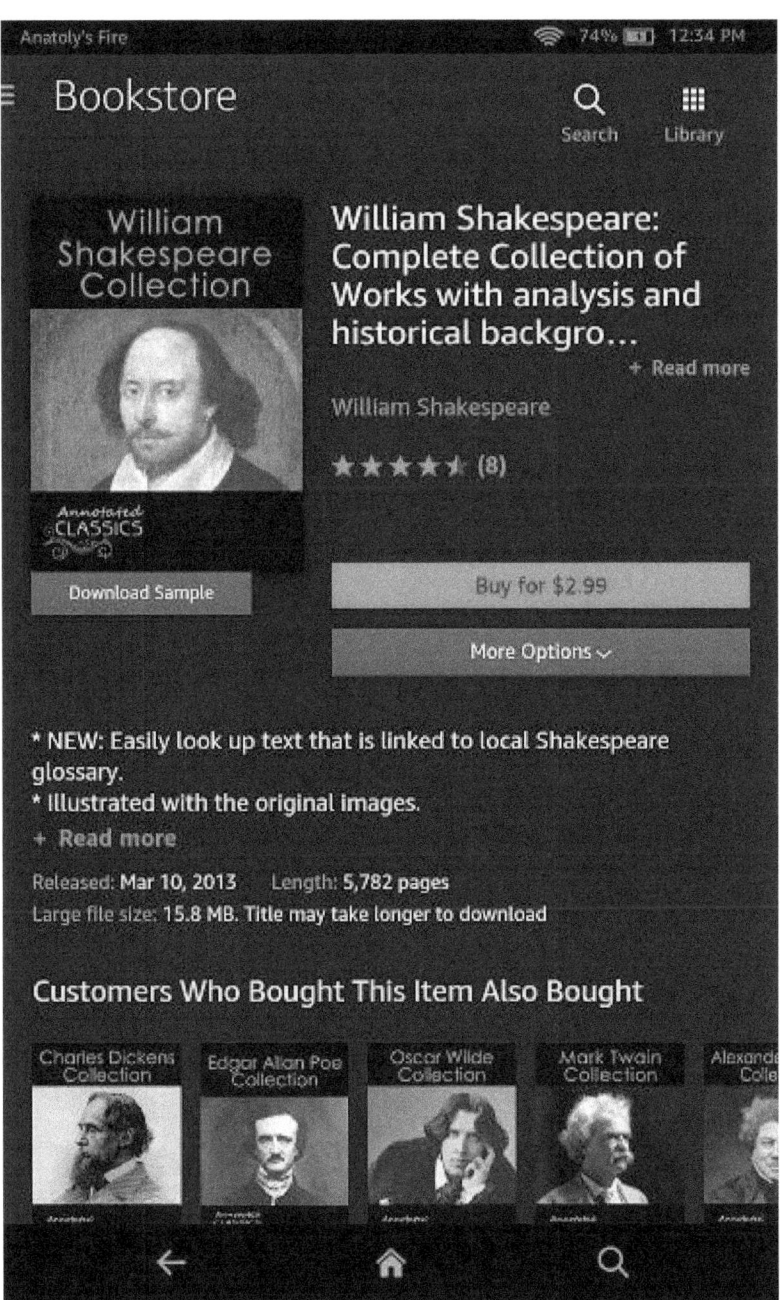

*Figure 3: eBook Description*

# 2. Buying or Subscribing to a Periodical

You can buy or subscribe to a newspaper or magazine from the Kindle Store using your Kindle Fire HD 6. To buy or subscribe to a periodical:

*Warning: Before touching the* **Buy Issue** *button or the* **Subscribe now** *button, make sure you want the periodical issue. The Kindle Store on the Kindle uses one-click purchasing. Unlike with eBook orders, you will not be given an opportunity to cancel a periodical order from the Confirmation screen.*

1. Touch **Shop** at the top of the screen. The Kindle Store opens.
2. Touch **Newsstand** on the left-hand side of the screen. The Newsstand Store opens, as shown in **Figure 4**.
3. Touch **Search** at the top of the screen. The virtual keyboard appears at the bottom of the screen.
4. Enter the name of a periodical and touch the 🔍 key. A list of matching periodical results appears, as shown in **Figure 5**.
5. Touch the title of a newspaper. The Periodical description appears, as shown in **Figure 6**.
6. Touch **Buy Issue** to purchase an issue, or touch **Start Your 14-Day Free Trial** to subscribe. A confirmation is shown and the periodical issue appears in the Library. You have 14 days to cancel your subscription before you are charged for the first time. The price of the subscription is listed next to 'Monthly Price'. Refer to *"Cancelling Your Newspaper or Magazine Free Trial"* on page 34 to learn how to cancel your subscription.

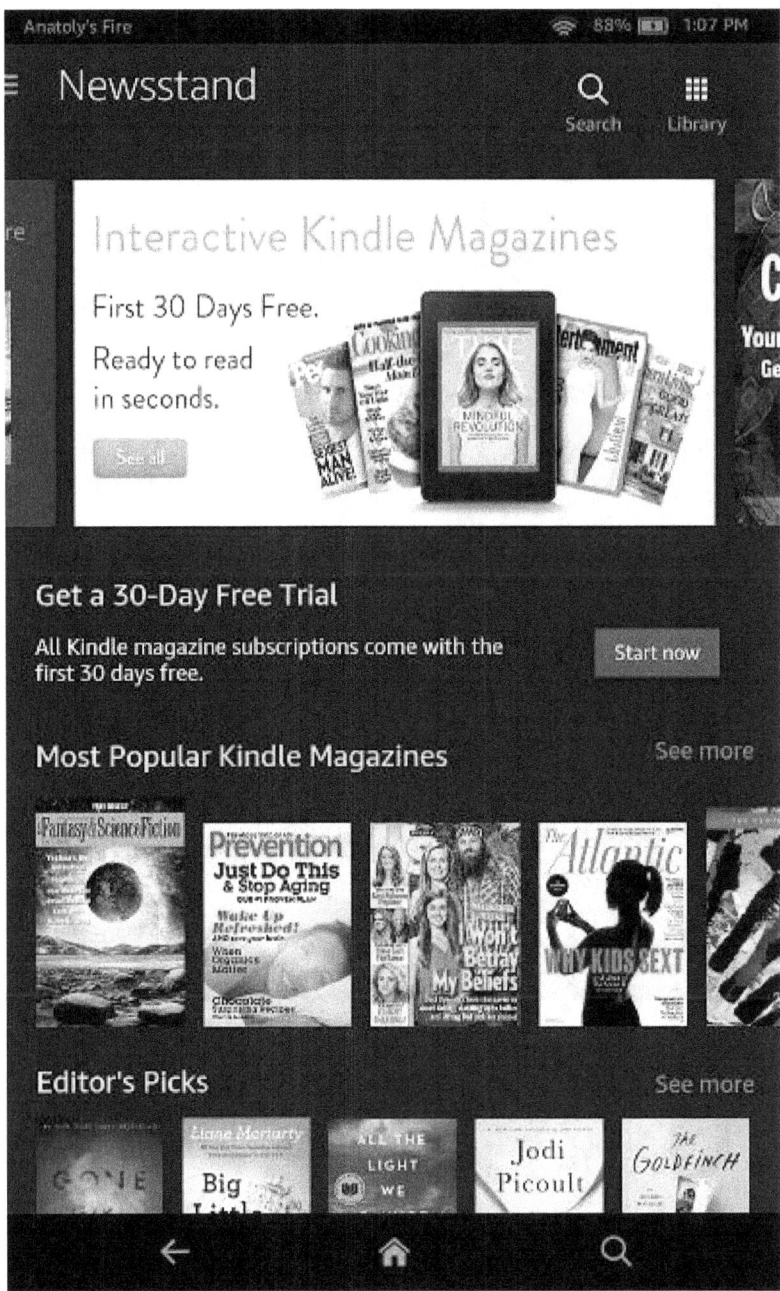

*Figure 4: Newsstand Store*

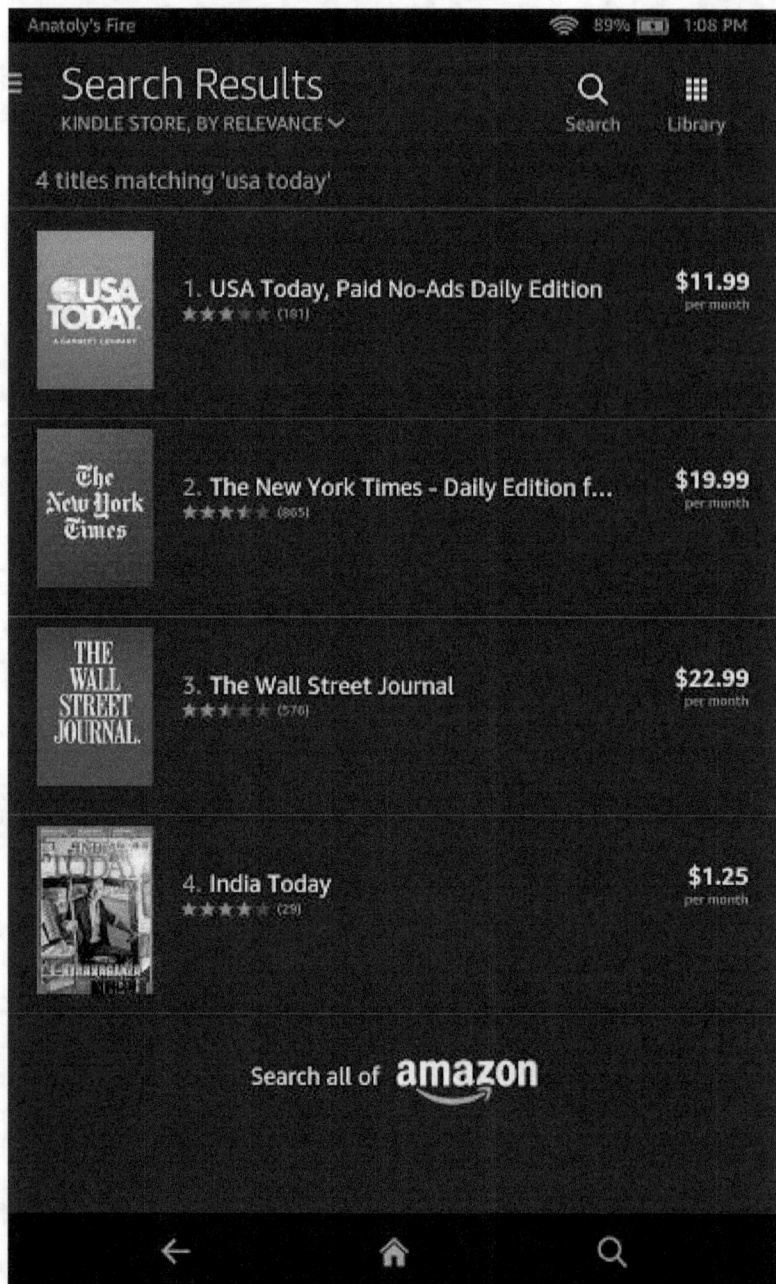

*Figure 5: List of Matching Periodical Results*

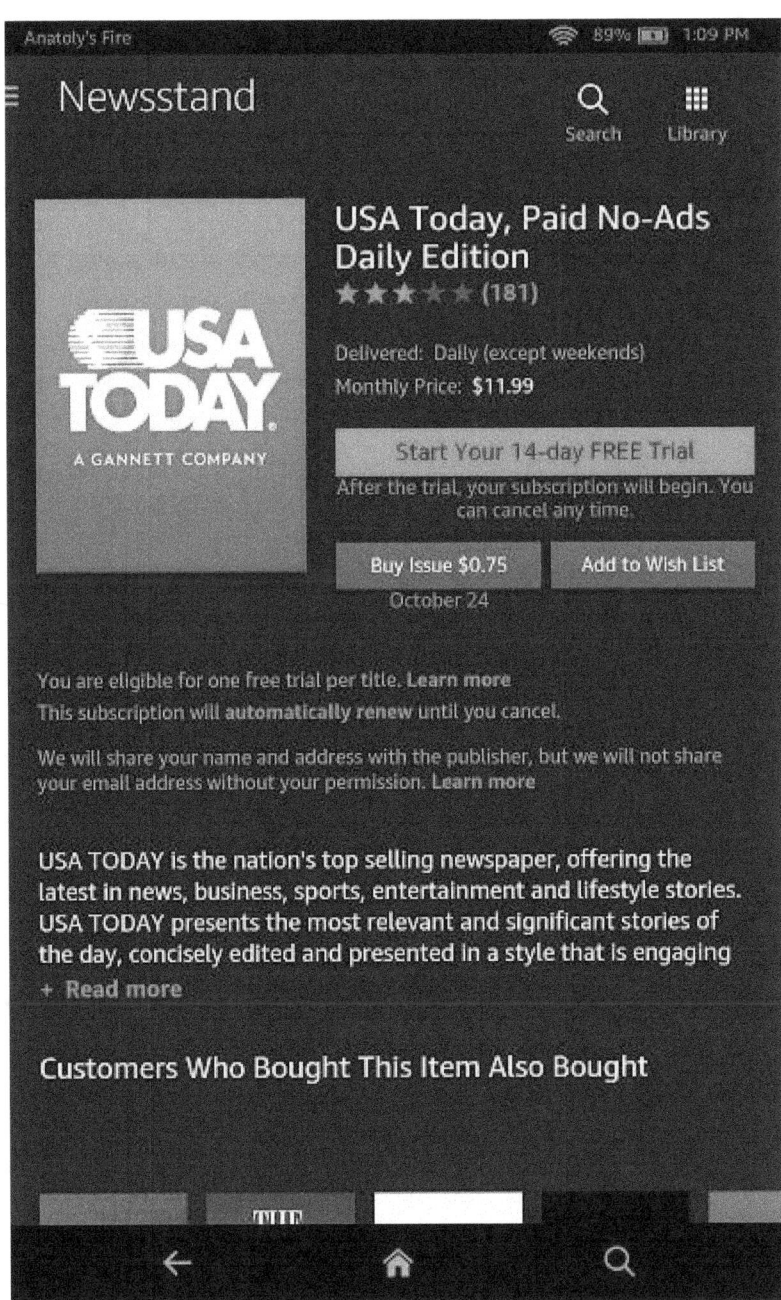

*Figure 6: Periodical Description*

# 3. Cancelling Your Newspaper or Magazine Free Trial

To cancel a subscription to a newspaper or magazine, use the Amazon website on your computer or Kindle Fire HD 6. To cancel a subscription:

1. Go to **www.amazon.com/myk** using your computer's internet browser or the Amazon Silk browser on the Kindle Fire HD 6. If you are signed in, the Content Management screen appears, as shown in **Figure 7**.
2. Click **Books** next to 'Show', as outlined in **Figure 7**. Select **Newspapers** from the list. A list of your purchased newspaper issues and subscriptions appears, as shown in **Figure 8**.
3. Click the [...] button next to the subscription that you wish to cancel. The Subscription options appear.
4. Click **Cancel Subscription**. A confirmation window appears.
5. Click **Cancel Subscription** again. The subscription is cancelled.

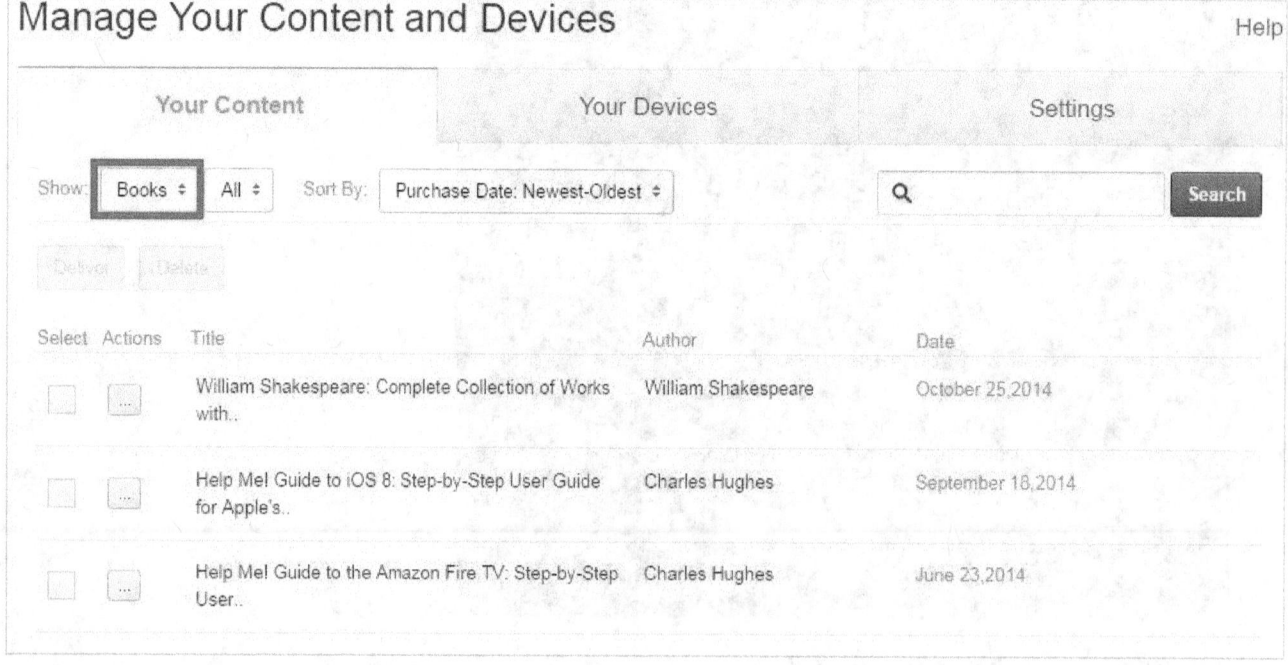

*Figure 7: Kindle Information Screen*

## Manage Your Content and Devices

Help

| | Your Content | | Your Devices | | Settings |

Newspapers ⇵    All ⇵    Purchase Date: Newest-Oldest ⇵

| Select | Actions | Title | Publisher | Purchase Date |
|---|---|---|---|---|
| | ... | USA Today, Paid No-Ads Daily Edition | USA TODAY | October 25,2014 |
| | ... | The New York Times - Daily Edition for Kindle (September.. | The New York Times Company | September 14,2010 |
| | ... | The Boston Globe (January 28.2010) | The Boston Globe | January 28.2010 |

*Figure 8: List of Purchased Newspaper Issues and Subscription*

# 4. Browsing Recommendations

Amazon makes recommendations based on the eBooks that you have viewed or purchased. Some recommendations appear when you view an eBook on the Home screen. These recommendations appear below the eBook cover. To view recommendations in the Kindle store:

*Note: Only the eBook store offers customized recommendations. The Newsstand Store does not have this feature.*

1. Touch **Shop** at the top of the Home screen. The Kindle Store opens.
2. Touch **Books** on the left-hand side of the screen. The Bookstore opens, as shown in **Figure 9**.
3. Touch **See more** next to 'Recommended for You'. A list of recommendations appears, as shown in **Figure 10**.

*Note: Refer to "Buying an eBook on the Kindle Fire HD 6" on page 26 to learn how to purchase an eBook.*

*Figure 9: Bookstore*

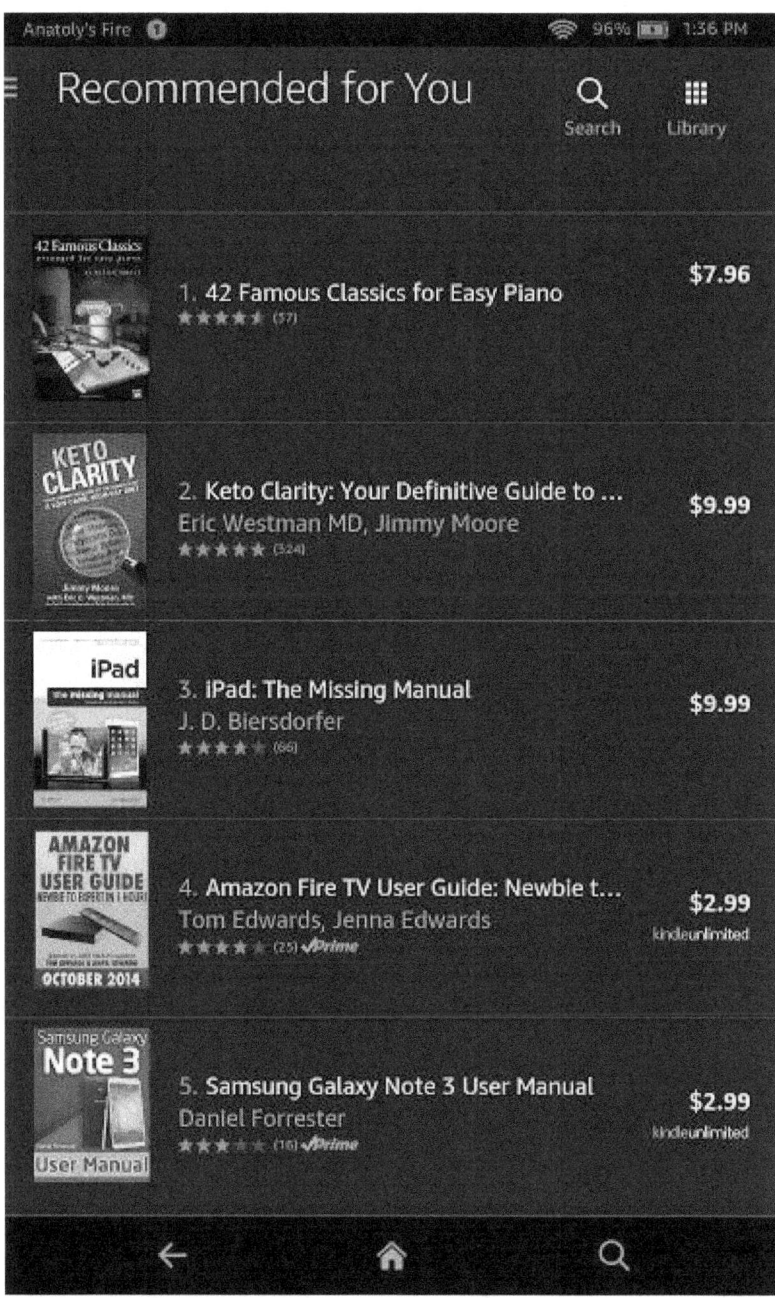

*Figure 10: List of Recommendations*

# 5. Archiving an eBook or Periodical

An eBook or periodical can be removed from your Kindle and placed in the Amazon Cloud where it does not take up space on your device. An archived eBook is retrievable using the wireless connection. To archive an eBook or periodical, touch and hold its cover on the Home screen or in the corresponding library. The Item menu appears, as shown in **Figure 11** (Home screen) and **Figure 12** (Books library). Touch **Remove from Device** in the Books library, or touch **Remove** if archiving from the Home screen. The eBook or periodical is archived in the Amazon Cloud.

*Note: To restore an archived eBook, touch* **Cloud** *in the Books or Newsstand library, and then touch the eBook or periodical cover.*

*Figure 11: Item Menu on the Home Screen*

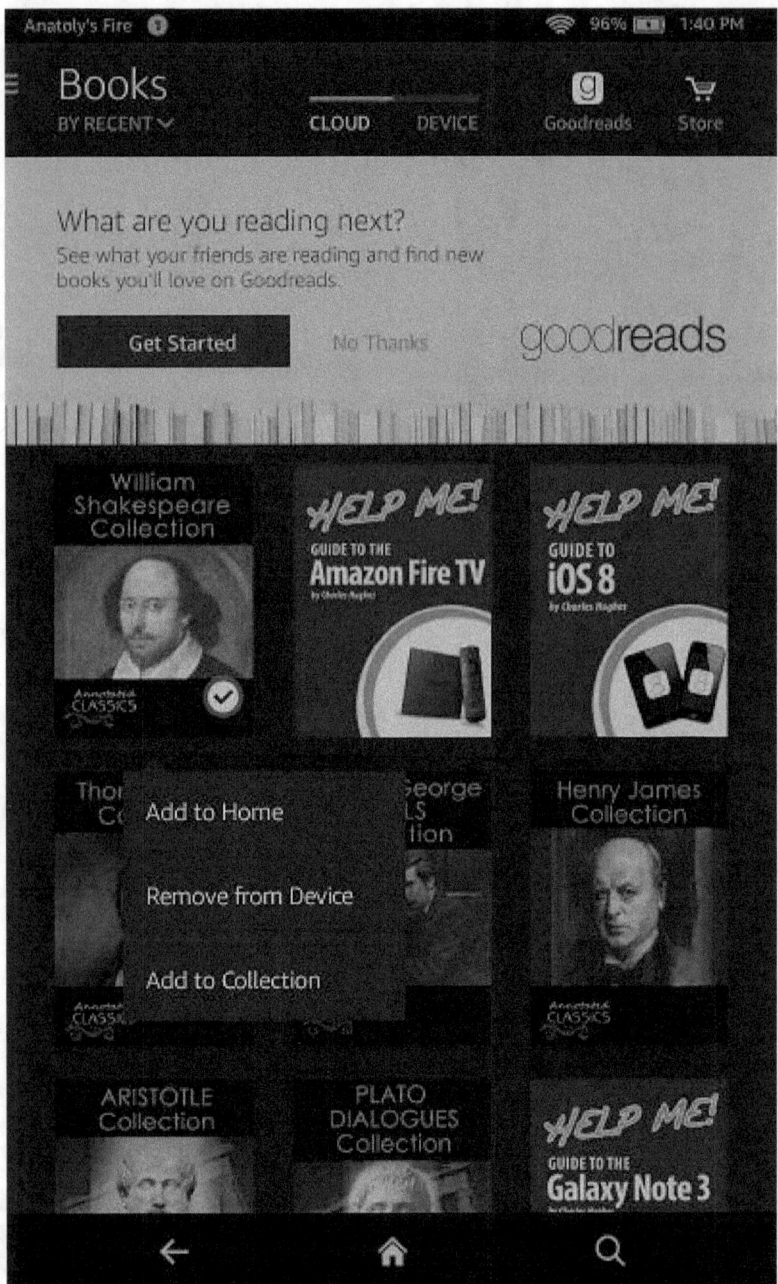

*Figure 12: Item Menu in the Books Library*

# 6. Keeping a Periodical Issue when a New Issue is Downloaded

When you have a subscription to a periodical, you can have the Kindle Fire HD 6 either delete the previous monthly issue every time a new one arrives or keep the issue. To retain the previous periodical issue, touch and hold the cover on the Home screen or in the Newsstand library. The Item menu appears. Touch **Keep**. The issue will be kept when a new one is downloaded. To automatically delete the current issue, touch and hold the cover again. The Item menu appears. Touch **Do not Keep**. The issue will be deleted when a new one is downloaded.

*Note: By default, the Kindle Fire HD 6 will automatically delete the previous issue when a new one is downloaded.*

# 7. Searching for an eBook in the Library

If you have a large number of eBooks on your Kindle Fire HD 6, you can find a specific eBook more easily by searching your library. To search for an eBook:

1. Touch **Books** at the top of the Home screen. The Books Library appears, as shown in **Figure 13**.
2. Touch the icon at the bottom of the screen. The virtual keyboard appears.
3. Enter the title or author of an eBook. A list of matching library results appears as you type, as shown in **Figure 14**. Touch the title of an eBook to read it.

*Figure 13: Books Library*

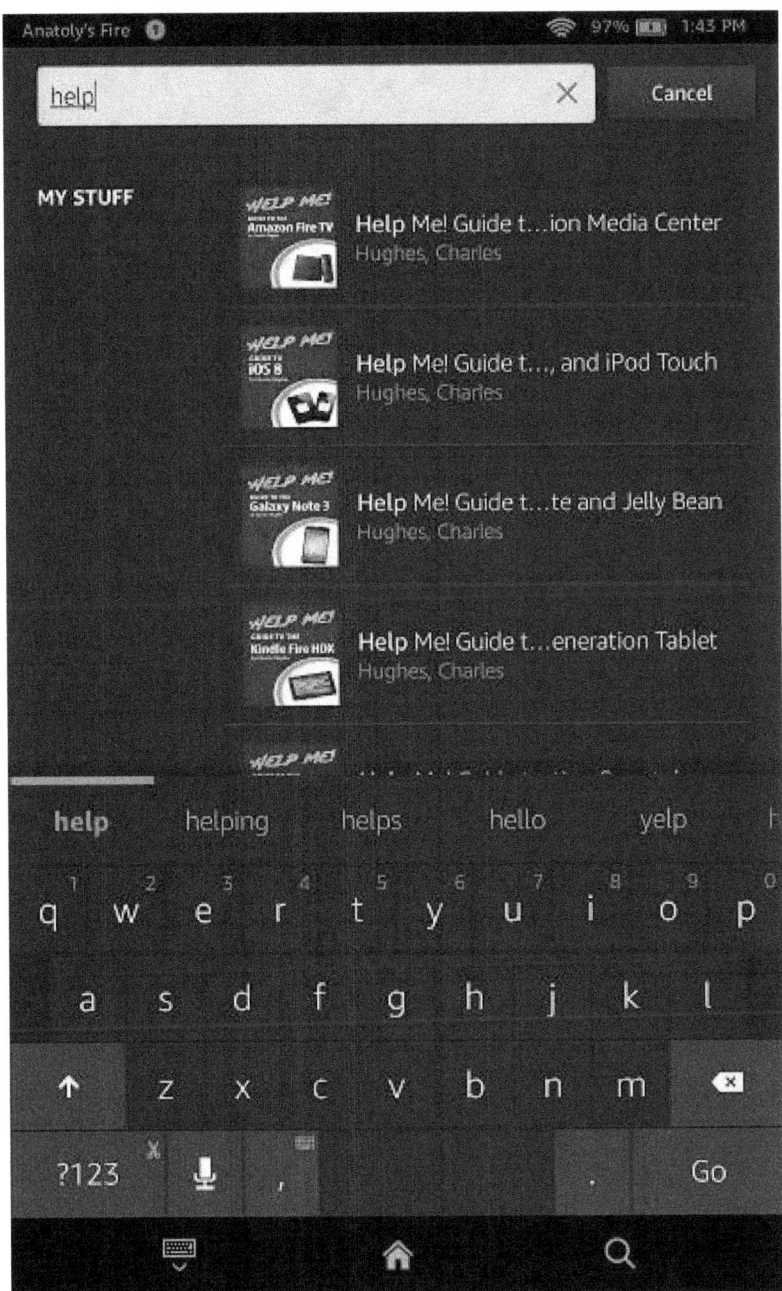

*Figure 14: List of Matching Library Results*

# 8. Sorting eBooks in the Library

You may organize the eBooks in your library chronologically by the download date, by author, or by the title. To sort your eBooks:

1. Touch **Books** at the top of the Home screen. The Books Library appears.
2. Touch **Books** in the upper left-hand corner of the screen. The Sort menu appears, as shown in **Figure 15**.
3. Touch **By Author**, **By Recent**, or **By Title**. The eBooks are sorted accordingly.

*Figure 15: Sort Menu*

# 9. Creating a Collection

If you have many eBooks on your Kindle Fire HD 6, you may want to create a collection of eBooks to organize them. Collections allow you to find eBooks more easily in your library.

1. Touch **Books** at the top of the Home screen. The Books Library appears.
2. Touch the left-hand side of the screen, and slide your finger to the right. The Library Navigation menu appears, as shown in **Figure 16**.
3. Touch **Collections**. The Collections screen appears, as shown in **Figure 17**.
4. Touch **Create a new collection**. The Create Collection window appears, as shown in **Figure 18**.
5. Enter a name for the new collection, and touch **Next**. A list of eBooks that are stored on your device appears.
6. Touch the eBooks that you would like to add to the collection. A check mark appears next to each selected eBook.
7. Touch **Add**. The new collection is created, and the selected eBooks are added to the collection.

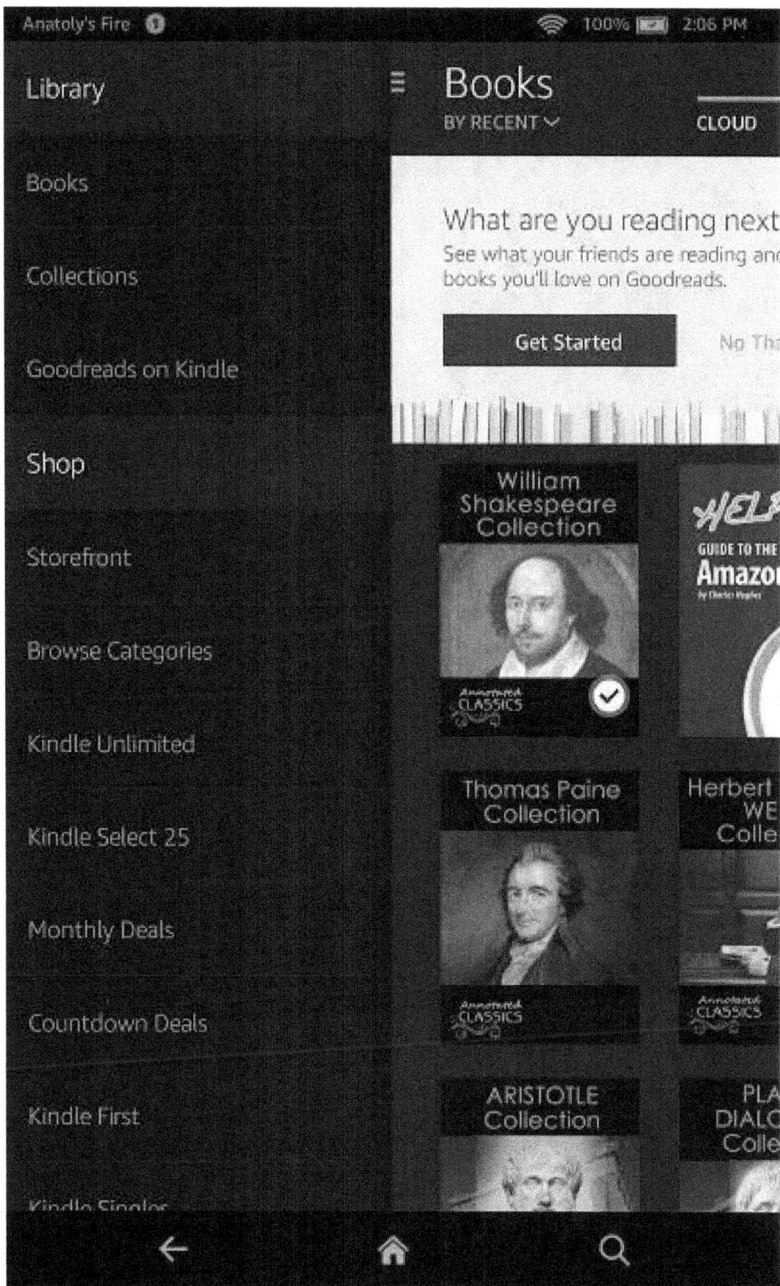

*Figure 16: Library Navigation Menu*

*Figure 17: Collections Screen*

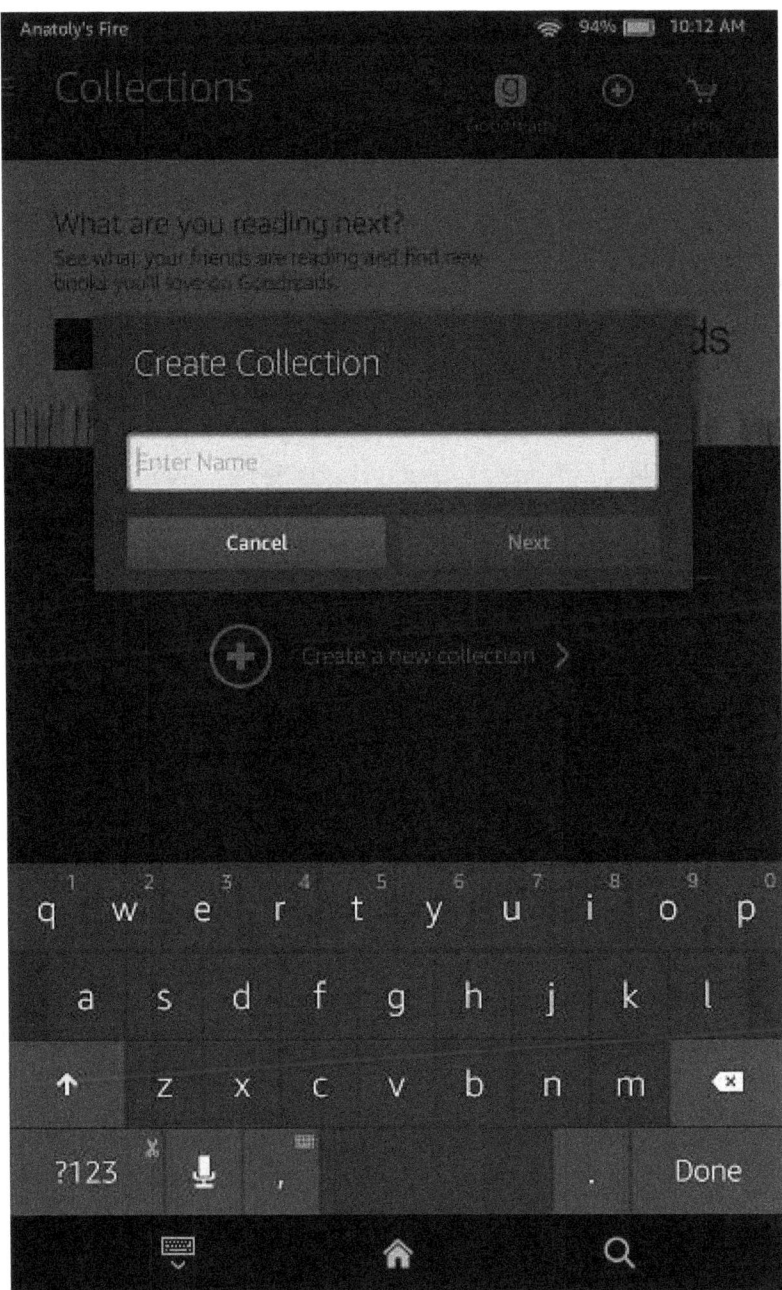

*Figure 18: Create Collection Window*

# 10. Editing a Collection

After you create a collection, you may add eBooks to or remove eBooks from the collection. To edit a collection:

1. Touch **Books** at the top of the Home screen. The Books Library appears.
2. Touch the left-hand side of the screen, and slide your finger to the right. The Library Navigation menu appears.
3. Touch **Collections**. The Collections screen appears.
4. Touch the collection that you want to edit. The eBooks stored in the collection appear, as shown in **Figure 19**.
5. Touch **Add** at the top of the screen. A list of eBooks stored on your device appears.
6. Touch the eBooks that you would like to add to the collection. A check mark appears next to each selected eBook.
7. Touch **Add**. The selected eBooks are added to the collection.

*Figure 19: eBooks Stored in a Collection*

# 11. Deleting a Collection

If you no longer need a collection, you may delete it from your device. Deleting a collection does not delete the eBooks that it contains. The eBooks are still found in the Books library. To delete a collection, touch and hold it on the Collections screen. Then touch **Delete**, and touch **Delete** again in the confirmation dialog. The collection is deleted.

*Note: Refer to* "Editing a Collection" *on page 50 to learn how to open the Collections screen.*

# Reading eBooks and Periodicals

## Table of Contents

## 1. Navigating an eBook or Periodical

The Kindle Fire HD 6 makes it easy to navigate an eBook or periodical. Use the following tips while reading:

- **Navigating the Pages** - Touch the screen and move your finger to the left to turn to the next page or to the right to turn to the previous one.
- **Navigating to a Specific Location** - Touch the screen anywhere (as long as it is not a link). The eBook menu appears at the top of the screen. Touch the        on the                                              bar at the bottom of the screen, and drag it to the left or right to select a specific location in the eBook or periodical. The last two visited locations on the book are marked as gray dots on the bar. Touch one of these dots to navigate to the location.

- **Sync to Furthest Page Read** - Touch the left edge of the screen and slide your finger to the right. The eBook menu appears, as shown in **Figure 1**. Touch **Sync to Furthest Page Read**. The device opens the furthest read page on all devices registered to the same Amazon account as the Kindle Fire HD 6.
- **View an Image in Full-Screen Mode** - Touch an image twice in quick succession.

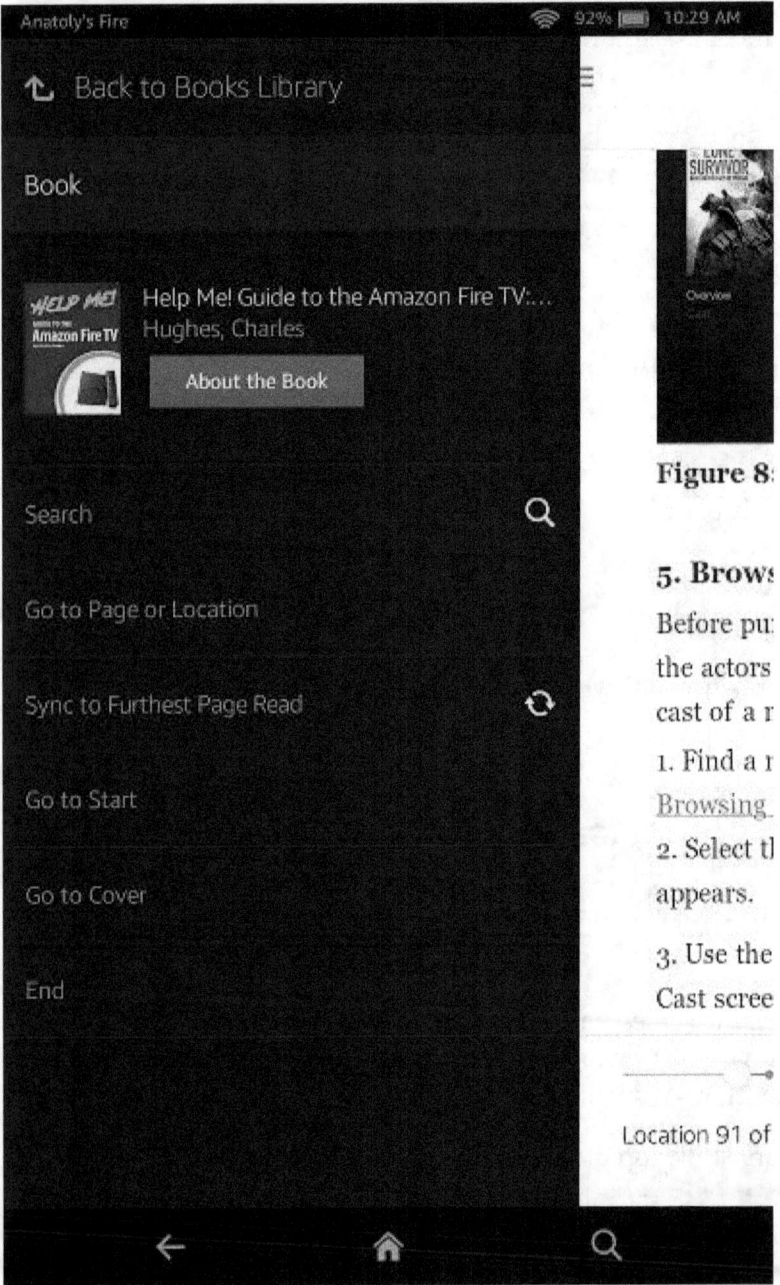

*Figure 1: eBook Menu*

## 2. Looking Up a Word in the Dictionary

While reading an eBook or periodical, use the built-in dictionary to look up word definitions. To look up a word, touch and hold it. A quick definition appears, as shown in **Figure 2**. Touch **Full Definition**. The full dictionary definition appears, as shown in **Figure 3**. Touch the ⬅button at the bottom of the screen to resume reading where you left off.

*Note: If you do not see a definition, touch the Wikipedia entry that appears, and move your finger to the left twice. Then, touch* **Download dictionary** *to install the English dictionary.*

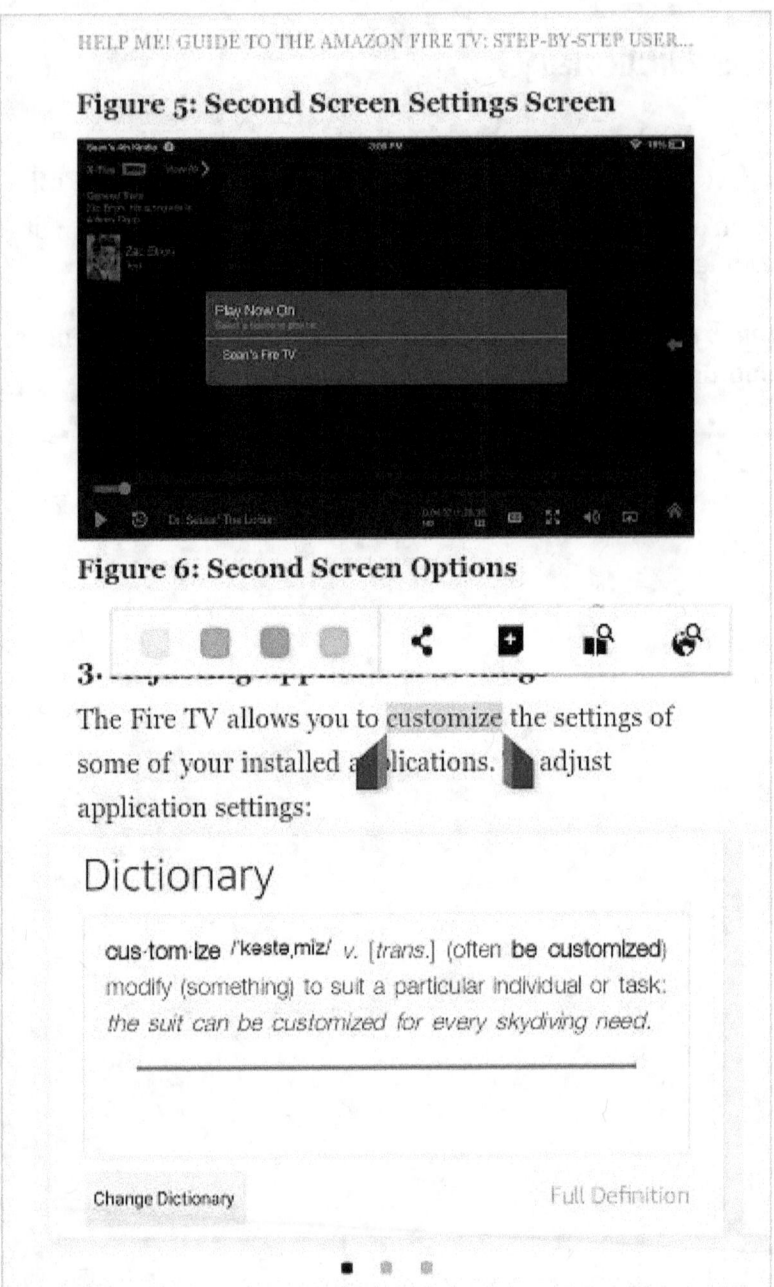

HELP ME! GUIDE TO THE AMAZON FIRE TV: STEP-BY-STEP USER...

**Figure 5: Second Screen Settings Screen**

**Figure 6: Second Screen Options**

3.

The Fire TV allows you to customize the settings of some of your installed applications. adjust application settings:

# Dictionary

cus·tom·ize /ˈkəstəˌmīz/ v. [trans.] (often be customized) modify (something) to suit a particular individual or task: the suit can be customized for every skydiving need.

Change Dictionary                    Full Definition

*Figure 2: Quick Definition*

THE NEW OXFORD AMERICAN DICTIONARY

cus·**tom·ize** /ˈkəstəˌmīz/ *v.* [*trans.*] (often **be customized**) modify (something) to suit a particular individual or task: *the suit can be customized for every skydiving need.*

_____

**cus·tom-made** *adj.* made to a particular customer's order.

_____

**cus·toms** /ˈkəstəmz/ *plural n.* the official department that administers and collects the duties levied by a government on imported goods: *cocaine seizures by customs have risen this year* | [as *adj.*] *a customs officer.*

   **<SPECIAL USAGE>**
- the place at a port, airport, or frontier where officials check incoming goods, travelers, or luggage: *arriving refugees were whisked through customs.*
- (usu. **customs duties**) the duties levied by a government on imported goods.

**<ORIGIN>** late Middle English: originally in the singular, denoting a customary due paid to a ruler, later duty levied on goods on their way to market.

_____

**cus·toms un·ion** *n.* a group of countries that have

*Figure 3: Full Dictionary Definition*

## 3. Translating a Word or Phrase

While reading, you can translate a single word, or an entire phrase, using Bing translate. To translate a word or phrase, touch and hold the word. A short definition of the word appears. If you want to select a phrase, drag your finger over the rest of the phrase. Touch the definition or Wikipedia window, and slide your finger to the left until 'Translation' appears. To change the language, touch the language on the right-hand side of the screen. You may also touch the 🔊 icon to hear a pronunciation of the translated word or phrase.

## 4. Highlighting a Word or Phrase

While reading an eBook or periodical, you can highlight words and phrases. You can then view a list of all of your highlights, and navigate to any highlight in the eBook. To highlight a word or phrase:

1. Touch and hold a single word until the magnifying glass appears, as shown in **Figure 4**. You may now select the text that you wish to highlight.
2. Drag your finger without letting go of the screen to select a phrase, or release the screen to highlight a single word. The phrase is selected, and the Text menu appears above the text, as outlined in **Figure 5**.
3. Touch one of the colors (pink, blue, yellow, or orange) in the menu. The word or phrase is highlighted, as shown in **Figure 6**.

*Note: Refer to* "Viewing Your Notes, Highlights, and Bookmarks" *on page 64 to learn how to view your list of highlights.*

possess the colonies in the present contest, the name of ancestors will be remembered by future generations with detestation.

The sun never om, but of a use of greater worth. 'Tis not the of the habit y, a county, a province, or a kingdom, but of a continent — of at least one eighth part of the habitable globe. 'Tis not the concern of a day, a ye or an ag posterity are virtually involved in the contest, and will be more or less affected, even to the end of time, by the proceedings now. Now is the seed-time of continental union, faith and honour. The least fracture now will be like a name engraved with the point of a pin on the tender rind of a young oak; the wound will enlarge with the tree, and posterity read it in full grown characters.

By referring the matter from argument to arms, a new aera for politics is struck; a new method of thinking hath arisen. All plans, proposals, &c. prior to the nineteenth of April, i. e. to the commencement of hostilities, are like the almanacs of the last year; which, though proper then are superseded and useless now. Whatever was advanced by the advocates on either side of the question then, terminated in one and the same point. viz. a union

*Figure 4: Magnifying Glass*

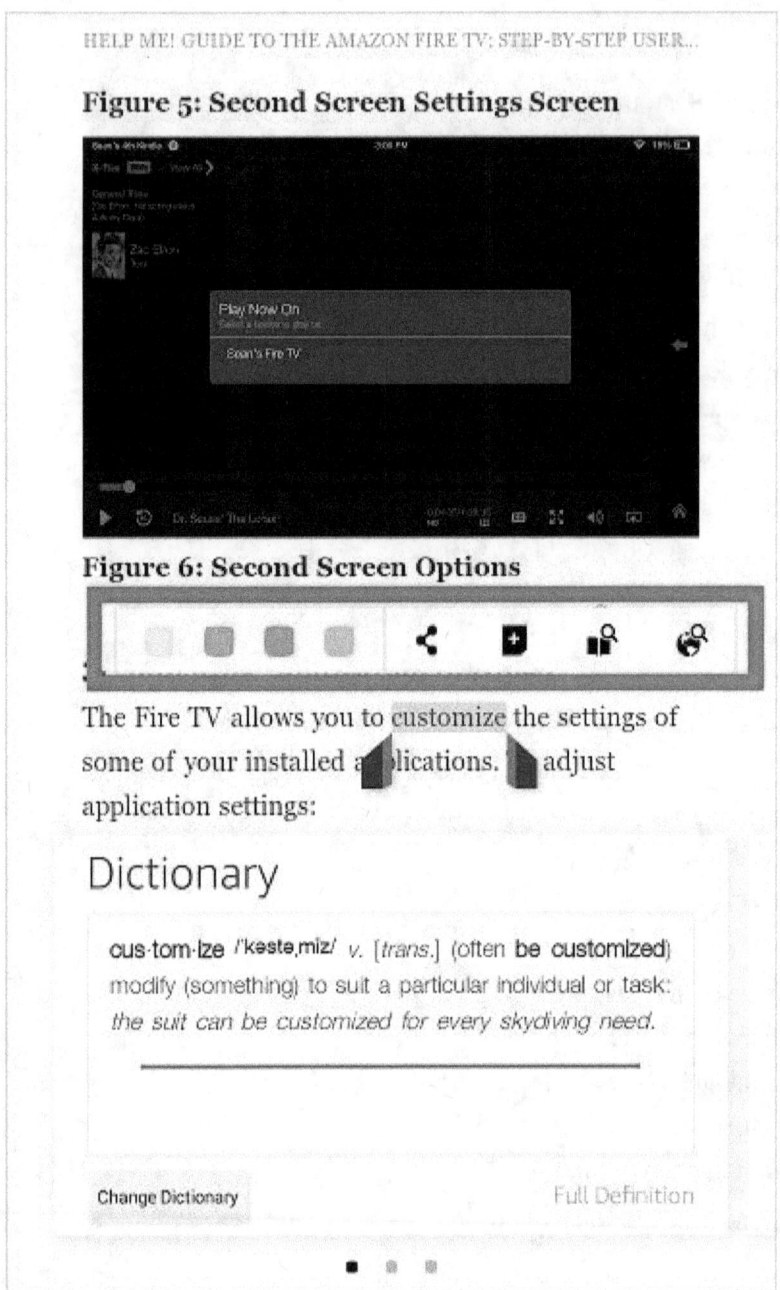

HELP ME! GUIDE TO THE AMAZON FIRE TV: STEP-BY-STEP USER...

**Figure 5: Second Screen Settings Screen**

**Figure 6: Second Screen Options**

The Fire TV allows you to customize the settings of some of your installed applications. To adjust application settings:

# Dictionary

cus·tom·ize /ˈkəstəˌmīz/ v. [trans.] (often be customized) modify (something) to suit a particular individual or task: *the suit can be customized for every skydiving need.*

Change Dictionary                          Full Definition

*Figure 5: Text Menu*

possess the colonies in the present contest, the name of ancestors will be remembered by future generations with detestation.

The sun never shined on a cause of greater worth. 'Tis not the affair of a city, a county, a province, or a kingdom, but of a continent — of at least one eighth part of the habitable globe. 'Tis not the concern of a day, a year, or an age; posterity are virtually involved in the contest, and will be more or less affected, even to the end of time, by the proceedings now. Now is the seed-time of continental union, faith and honour. The least fracture now will be like a name engraved with the point of a pin on the tender rind of a young oak; the wound will enlarge with the tree, and posterity read it in full grown characters.

By referring the matter from argument to arms, a new aera for politics is struck; a new method of thinking hath arisen. All plans, proposals, &c. prior to the nineteenth of April, i. e. to the commencement of hostilities, are like the almanacs of the last year; which, though proper then are superseded and useless now. Whatever was advanced by the advocates on either side of the question then, terminated in one and the same point. viz. a union

2 mins left in book

*Figure 6: Highlighted Phrase*

# 5. Making a Note

While reading an eBook or periodical, notes can be added. To add a note:

1.  Touch and hold a single word until the magnifying glass appears. The location where the note will be added is selected. If you want to select a phrase, drag your finger over the rest of the phrase.
2.  Release the screen. The Text menu appears.
3.  Touch the ![icon] icon. The virtual keyboard appears at the bottom of the screen.
4.  Enter a note and touch **Save**. A ![icon] icon appears next to the word or phrase, and the word is highlighted to signify that a note is attached.

To remove a note:

1.  Touch the ![icon] icon that corresponds to the note that you wish to remove. The Note appears.
2.  Touch **Delete**. A confirmation dialog appears.
3.  Touch **Delete** again. The note is removed.

*Note: Refer to* "Viewing Your Notes, Highlights, and Bookmarks" *on page 64 to learn how to view your list of notes.*

# 6. Adding a Bookmark

While reading an eBook or periodical, the media can be bookmarked in order to quickly find the same location in the future. To add a bookmark, touch the upper right-hand corner of the screen.

A ![icon] appears in the upper right-hand corner of the screen to indicate that the page is bookmarked, as shown in **Figure 7**.

*Note: Refer to* "Viewing Your Notes, Highlights, and Bookmarks" *on page 64 to learn how to view your list of bookmarks.*

THOMAS PAINE: COMPLETE WORKS, HISTORICAL BACKGROUN...

with Great-Britain: the only difference between the parties was the method of effecting it; the one proposing force, the other friendship; but it hath so far happened that the first hath failed, and the second hath withdrawn her influence.

As much hath been said of the advantages of reconciliation which, like an agreeable dream, hath passed away and left us as we were, it is but right, that we should examine the contrary side of the argument, and inquire into some of the many material injuries which these colonies sustain, and always will sustain, by being connected with, and dependent on Great Britain: To examine that connection and dependence, on the principles of nature and common sense, to see what we have to trust to, if separated, and what we are to expect, if dependant.

I have heard it asserted by some, that as America hath flourished under her former connection with Great Britain that the same connection is necessary towards her future happiness, and will always have the same effect. Nothing can be more fallacious than this kind of argument. We may as well assert that because a child has thrived upon milk that it is never to have

2 mins left in book                                          1%

*Figure 7: Bookmarked Page*

# 7. Viewing Your Notes, Highlights, and Bookmarks

While reading an eBook or periodical, you may view a list of all of your bookmarks, notes, and highlights in order to navigate to each directly. To view a list of your bookmarks, notes, and highlights:

1. Touch anywhere on the screen (as long as it is not a link). The eBook options appear at the top of the screen, as shown in **Figure 8**.
2. Touch **Notes**. The Notebook appears, as shown in **Figure 9**. Each item is labeled as "highlight", "bookmark", or "note." Alternatively, touch **Bookmarks** in the eBook options to view a list containing only bookmarks, as shown in **Figure 10**
3. Touch an item in the list. The Kindle Fire HD 6 navigates to its location. Alternatively, touch the button at the bottom of the screen to resume reading where you left off. When viewing the bookmark list, you may also touch outside of the list to hide it.

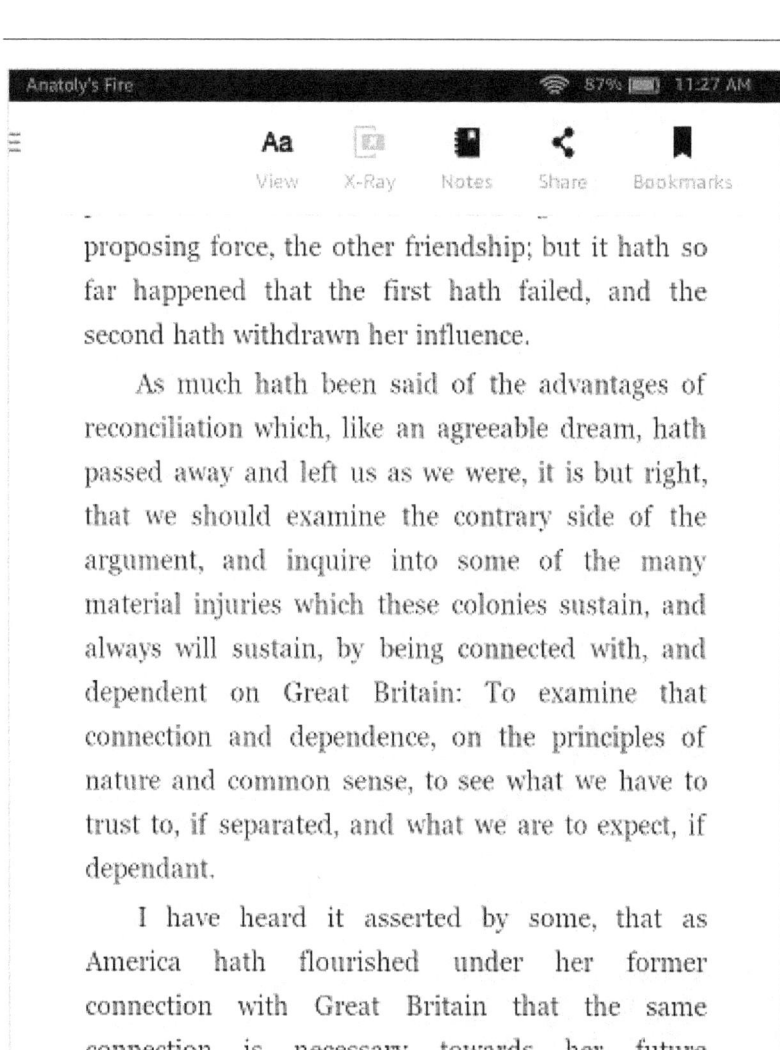

proposing force, the other friendship; but it hath so far happened that the first hath failed, and the second hath withdrawn her influence.

As much hath been said of the advantages of reconciliation which, like an agreeable dream, hath passed away and left us as we were, it is but right, that we should examine the contrary side of the argument, and inquire into some of the many material injuries which these colonies sustain, and always will sustain, by being connected with, and dependent on Great Britain: To examine that connection and dependence, on the principles of nature and common sense, to see what we have to trust to, if separated, and what we are to expect, if dependant.

I have heard it asserted by some, that as America hath flourished under her former connection with Great Britain that the same connection is necessary towards her future happiness, and will always have the same effect.

Location 265 of 39771 | 1%

*Figure 8: eBook Options*

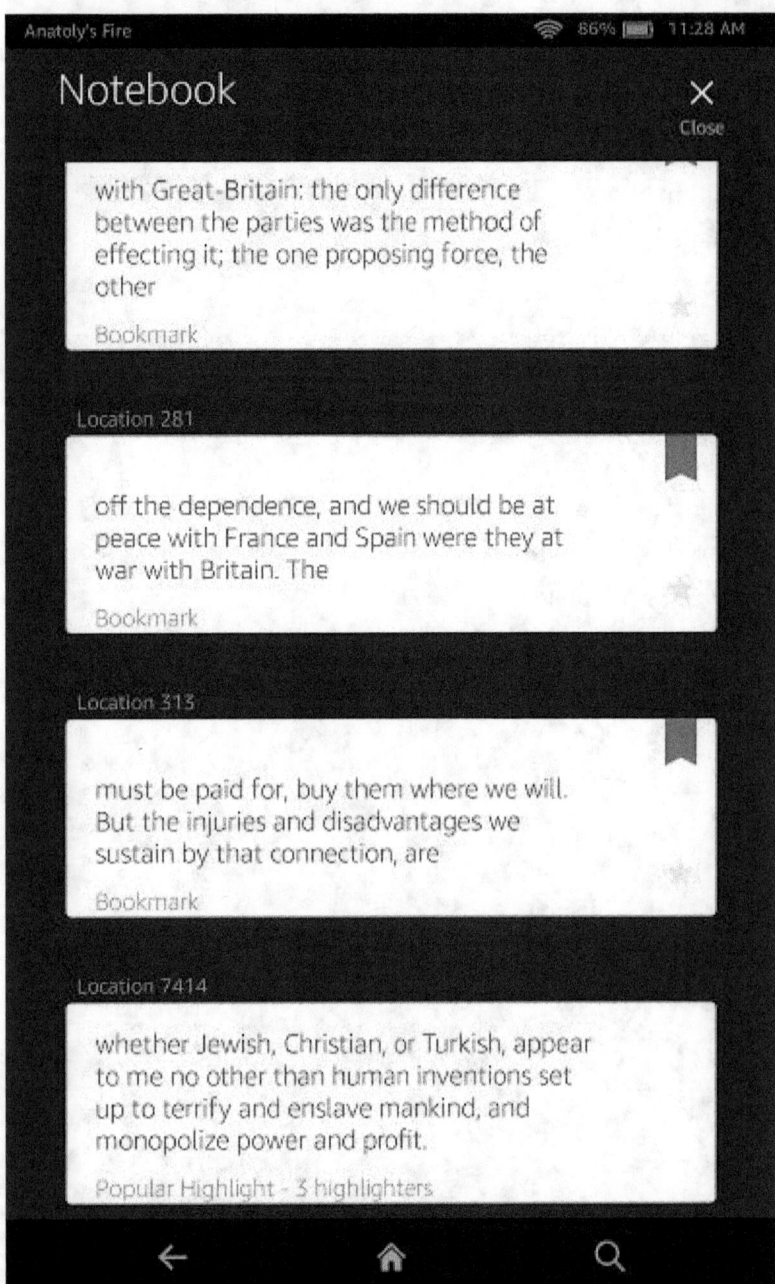

*Figure 9: My Notes & Marks Screen*

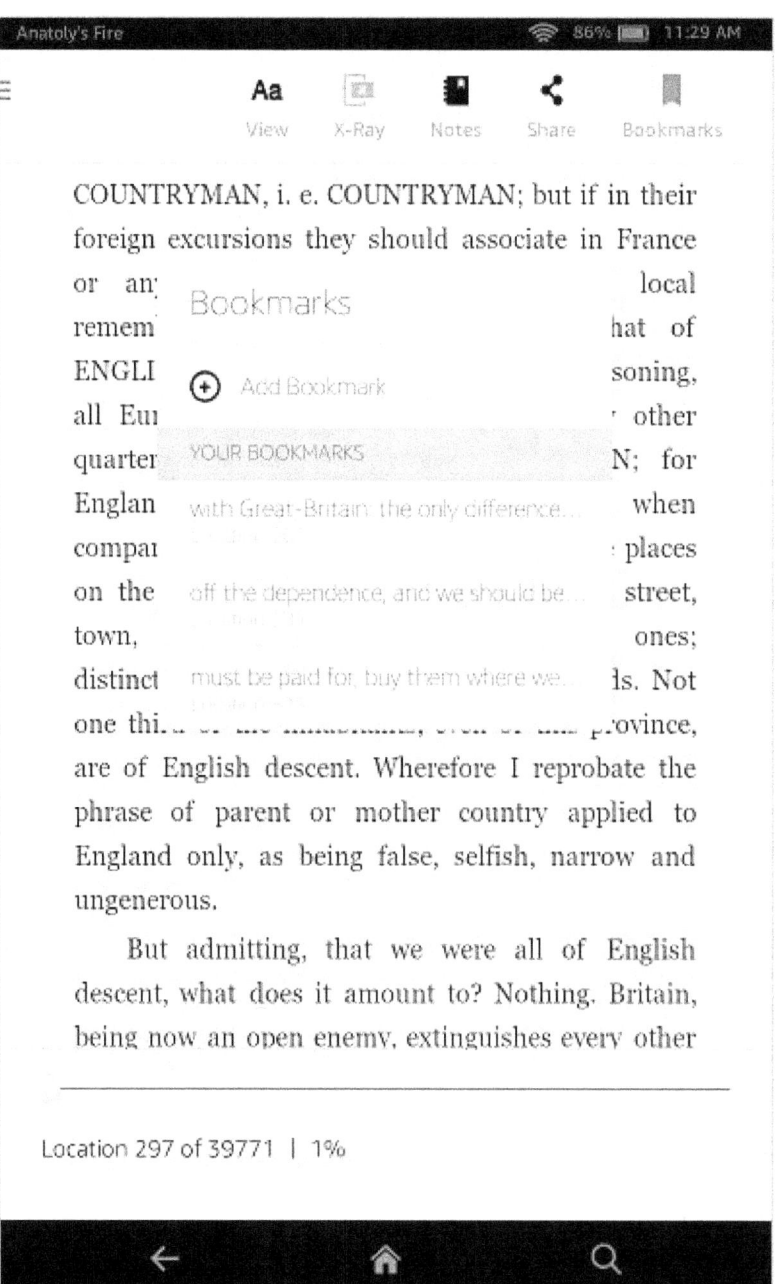

*Figure 10: List of Bookmarks*

# 8. Changing the Font Size

While reading an eBook, the size of the font can be changed. To change the font size:

1. Touch anywhere on the screen (as long as it is not a link). The eBook options appear at the top of the screen.
2. Touch **Aa** at the top of the screen. The Font menu appears, as shown in **Figure 11**.
3. Touch the [Aa▲] button to increase the font size, or touch the [Aa▼] button to decrease it. The font size is changed. Touch anywhere outside of the Font menu to return to reading where you left off.

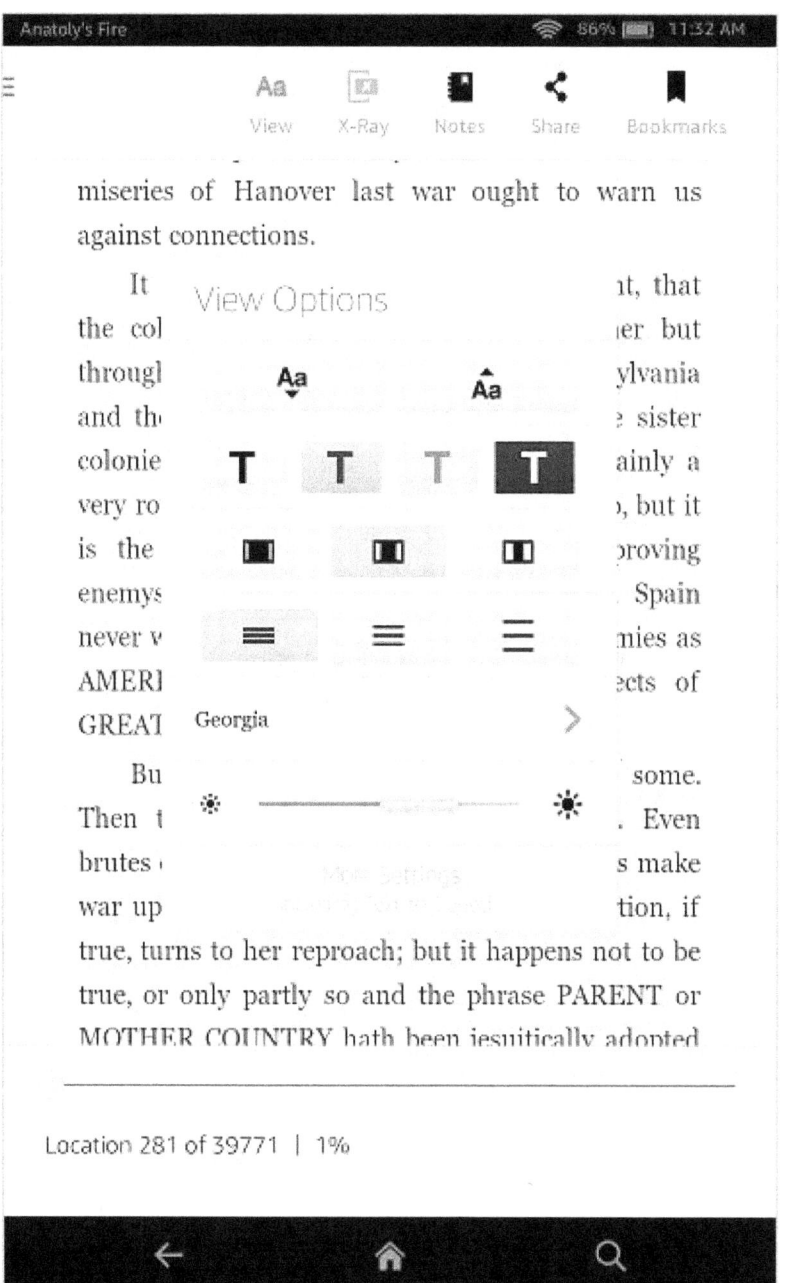

miseries of Hanover last war ought to warn us against connections.

It　　　　　　　　　　　　　　it, that the col　　　　　　　　　　　　er but throug　　　　　　　　　　　　ylvania and th　　　　　　　　　　　　e sister colonie　　　　　　　　　　　ainly a very ro　　　　　　　　　　), but it is the　　　　　　　　　　proving enemys　　　　　　　　　　. Spain never v　　　　　　　　　　mies as AMERI　　　　　　　　　　cts of GREAT

Bu　　　　　　　　　　　　　some. Then t　　　　　　　　　　. Even brutes　　　　　　　　　　　s make war up　　　　　　　　　　tion, if true, turns to her reproach; but it happens not to be true, or only partly so and the phrase PARENT or MOTHER COUNTRY hath been jesuitically adopted

*Figure 11: Font Menu*

# 9. Changing the Font Style

While reading an eBook, the type of font displayed can be changed. To change the font style:

1. Touch anywhere on the screen (as long as it is not a link). The eBook options appear at the top of the screen.
2. Touch **Aa** at the top of the screen. The Font menu appears.
3. Touch **Georgia**. The Font Style menu appears. Touch the menu and move your finger up or down to scroll through the available styles.
4. Touch a style in the list. The font style is changed. Touch anywhere outside of the Font Style menu to return to reading where you left off.

# 10. Changing the Color Mode

While reading an eBook, you may change the Color mode. The available options are black text on a white background (the default), white on black, brown on sepia, and black on green. To change the Color mode:

1. Touch anywhere on the screen (as long as it is not a link). The eBook options appear at the top of the screen.
2. Touch **Aa** at the top of the screen. The Font menu appears.
3. Touch the ⊤ button, ⊤ button, ⊤ button, or the ⊤ . The new Color mode is applied. Touch anywhere outside of the Font menu to return to reading where you left off.

# 11. Adjusting the Number of Words per Line

While reading an eBook, you may change the number of words that appear on one line, which changes the size of the left and right margins. To change the number of words per line:

1. Touch anywhere on the screen (as long as it is not a link). The eBook options appear at the top of the screen.
2. Touch **Aa** at the top of the screen. The Font menu appears.
3. Touch the ▮▯, ▮▮, or ▯▮ button. The number of words per line is adjusted accordingly.

## 12. Adjusting the Line Spacing

While reading an eBook, the amount of space between each line can be altered for easier reading. To change the line spacing:

1. Touch anywhere on the screen (as long as it is not a link). The eBook options appear at the top of the screen.
2. Touch **Aa** at the top of the screen. The Font menu appears.
3. Touch the ▦ , ▤ , or ▧ button. The line spacing is adjusted accordingly.

## 13. Changing the Screen Orientation

While reading an eBook, the screen can be rotated. To change the screen orientation, rotate the Kindle to the left or right. If the Kindle is upside down, the screen will still orient correctly. If the screen does not rotate, refer to *"Screen does not rotate"* on page 258 to learn how to resolve the problem.

## 14. Searching an eBook

You may search an eBook for a particular word or phrase. To search an eBook:

1. Touch anywhere on the screen (as long as it is not a link). The eBook controls appear at the bottom of the screen.
2. Touch the 🔍 button at the bottom of the screen. The Search field appears at the top of the screen.
3. Enter a search word or phrase and touch **Go**. A list of matching results appears, as shown in **Figure 12**. Touch a search result to navigate to its location.

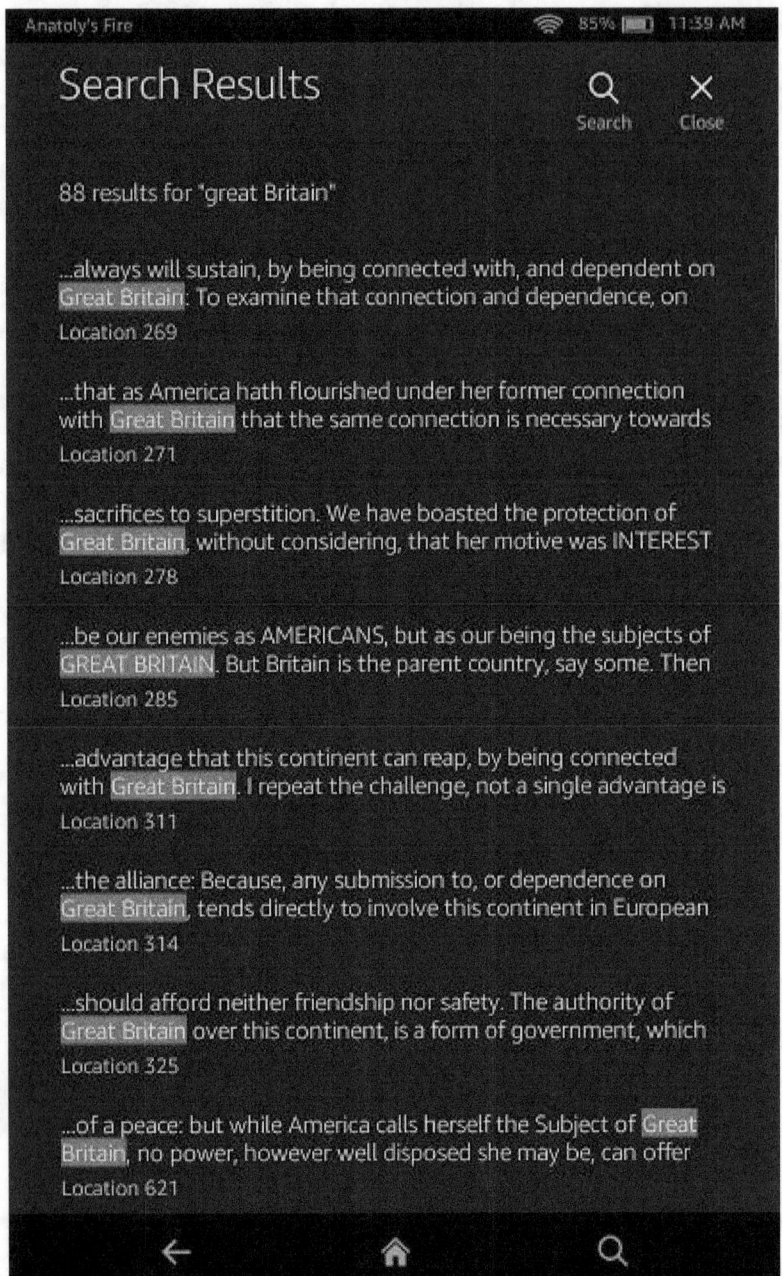

*Figure 12: List of Matching Results*

# 15. Sharing a Passage on a Social Network

You may share passages contained in eBooks with your friends on Facebook. To share a passage:

1. Touch and hold a single word until the magnifying glass appears. You may now select the text that you wish to highlight.
2. Drag your finger without letting go of the screen to select a phrase. The phrase is selected and the Text menu appears.
3. Touch **Share**. The Sharing menu appears, as shown in **Figure 13**.
4. Touch the **Facebook** or **Twitter** to select where the passage will be shared. The corresponding sharing screen appears. If you are not already signed in to your social networks, refer to *"Logging In to Your Facebook and Twitter Accounts"* on page 249 to learn how to log in.
5. Add an optional message to your post, and touch **Post**. The selected passage is shared on the selected social network.

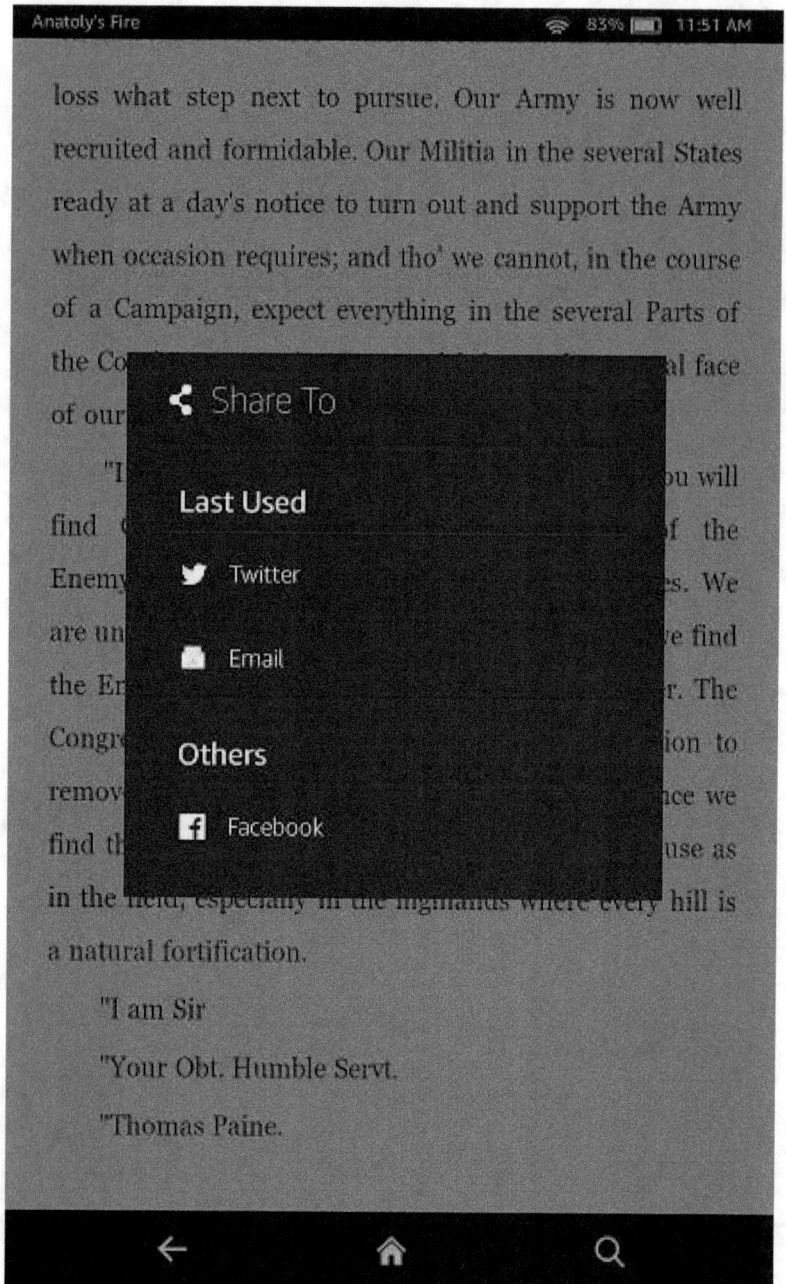

*Figure 13: Sharing Menu*

# 16. Looking Up Characters or Terms in a Story

The Kindle Fire HD 6 has a built-in feature, called X-Ray, which allows you to look up the names and descriptions of characters, terms, and images in a story. Only eBooks compatible with X-Ray will work with this feature. The X-Ray icon is grayed out in eBooks that are not compatible. To look up characters or terms:

1. Touch anywhere on the screen (as long as it is not a link). The eBook options appear at the top of the screen.
2. Touch **X-Ray**. A list of characters and terms appears, as shown in **Figure 14**.
3. Touch **People**, **Terms**, or **Images** at the top of the screen. The corresponding list of items appears.
4. Touch a character or term in the list. The device navigates to the specified location. You can also touch **Read More** when viewing a term to read more about it.

*Figure 14: List of Characters and Terms*

# Managing and Listening to Audiobooks

## Table of Contents

## 1. Purchasing an Audiobook

In addition to reading eBooks on the Kindle Fire HD 6, you may listen to audiobooks. To purchase an audiobook:

1. Touch **Shop** at the top of the Home screen. The Kindle Store opens, as shown in **Figure 1**.
2. Touch **Audiobooks** on the left-hand side of the screen. The Audiobooks Store opens, as shown in **Figure 2**.
3. Touch **Search** at the top of the screen. The virtual keyboard appears.
4. Enter the name of an audiobook or author, and touch the ⬚ button. A list of matching audiobook results appears, as shown in **Figure 3**.
5. Touch an audiobook in the list. The Audiobook description appears, as shown in **Figure 4**.
6. Touch **Buy for $##.##**, where ##.## represents the price of the audiobook. The audiobook is purchased and downloaded to your device. The audiobook will appear as the first item in your library when you touch the ⬚ button.

*Note: Purchasing the eBook version of the audiobook, where available, allows you to purchase the audiobook at a reduced price.*

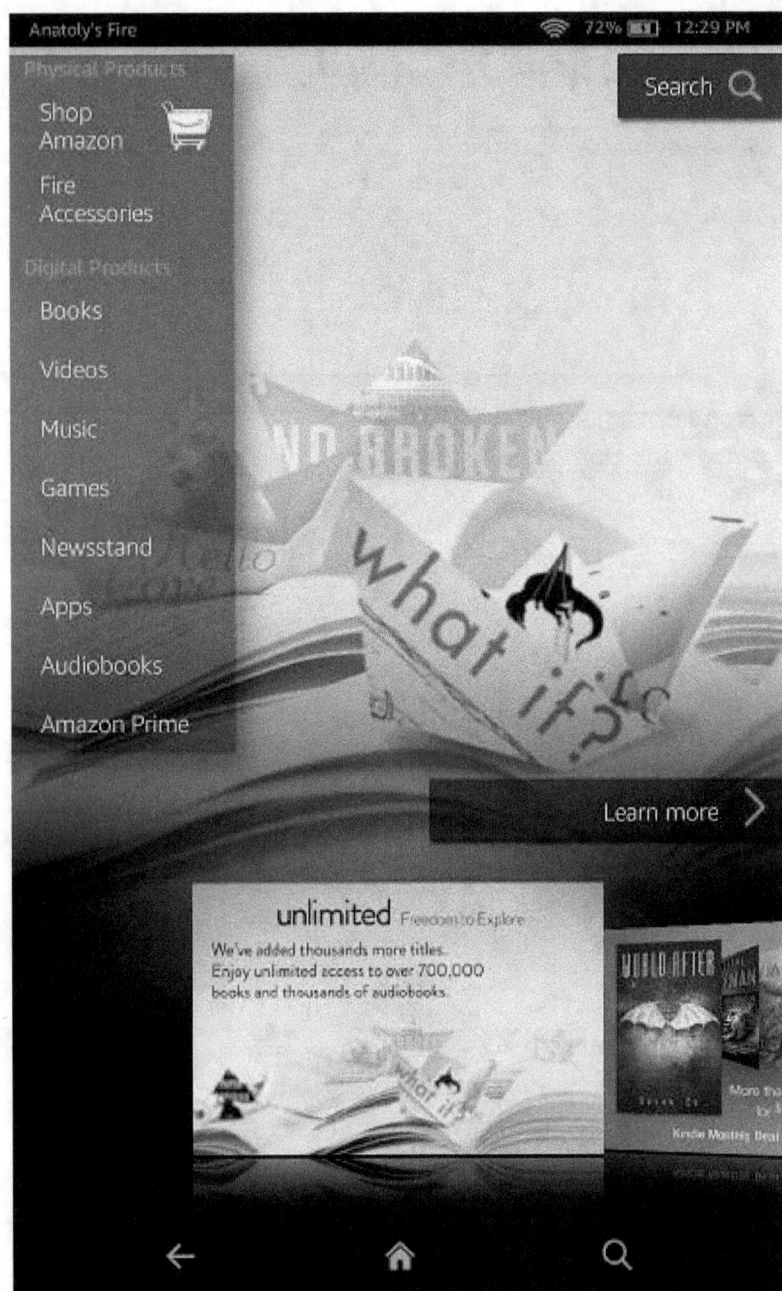

*Figure 1: Kindle Store*

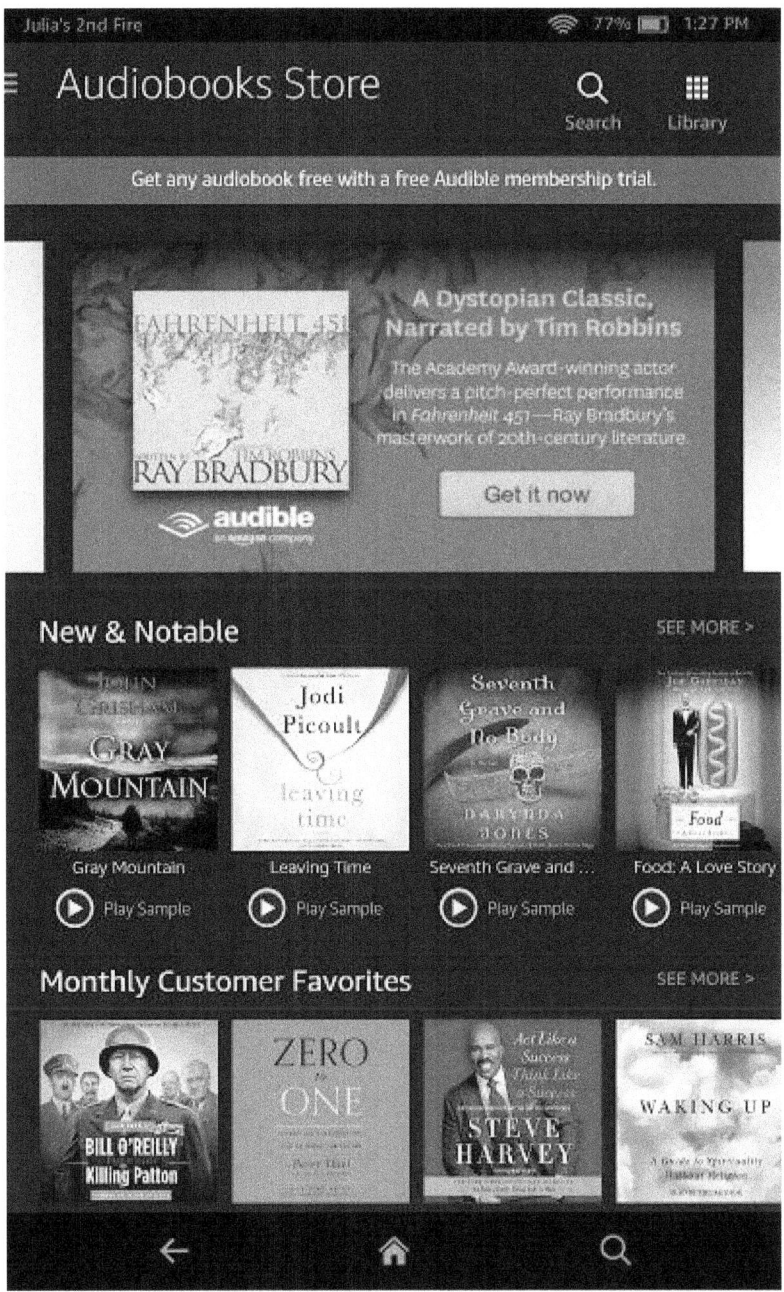

*Figure 2: Audiobooks Store*

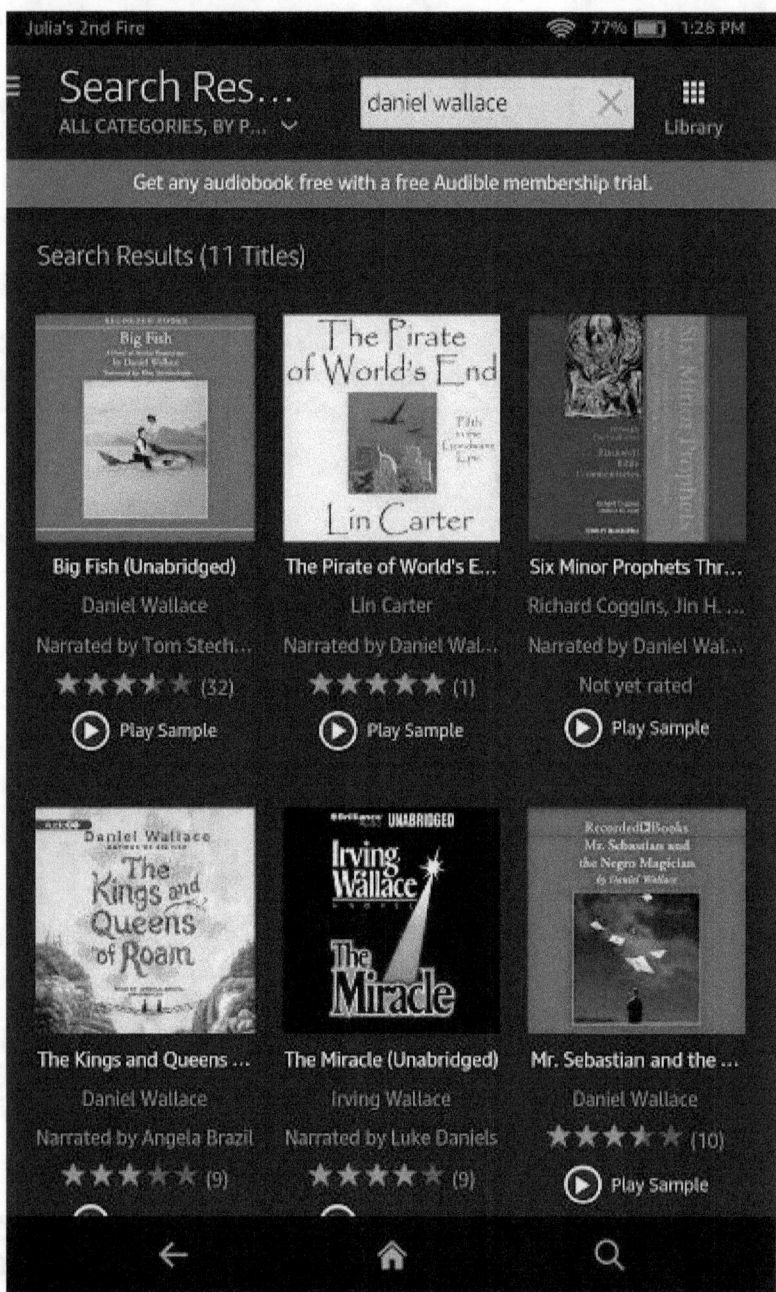

*Figure 3: List of Matching Audiobook Results*

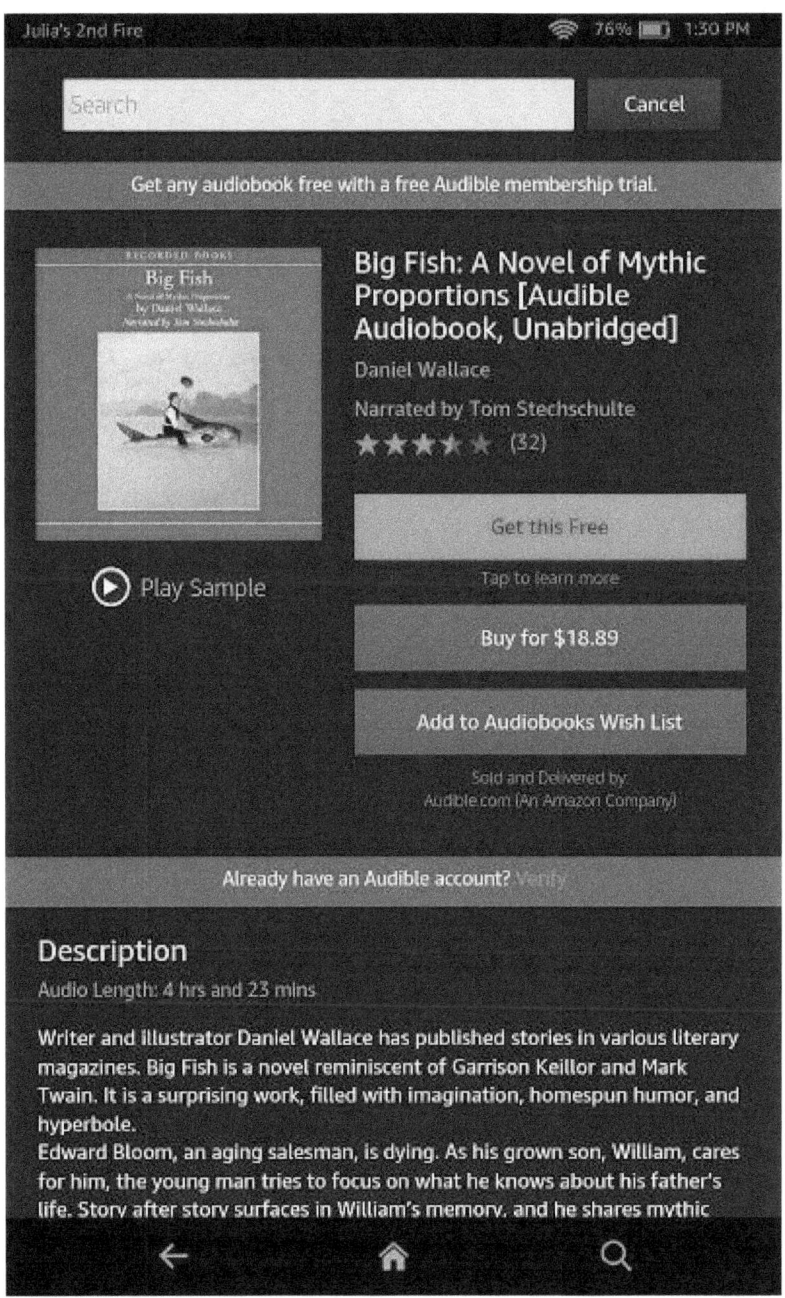

*Figure 4: Audiobook Description*

# 2. Listening to an Audiobook

You may listen to audiobooks right on your Kindle Fire HD 6. To listen to an audiobook:

1. Touch **Audiobooks** at the top of the Home screen. The Audiobooks library appears, as shown in **Figure 5**.
2. Touch the cover of an audiobook. The audiobook begins to play, and the cover appears in full screen, as shown in **Figure 6**. Touch the button if the audiobook does not begin to play automatically.
3. Use the following controls at the bottom of the screen while listening to an audiobook:

- Rewind the audiobook by 30 seconds.

- Pause the audiobook.

- Resume a paused audiobook.

- Add a bookmark at the current location. Touch and hold to add a note. Touch the icon in the upper right-hand corner of the screen to view a list of your audiobook notes and bookmarks.

- Set a sleep timer, which will turn off the audiobook after a certain period of time.

- Change the reading speed.

- Adjust the volume. You can also use the volume buttons. Refer to *"Button Layout"* on page 7 to learn where the volume buttons are located.

*Figure 5: Audiobooks Library*

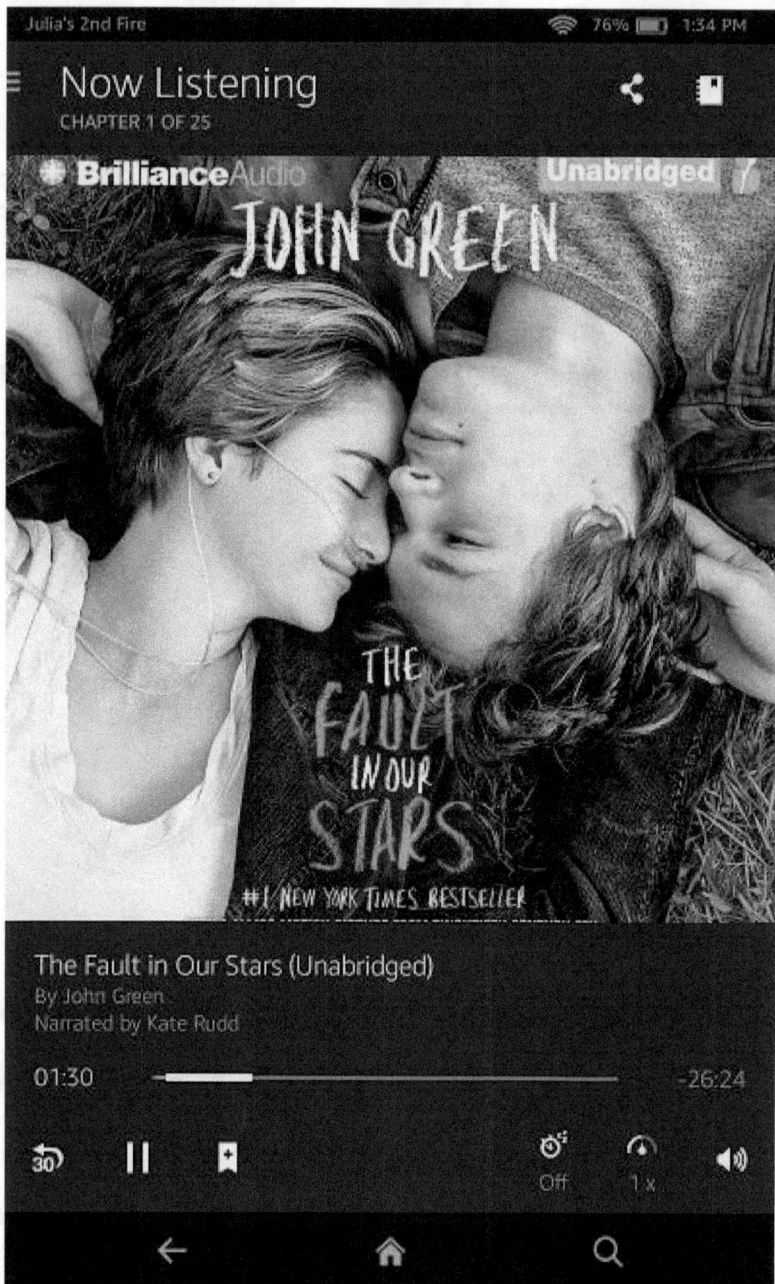

*Figure 6: Audiobook*

# 3. Navigating to a Specific Chapter in an Audiobook

To skip to a specific chapter while listening to an audiobook, touch the left edge of the screen and move your finger to the right. A list of chapters appears, as shown in **Figure 7**. Touch a chapter in the list. The audiobook skips to the selected chapter and begins to play.

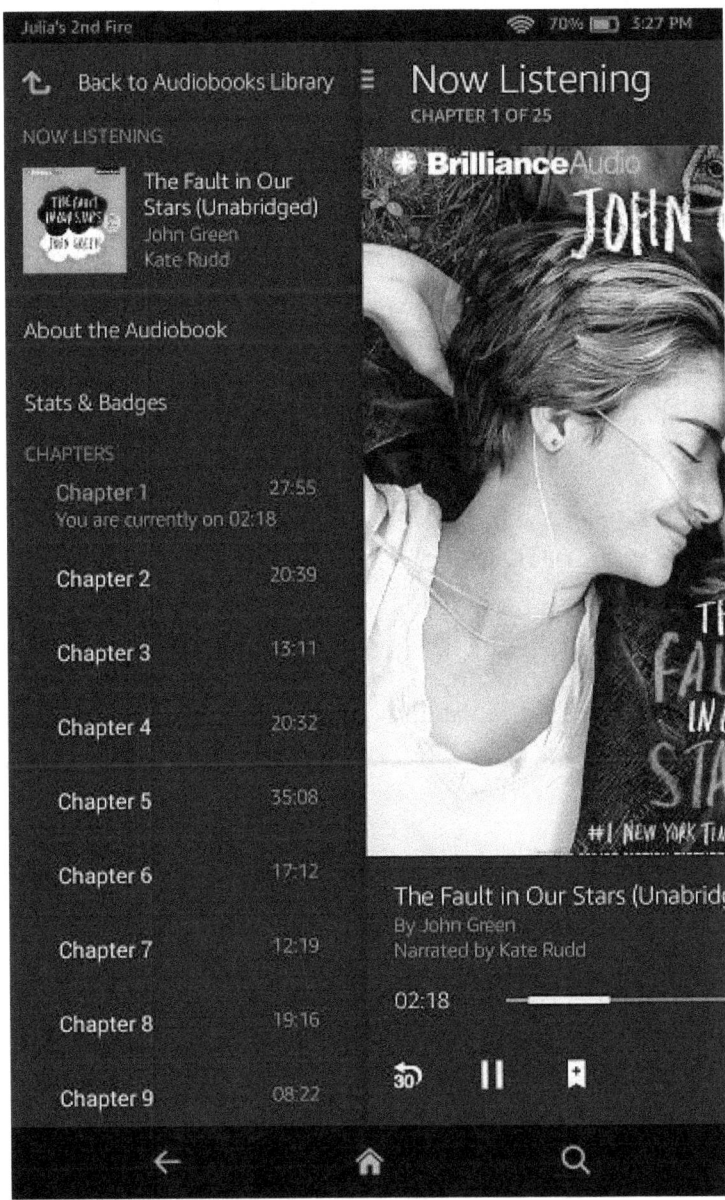

*Figure 7: List of Chapters*

# 4. Reading an eBook while Listening to the Companion Audiobook

The Kindle Fire HD 6 allows you to listen to an audiobook while reading the companion Kindle eBook. Make sure that you own both the audiobook and the companion Kindle eBook before proceeding. Refer to *"Buying an eBook on the Kindle Fire HD 6"* on page 26 to learn how to purchase an eBook. Refer to *"Purchasing an Audiobook"* on page 77 to learn how to purchase an audiobook. To listen to an audiobook while reading an eBook, touch anywhere on the page (except for a link), and then touch the ▶ icon in the lower left-hand corner of the screen. The audiobook turns on, and words are highlighted in gray as they are read. Refer to *"Reading eBooks and Periodicals"* on page 53 to learn more about eBooks.

# 5. Archiving and Restoring an Audiobook

An audiobook can be removed from your Kindle Fire HD 6 and placed in the Amazon Cloud where it does not take up space on your device. An archived audiobook is retrievable using the wireless connection. To archive an audiobook:

1. Touch **Audiobooks**. The Audiobooks library appears.
2. Touch and hold the audiobook that you wish archive. The item menu appears, as shown in **Figure 8**.
3. Touch **Remove from Device**. The selected audiobook is archived. You can always download the audiobook back to your device by touching **Cloud** at the top of the Audiobook library, and then touching the cover of the audiobook.

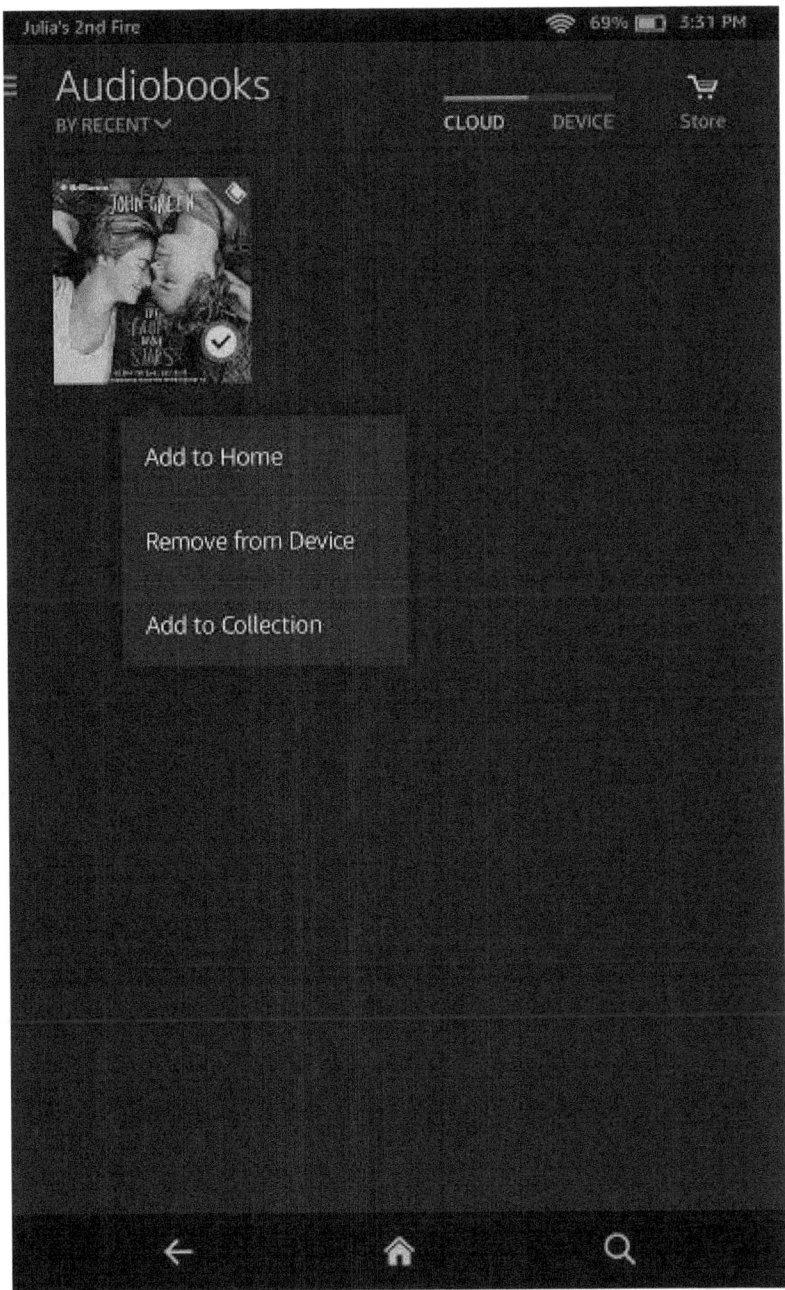

*Figure 8: Item Menu*

# Managing Movies and TV Shows

## Table of Contents

## 1. Browsing Movies and TV Shows in the Video Store

You can browse the Amazon library of movies and TV shows right on your Kindle Fire HD 6. To browse movies and TV shows:

1. Touch **Shop** at the top of the Home screen. The Kindle Store opens, as shown in **Figure 1**.
2. Touch **Videos** on the left-hand side of the screen. The Video store opens, as shown in **Figure 2**.
3. Touch **Search** at the top of the screen. The virtual keyboard appears.

4. Enter the name of a movie or TV show, and touch the ![search] button. A list of matching results appears, as shown in **Figure 3**. You can also browse by category by touching the left edge of the screen and sliding your finger to the right.

*Figure 1: Kindle Store*

*Figure 2: Video Store*

*Figure 3: List of Matching Results*

## 2. Buying or Renting a Movie

You can purchase or rent movies from the Amazon library using your Kindle Fire HD 6. To buy or rent a movie:

1. Find the movie that you wish to buy or rent. Refer to *"Browsing Movies and TV Shows in the Video Store"* on page 88 to learn how.
2. Touch the movie thumbnail. The Movie description appears, as shown in **Figure 4**.
3. Touch **Rent** or **Buy**. The orange button turns green.
4. Touch **Rent** or **Buy** again. The movie is purchased and downloaded to your Kindle Fire HD 6. Touch **Download** to load the movie onto your Kindle Fire HD 6 or **Watch Now** to stream it using a Wi-Fi connection.

*Note: When renting a movie, you have 30 days to begin to watch it, with the movie expiring 24 hours after you touch 'Watch Now' or 'Download'. Downloading a movie to the Kindle Fire HD 6 allows you to watch it while not connected to the internet. However, you may only download the movie to one device at a time and cannot stream it on another device registered to your Amazon account while it is loaded onto the Kindle Fire HD 6.*

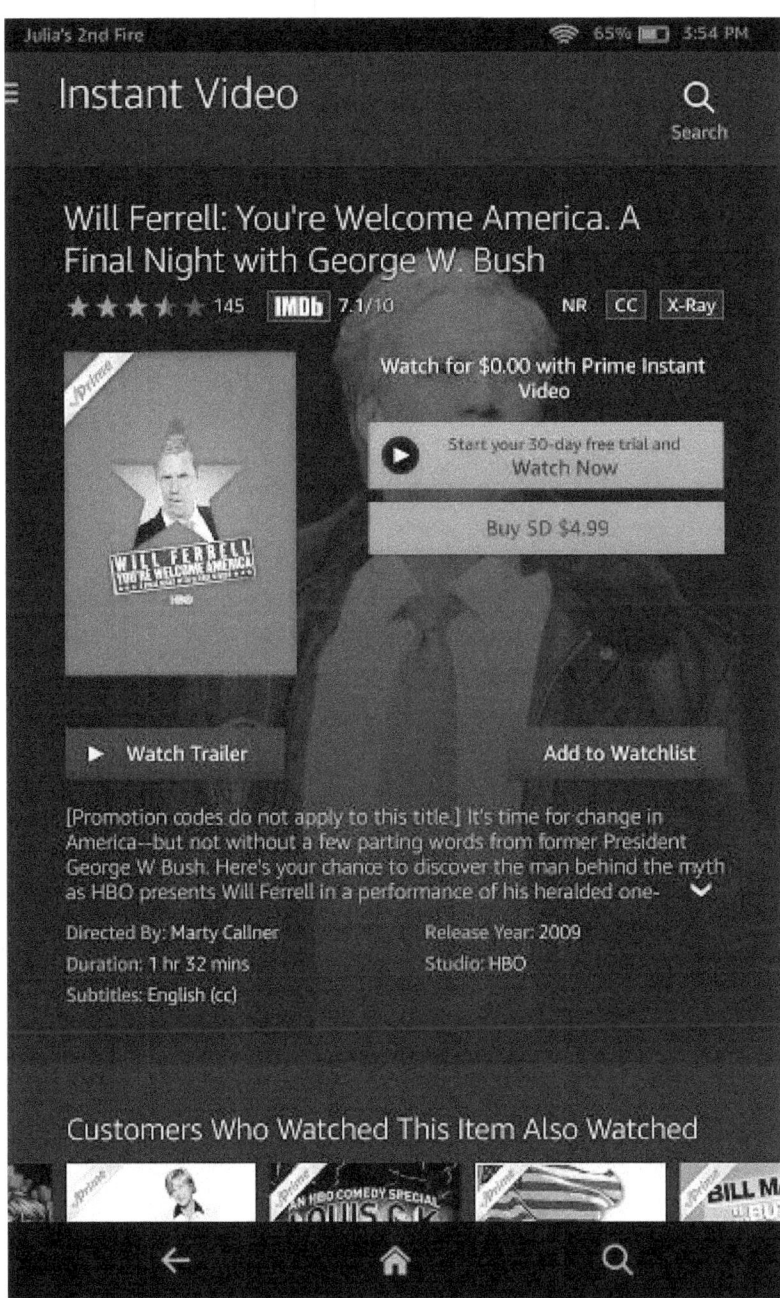

*Figure 4: Movie Description*

# 3. Buying or Renting a TV Show

You can purchase or rent TV shows from the Amazon library using your Kindle Fire HD 6. To buy or rent a TV show:

1. Find the TV show that you wish to buy or rent. Refer to *"Browsing Movies and TV Shows in the Video Store"* on page **88** to learn how.
2. Touch the movie thumbnail. The TV Show description and a list of episodes appear, as shown in **Figure 5**.
3. Touch the **Buy Episode** or **Buy Season** to purchase the corresponding item. The orange 'Buy' button turns green.
4. Touch **Buy Episode** or **Buy Season** again. The episode or season is purchased. Touch **Watch** to stream the TV show.

*Note: Downloading a TV show to the Kindle Fire HD 6 allows you to watch it while not connected to the internet. However, you may only download the TV show to one device at a time and cannot stream it on another device registered to your Amazon account while it is loaded onto the Kindle Fire HD 6.*

*Figure 5: TV Show Description*

# 4. Playing a Movie or TV Show

The Kindle Fire HD 6 can play movies and TV shows from the library. To play a movie or TV show:

1. Touch **Videos** at the top of the Home screen. The Video store opens.
2. Touch **Library** in the upper right-hand corner of the screen. The Video library opens, as shown in **Figure 6**.
3. Touch **Movies** or **TV**. The corresponding library opens.
4. Touch a video thumbnail. The video description appears, as shown in **Figure 7**.
5. Touch **Watch Now**. The video begins to play.
6. Use the following tips to control the playback of a video:

   - **Controlling the Volume -** Use the volume buttons to control the volume. Refer to *"Button Layout"* on page 7 to learn where the volume buttons are located.
   - **Pausing and Resuming the Video -** Touch the screen anywhere. The Video controls appear, as shown in **Figure 8**. Touch the button. The video is paused. Touch the button. Video playback resumes.
   - **Rewinding by Ten Seconds -** Touch the screen anywhere. The Video controls appear. Touch the button. The video rewinds by ten seconds and resumes playing. You can also rewind while the movie is paused. When you touch the button, the movie will resume from the new location.
   - **Navigating to a Specific Location -** Touch the screen anywhere. The Video controls appear. Touch the on the bar and drag it to the desired location. The video skips to the location and continues to play.

*Note: If a video has not downloaded or buffered completely, you will not be able to navigate to a location that has not yet finished loading.*

*Figure 6: Video Library*

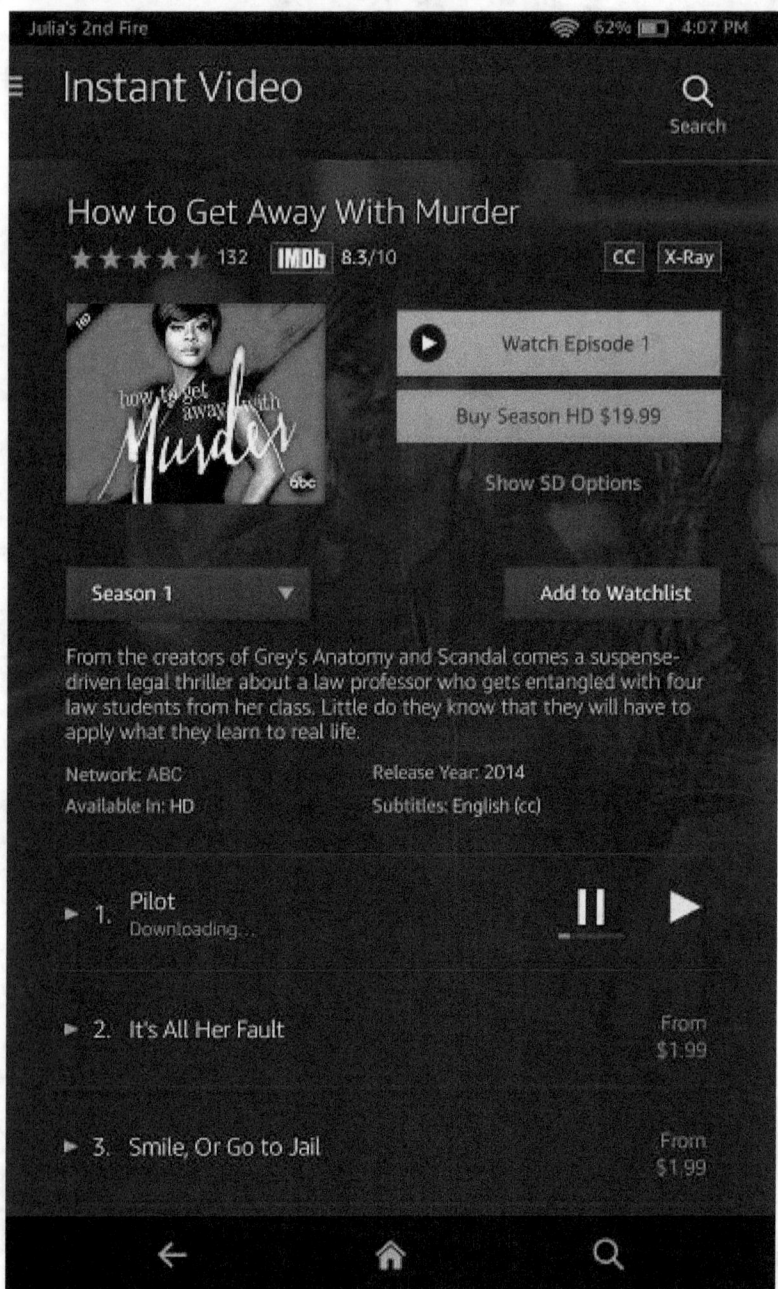

*Figure 7: Video Description*

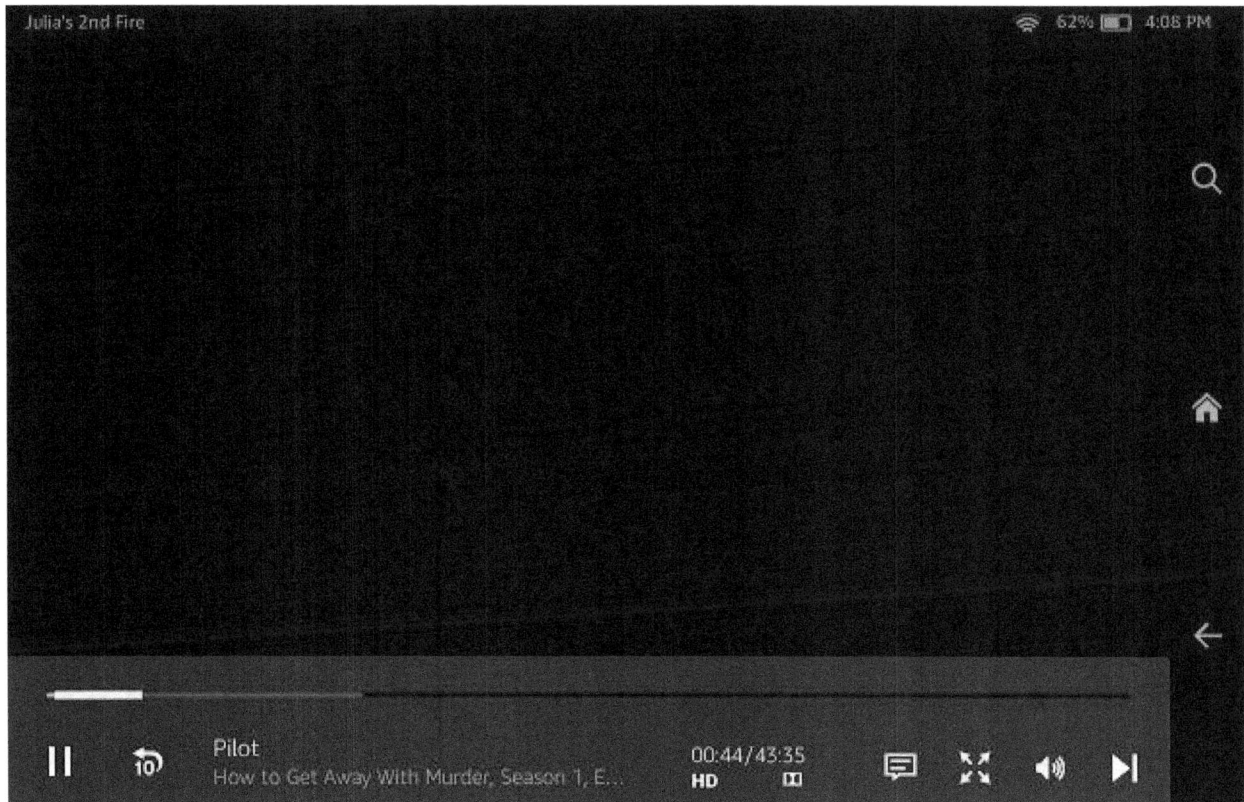

*Figure 8: Video Controls*

# 5. Using X-Ray for Movies

While watching a movie, you can use X-Ray to look up the names of the actors that are in the current scene, as well as the song that is currently playing. To use X-Ray for movies, touch the screen anywhere while a movie is playing. A list of actors and the current song, if any, appears on the left-hand side of the screen. Touch the name of an actor to look up his or her biography and filmography. Touch the name of the song to view a list of all songs that can be heard in the movie. Touch **Jump to Scene** if you wish to skip to a scene where a particular song is played.

# 6. Archiving Movies and TV Shows

Any movies or TV shows that are stored on your Kindle Fire HD 6 can be archived and stored in the Amazon Cloud where they do not take up space on your device. To archive movies and TV shows:

1. Touch **Videos** at the top of the Library. The Video store opens.
2. Touch **Library** in the upper right-hand corner of the screen. The Video library opens.
3. Touch **Movies** or **TV** to find the video that you wish to archive. The corresponding video library opens.
4. Touch and hold a video thumbnail. The Video menu appears.
5. Touch **Delete Download**. The video is archived in the Amazon Cloud.

# 7. Importing Movies from an Outside Source Using Your PC or Mac

Movies that you have purchased or downloaded elsewhere can be imported to the Kindle Fire HD 6. Supported video formats include MP4, 3GP, and VP8. To import movies:

1. Connect the Kindle Fire HD 6 to your computer using the provided USB cable.
2. Open **My Computer** on a PC and double-click the 'KINDLE' removable drive. On a Mac, you will need to download the Android File Transfer utility, which can be found at **https://www.android.com/filetransfer**. The Kindle Folders open on a PC, as shown in **Figure 9**, or on a Mac, as shown in **Figure 10**.
3. Double-click the **Movies** folder. The Video folder opens.
4. Drag and drop a video into the Video folder. The video is copied and will appear in the Photos application on your Kindle Fire HD 6, given that it is of the correct format.

*Note: To access the transferred video, touch **Photos** at the top of the screen, touch **All**, and then touch **Videos**.*

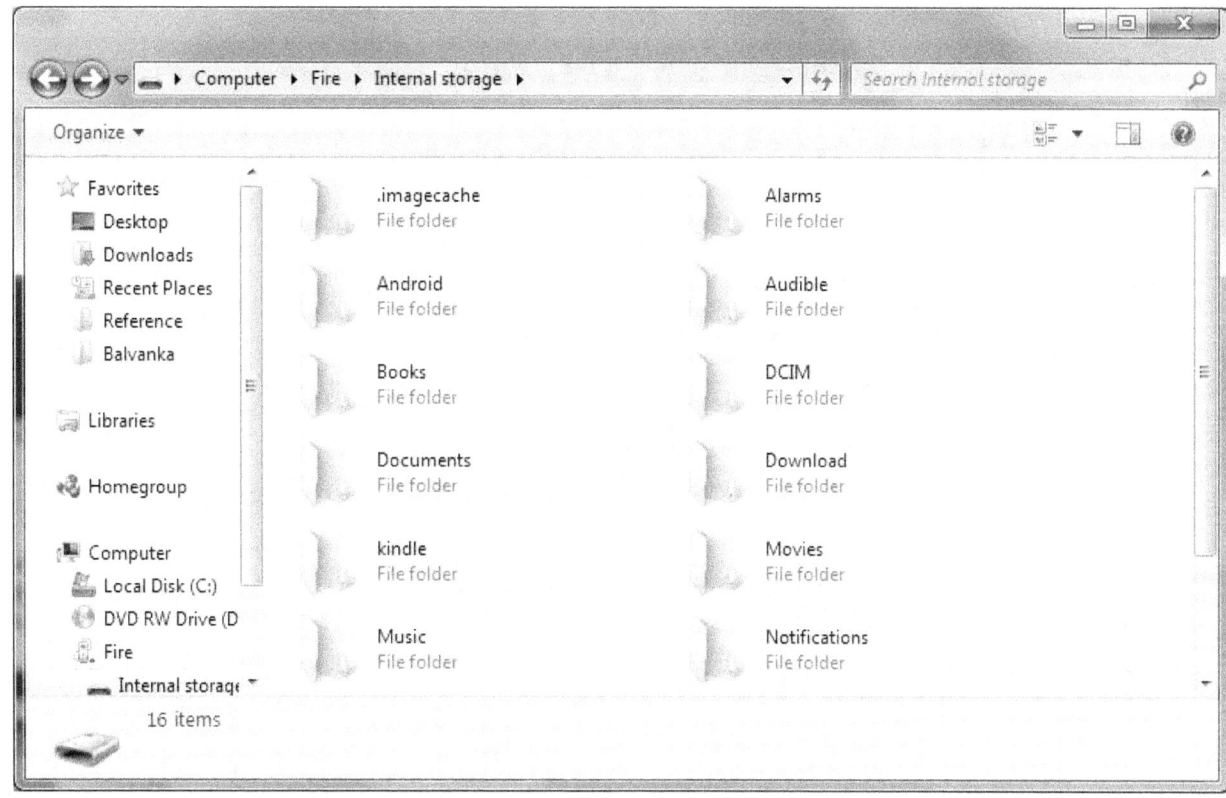

*Figure 9: Kindle Folders on a PC*

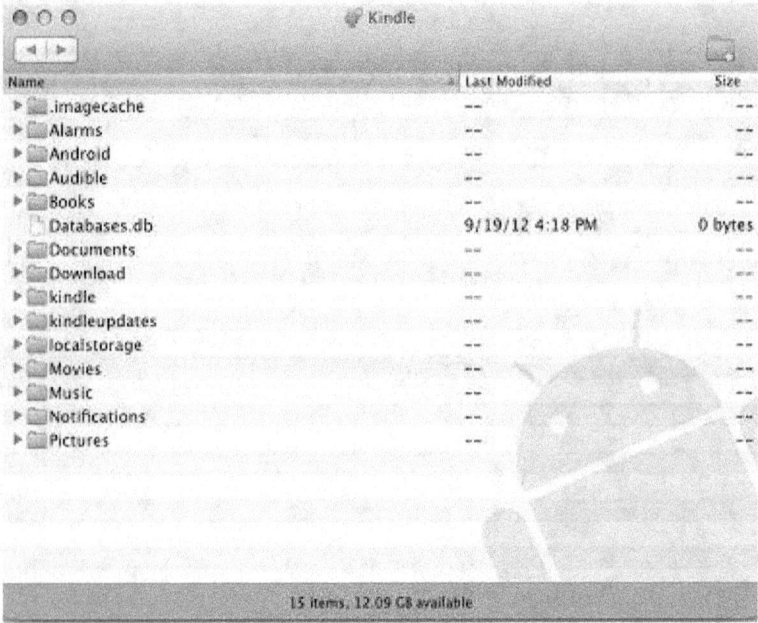

*Figure 10: Kindle Folders on a Mac*

# Managing Music

## Table of Contents

## 1. Browsing the Music Store

You can browse the Amazon music store right on your Kindle Fire HD 6. To browse music:

1.  Touch **Shop** at the top of the Home screen. The Kindle Store opens, as shown in **Figure 1**.
2.  Touch **Music** on the left-hand side of the screen. The Music store opens, as shown in **Figure 2**.
3.  Touch **Search** at the top of the screen. The virtual keyboard appears.
4.  Enter the name of an artist, song, or album, and touch the [icon] button. A list of matching results appears, as shown in **Figure 3**.
5.  Touch a result in the list. The music description appears, as shown in **Figure 4** (album description). You can also touch an artist's name to see all available albums by that artist.

*Note: Refer to* "Buying a Song or Album" *on page 108 to learn how to purchase a song or album.*

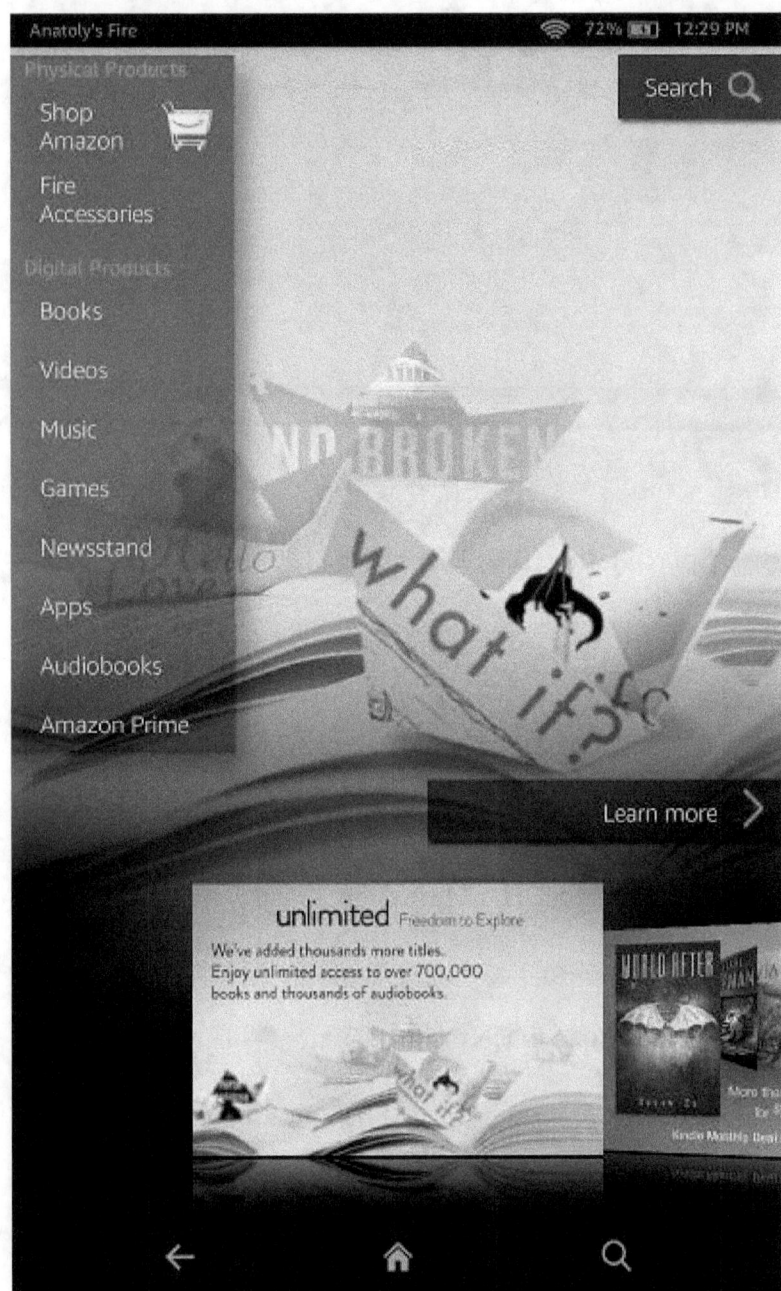

*Figure 1: Kindle Store*

*Figure 2: Music Store*

*Figure 3: Matching Music Results*

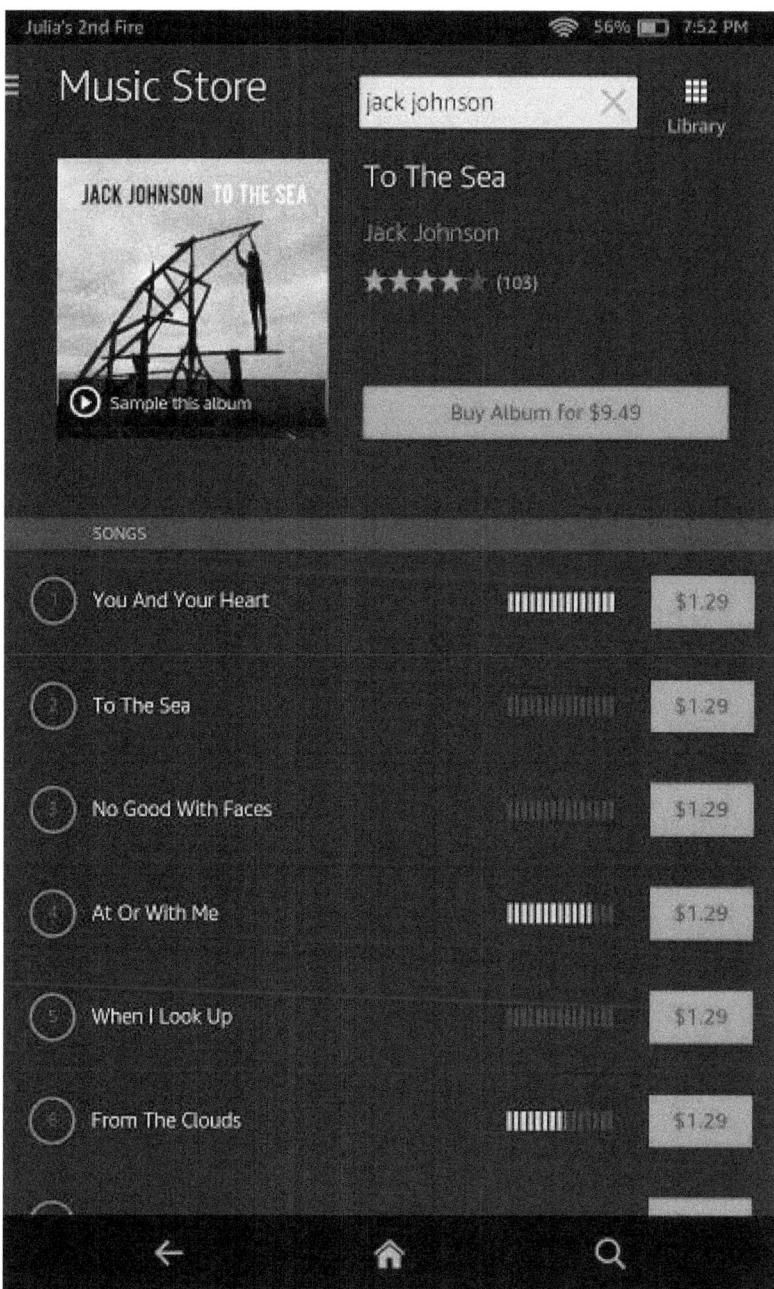

*Figure 4: Album Description*

# 2. Buying a Song or Album

You can purchase music from the Amazon store using your Kindle Fire HD 6. To buy a song or album:

1. Find the album containing the song that you wish to download. Refer to *"Browsing the Music Store"* on page 103 to learn how.

2. Touch the name of the album. The list of songs appears. Touch the button next to a song to preview it.
3. Touch **Buy Album**. 'Buy Now' appears.
4. Touch **Buy Now**. The album is purchased and stored in your Amazon Cloud. To purchase a single song, touch the price of the song, and then touch **Buy**.

*Note: Refer to "Tips and Tricks" on page 252 to learn how to set the Kindle Fire HD 6 to automatically store a song to the cloud or device when buying music.*

# 3. Playing a Song

You can play music using your Kindle Fire HD 6. To play a song:

1. Touch **Music** at the top of the Home screen . The Music library appears, as shown in **Figure 5**.
2. Touch **Cloud** or **Device**, depending on where your music is stored. The corresponding storage location opens.
3. Touch an album cover. A list of the songs in the album appears.
4. Touch a song. The song begins to play, as shown in **Figure 6**. The next song in the album automatically plays when the current one has ended.

*Note: To add an entire artist or album to the 'Now Playing' list, touch and hold the corresponding item and touch **Add to Playlist**.*

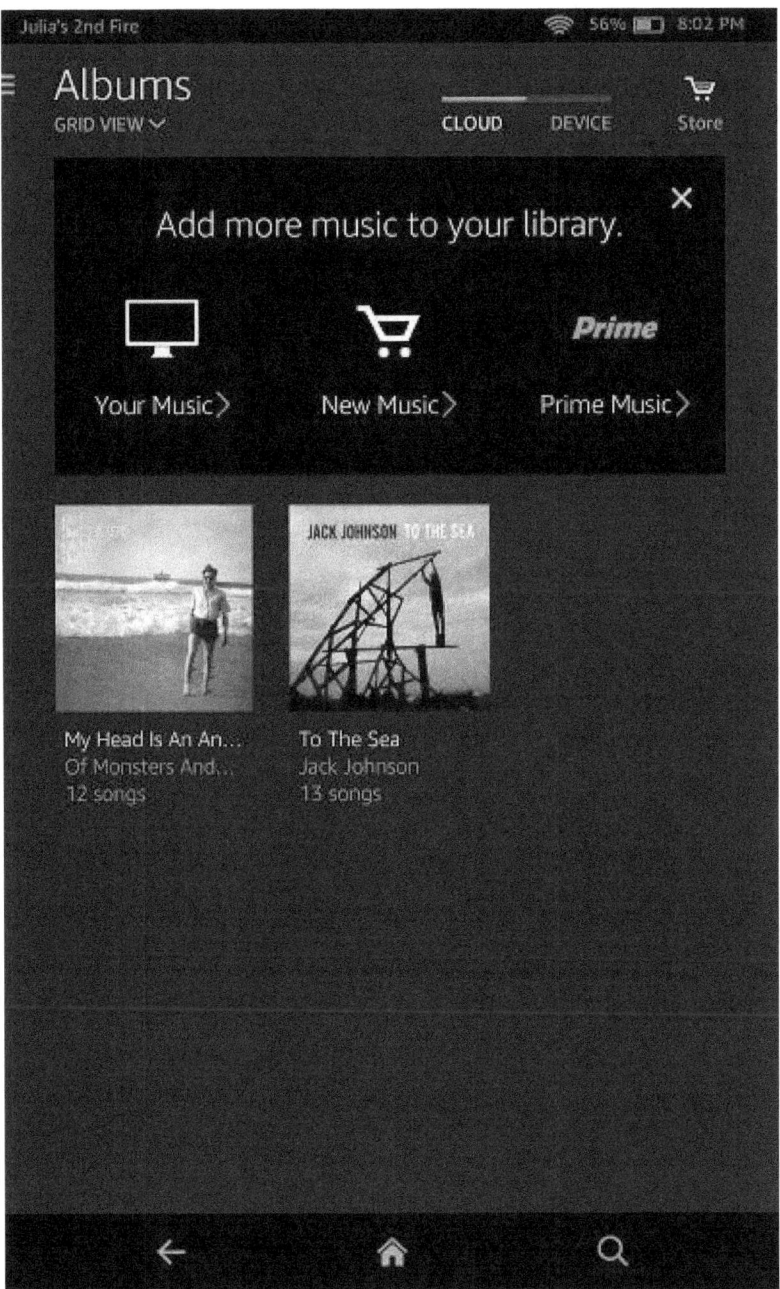

*Figure 5: Music Library*

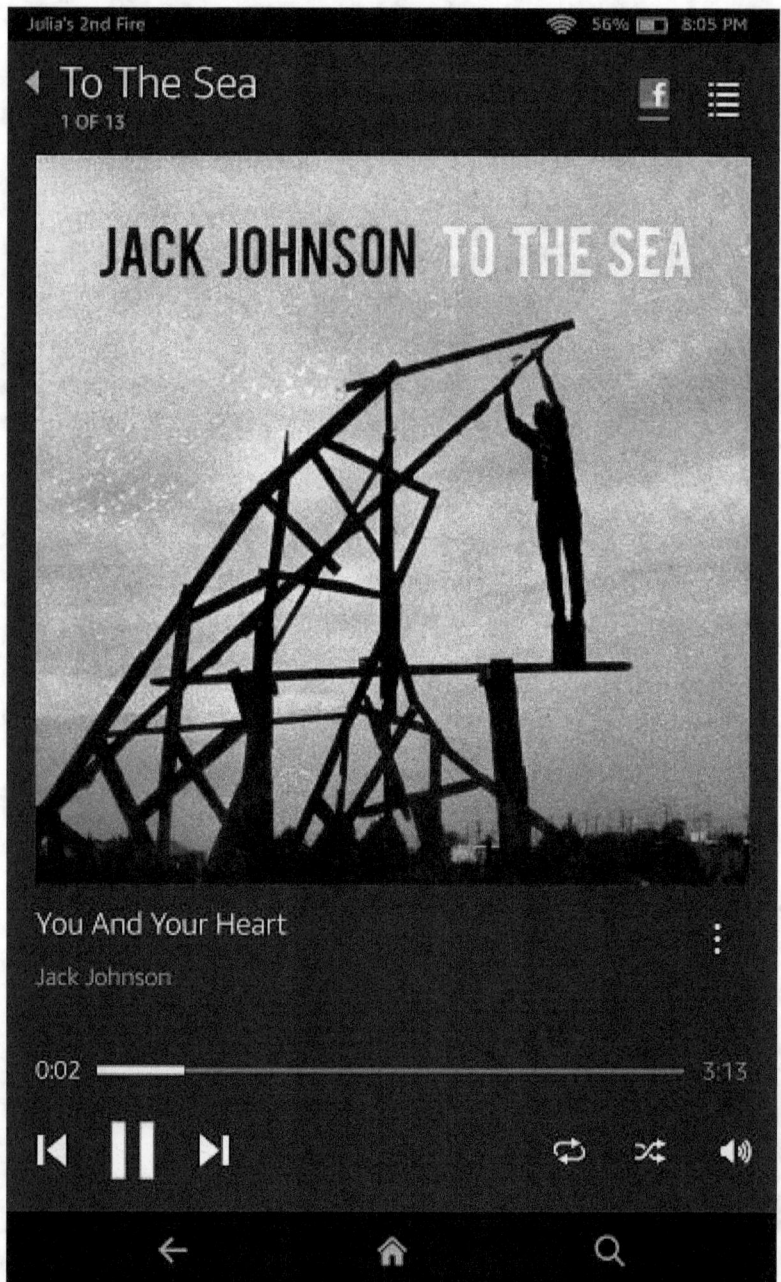

*Figure 6: Song Playing*

# 4. Controlling the Music

While a song is playing, touch one of the following buttons to perform the associated action:

- Pauses the current song.

- Resumes the current song when it is paused.

- Shuffles the songs in the current playlist or album.

- Repeats the current playlist or album. If only one song is enqueued, the song will repeat.

- Navigates to the beginning of the current song. If already at the beginning of a song, touching this button will navigate to the previous song.

- Skips the current song. If more than one song is enqueued, the next song begins to play.

**Name of the album (upper left-hand corner)** - Returns to the album contents. Touch the name of the song at the bottom of the screen to return to the 'Now Playing' screen at any time.

*Note: Refer to "Tips and Tricks" on page 252 to learn how to make music controls appear on the Lock screen.*

# 5. Creating and Editing a Playlist

Playlists can be created and edited right on the Kindle Fire HD 6. You can only create a playlist with the music on your device.
To create a playlist:

1. Touch **Music** at the top of the Home screen. The Music library appears
2. Touch **Device** at the top of the screen. The music stored on your device appears.
3. Touch the left edge of the screen and slide your finger to the right. The Music menu appears, as shown in **Figure 7**.
4. Touch **Playlists**. The existing playlists appear, as shown in **Figure 8**.
5. Touch the ➕ icon at the top of the screen. The New Playlist window appears, as shown in **Figure 9**.
6. Enter a name for the new playlist and touch **Save**. The new playlist is created and a list of songs appears.
7. Touch the ⊕ button next to a song. The song is added to the playlist. Touch the ⊖ icon to remove a song from the playlist.

8. Touch **Done** in the upper right-hand corner of the screen. The playlist is saved.

To edit a playlist:

1. Follow steps 1-4 above. The existing playlists appear.
2. Touch a playlist. The songs within the playlist appear.
3. Touch **Edit**. The Playlist Editing screen appears, as shown in **Figure 10**.
4. Use the following tips to edit a playlist:

   - Touch the ⊖ button to the right of a song to remove it from the playlist.
   - Touch **Add Songs** at the top of the screen to add a song to the playlist. A list of songs appears. Touch the ⊕ button next to a song to add it to the playlist.
   - Touch the ☰ icon to the left of a song, and drag it up or down to change the order of the songs.
   - Touch **Rename** to rename the playlist.

5. Touch **Done** in the upper right-hand corner. Your playlist edits are saved.

*Note: You can only create a playlist with music downloaded to your device.*

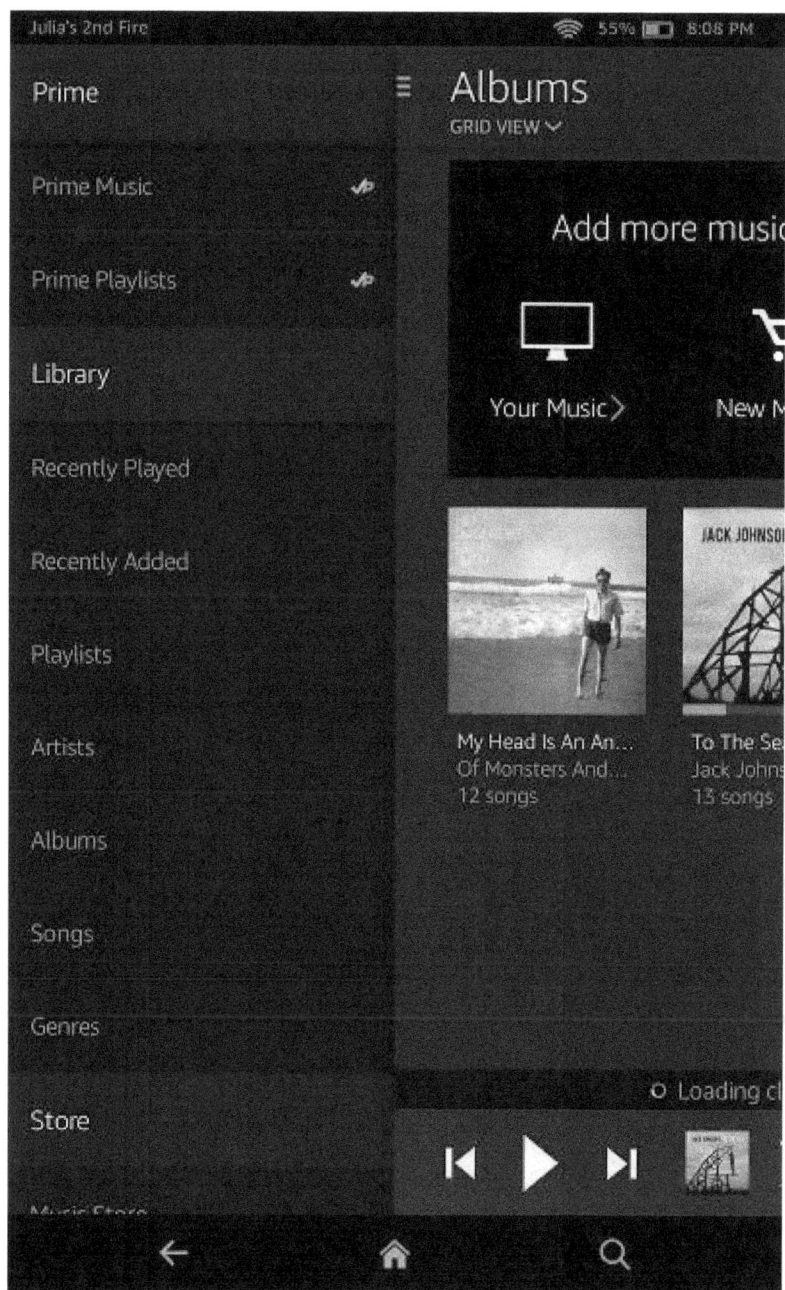

*Figure 7: Music Menu*

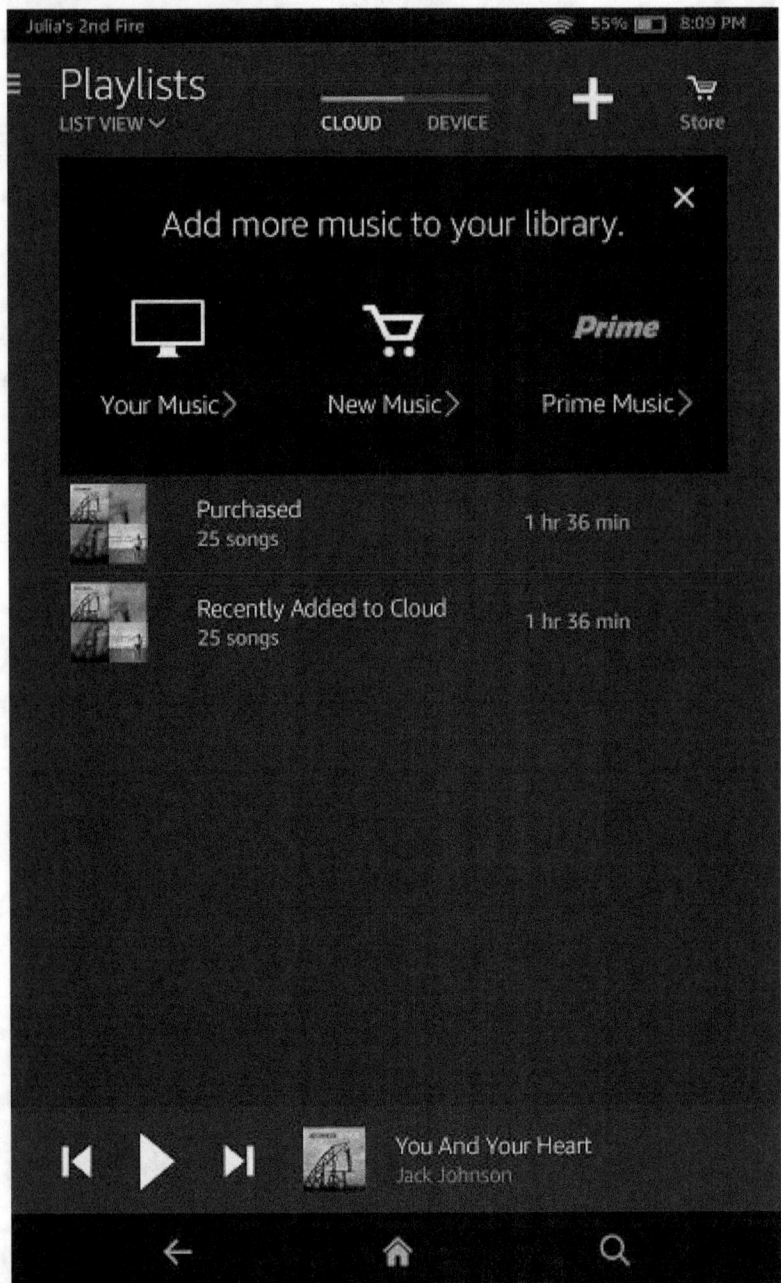

*Figure 8: Existing Playlists*

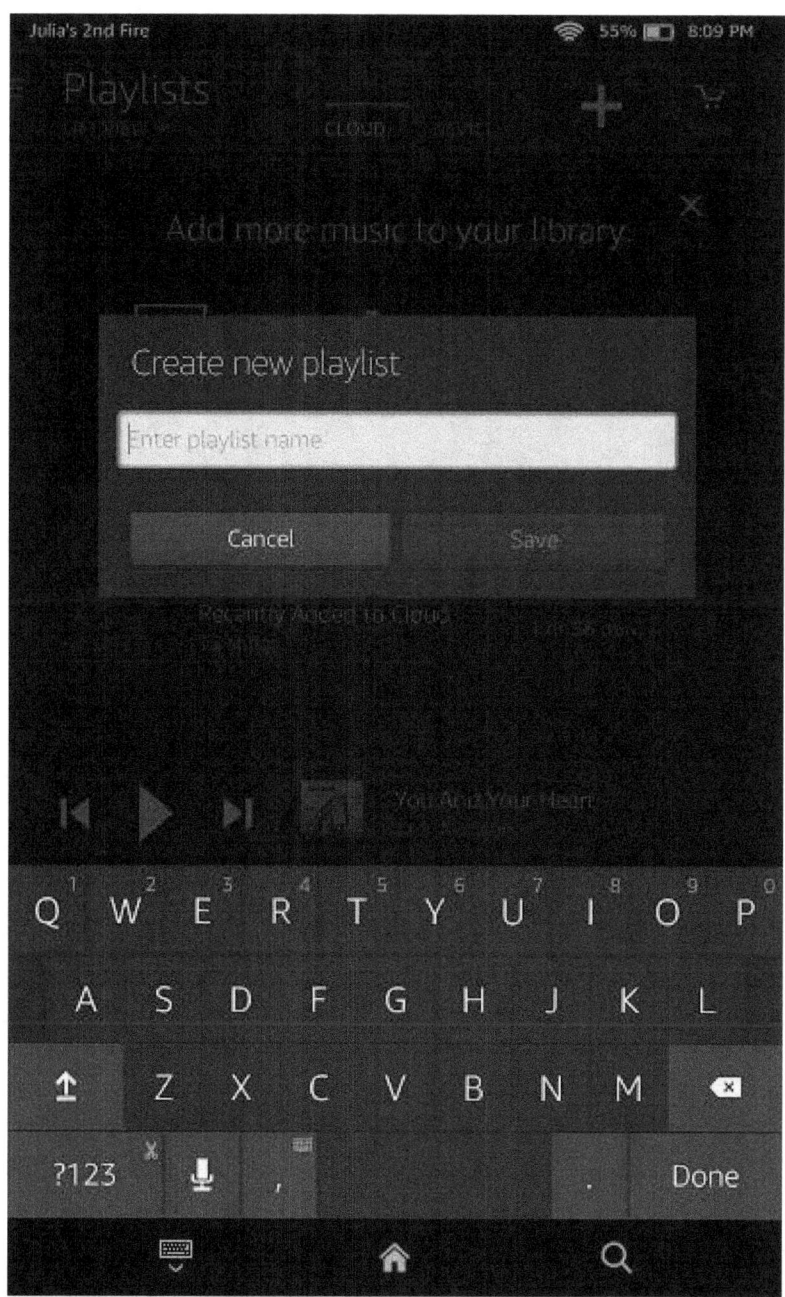

*Figure 9: New Playlist Window*

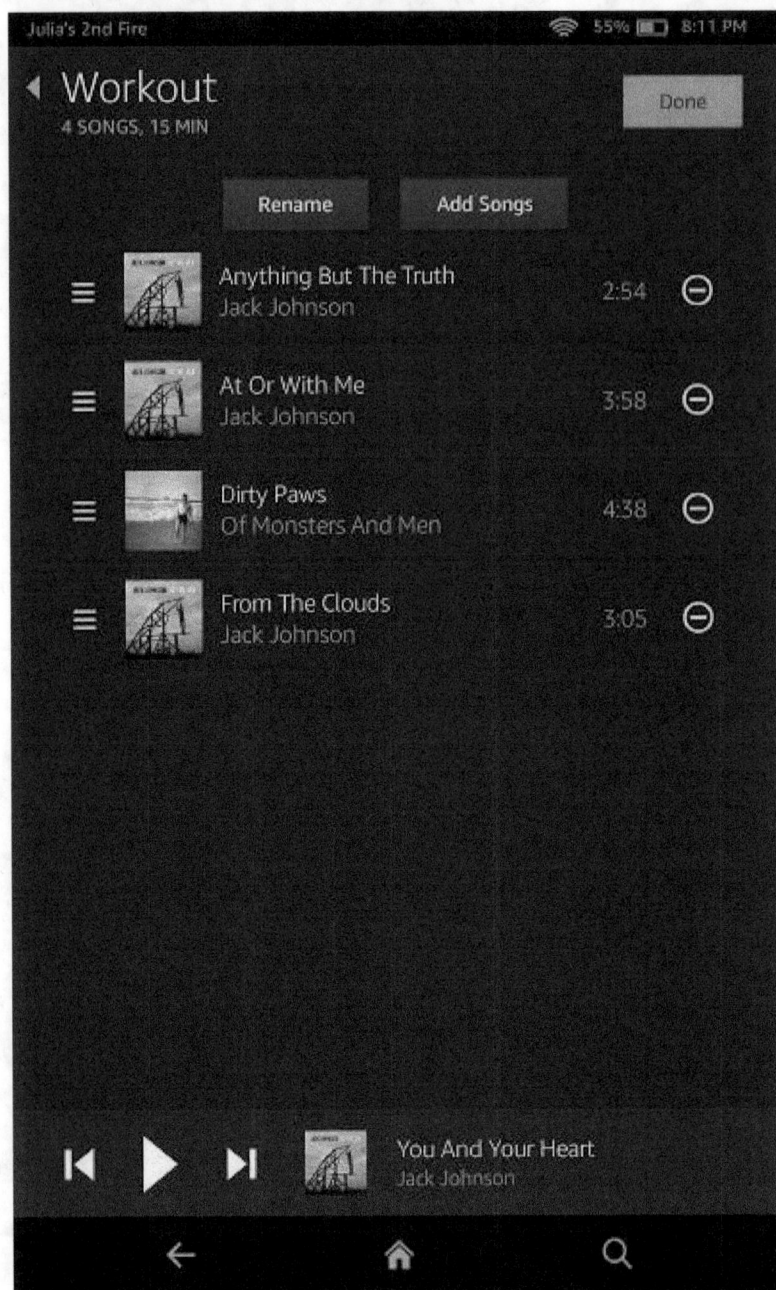

*Figure 10: Playlist Editing Screen*

# 6. Archiving Music

Any music that is stored on your Kindle Fire HD 6 can be removed from your device and stored in the Amazon Cloud. To archive music:

1. Touch **Music** at the top of the Library. The Music library appears
2. Touch **Device**. The music stored on your device appears.
3. Touch and hold an artist, album, or song. The Music Management options appear, as shown in **Figure 11**.
4. Touch **Remove from device**. The selected music is removed from your device and stored in the Cloud.

*Note: Any music purchased from the Amazon store is automatically stored in the Amazon cloud. You will not lose your music when you remove it from your device.*

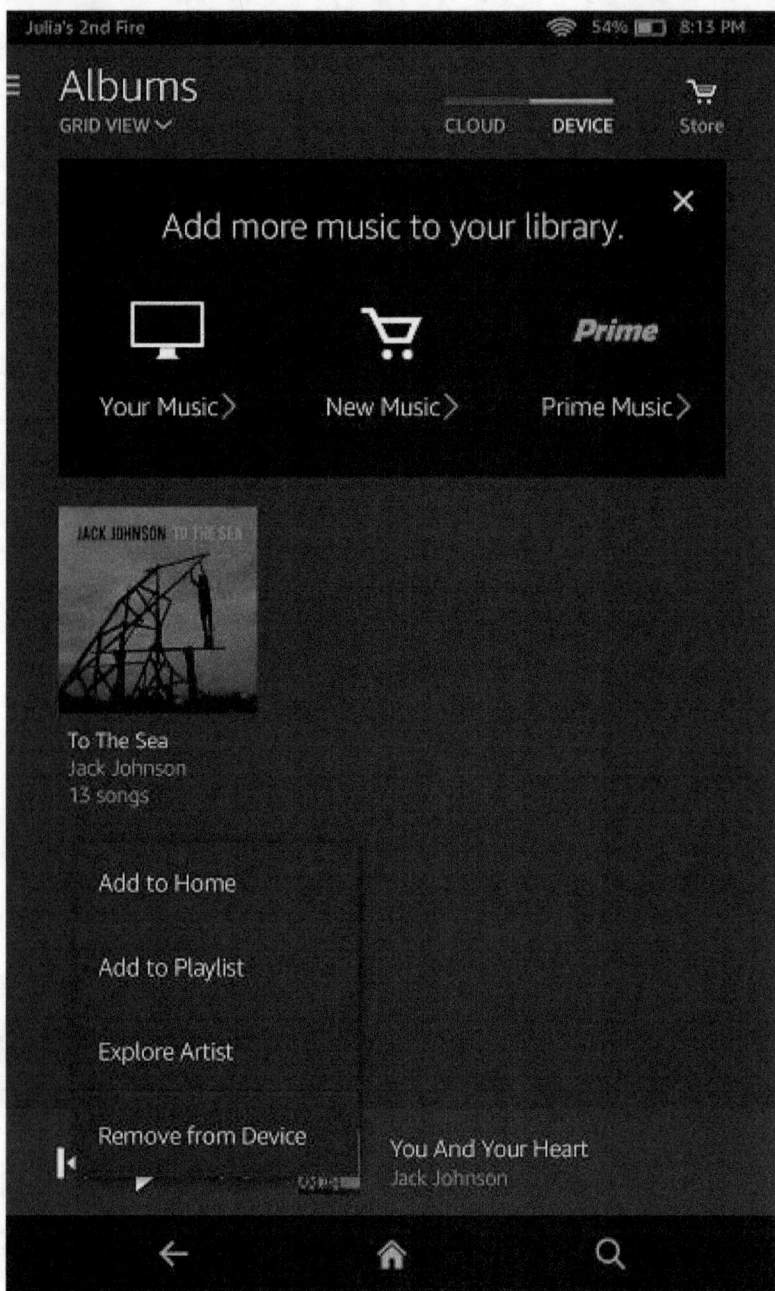

*Figure 11: Music Management Options*

# 7. Importing Music from an Outside Source Using Your PC or Mac

Music that you have purchased or downloaded elsewhere can be imported to the Kindle Fire HD 6. Supported audio formats include non-DRM AAC, MP3, OGG, WAV, and MP4. To import music:

1. Connect the Kindle Fire HD 6 to your computer using the provided USB cable. The USB Connected screen appears.
2. Open **My Computer** on a PC and double-click the 'KINDLE' removable drive. On a Mac, you will need to download the Android File Transfer utility, which can be at **https://www.android.com/filetransfer**. The Kindle Folders open on a PC, as shown in **Figure 12**, or on a Mac, as shown in **Figure 13**.
3. Double-click the **Music** folder. The Music folder opens.
4. Drag and drop a song or folder of music into the Video folder. The music is copied and will appear in the Music library.

*Note: You can also transfer any music from the Kindle Fire HD 6 to your computer by dragging and dropping it from the Music folder to your computer. Even songs purchased in the Amazon Music Store can be transferred.*

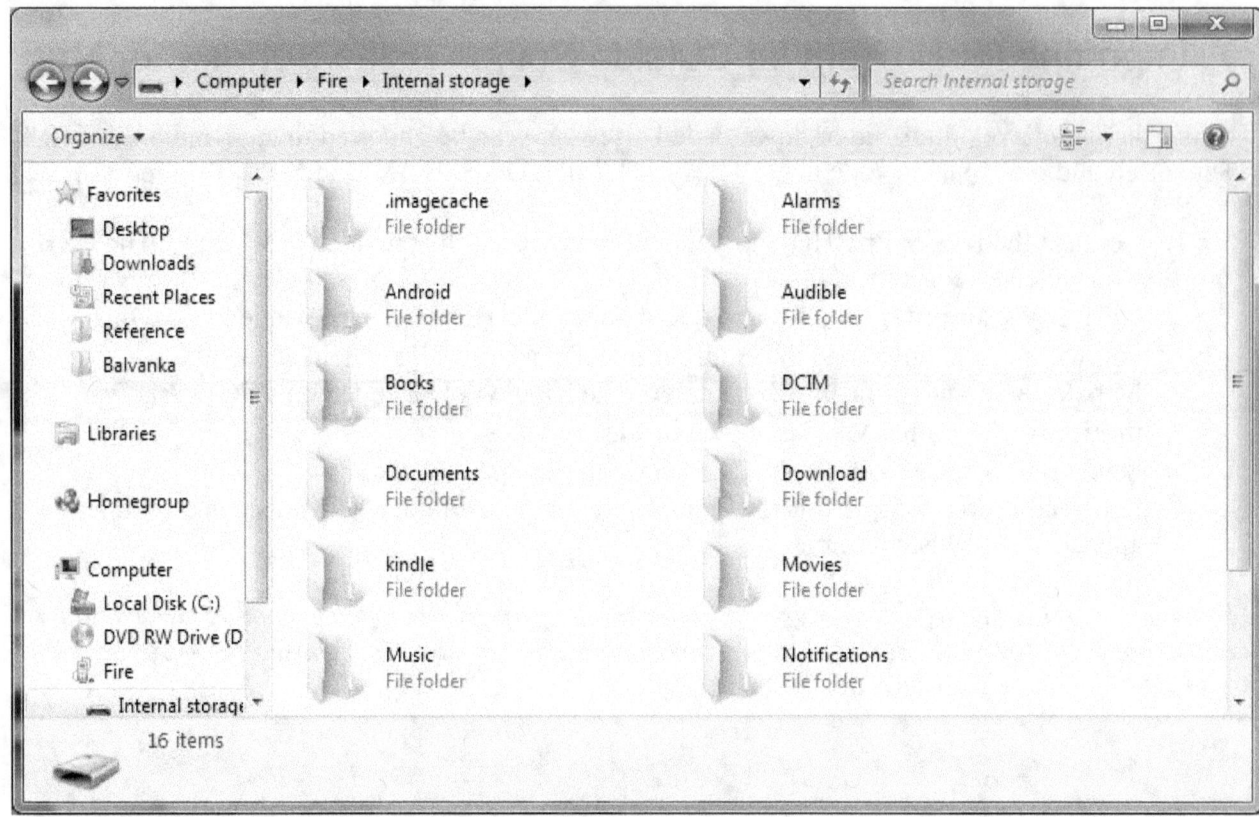

*Figure 12: Kindle Folders on a PC*

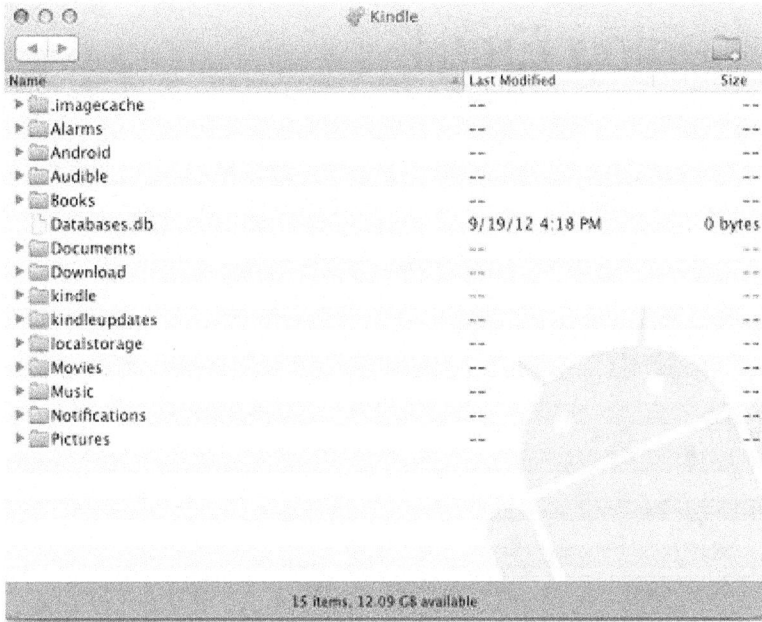

*Figure 13: Kindle Folders on a Mac*

# Managing Email

## Table of Contents

## 1. Adding an Email Account to the Kindle Fire HD 6

Before you can send and receive email using the Email application, you must add an email account to the device. The first time that you open the email application, the device allows you to add an account. To add an email account:

1. Touch the icon at the bottom of the Home screen. The Email application opens, and the Add Account screen appears, as shown in **Figure 1**.
2. Enter your email address and touch **Next**. The password field appears. If you have a Google account, the Google Account screen appears, where you can enter your password.
3. Enter your password and touch **Sign In**. Your email account is added to the Kindle Fire HD 6. You will need to touch **Accept** on the following screen if you are adding a Google account.
4. Touch **Go to Inbox**. Your email inbox appears.

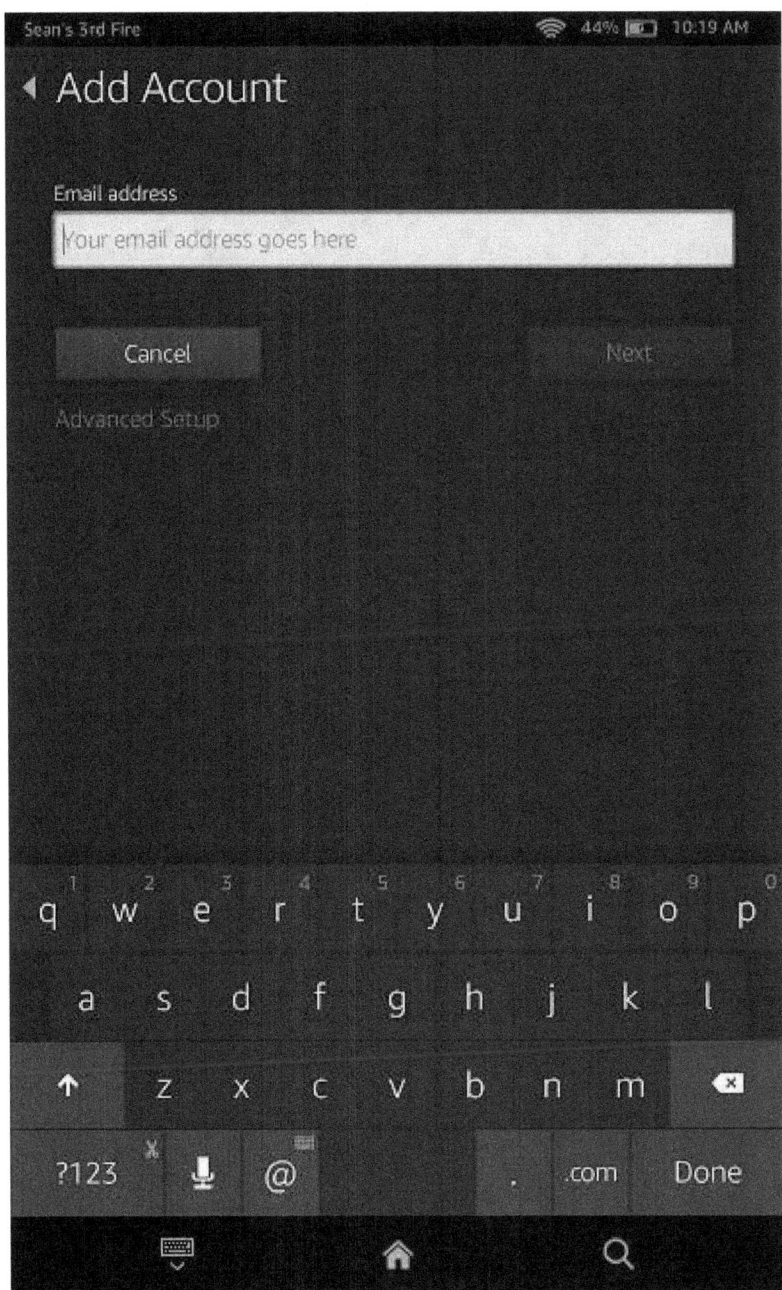

*Figure 1: Add Account Screen*

# 2. Reading Email

You can read the email in your Email inbox on the Kindle Fire HD 6. To read email:

1.  Touch the ![icon] icon. The Email application opens, and the Inbox appears, as shown in **Figure 2**.
2.  Touch an email in the list. The email opens, as shown in **Figure 3**.
3.  Touch the email anywhere and slide your finger to the left or right. The previous or next email appears, respectively.
4.  Touch **Inbox** in the upper left-hand corner of the screen. The Inbox appears.

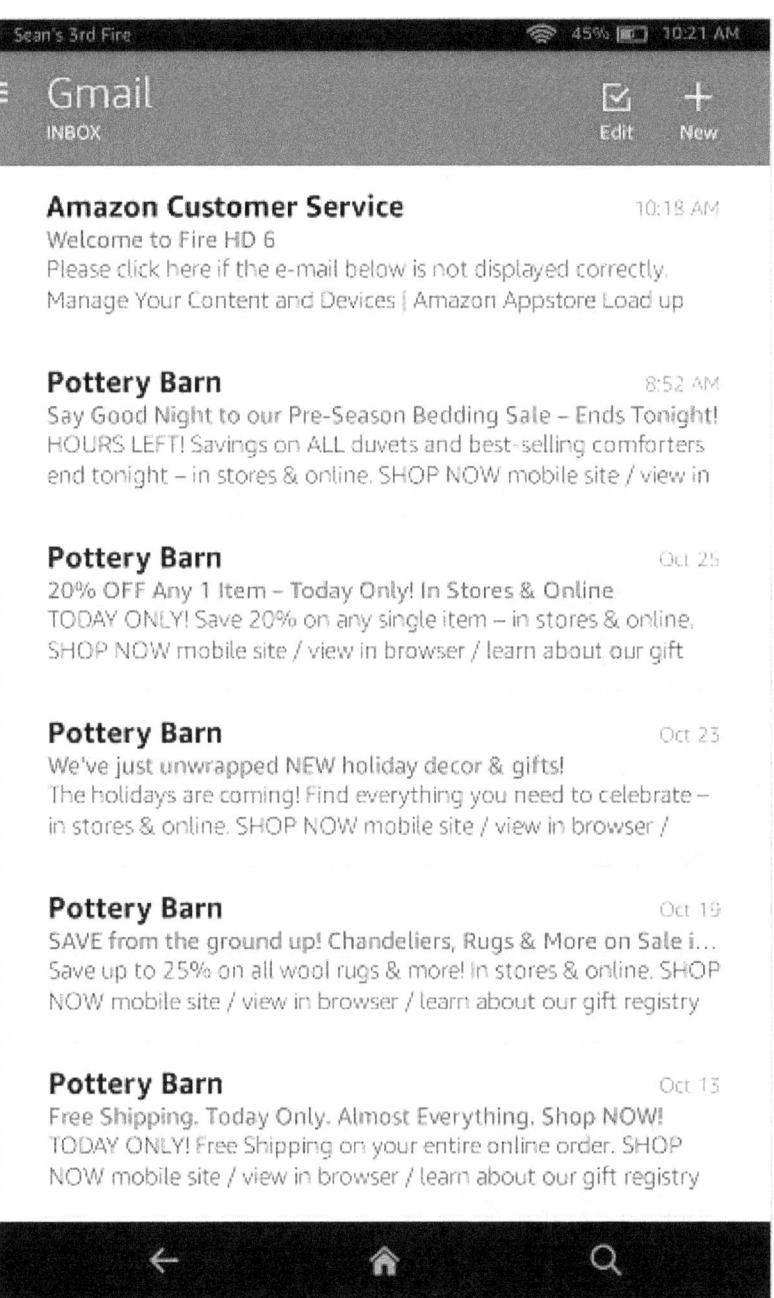

*Figure 2: Email Inbox*

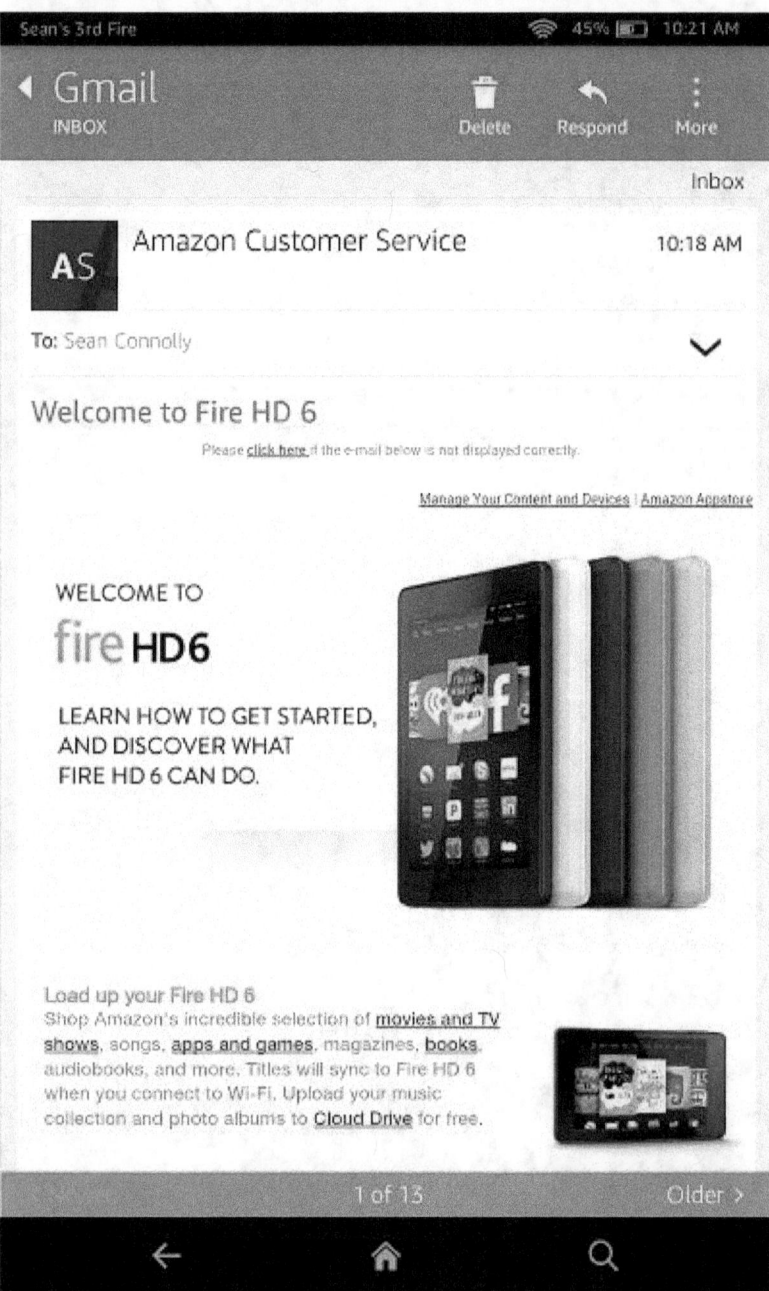

*Figure 3: Email Open*

# 3. Writing an Email

Compose email directly from the Kindle Fire HD 6 using your email account. To write an email:

1. Touch the icon. The Email application opens.
2. Touch the icon in the upper right-hand corner of the screen. The Compose screen appears, as shown in **Figure 4**.
3. Enter the recipient's email address in the 'To:' field. Enter an optional subject. Touch the white space below 'Subject' and enter your message.
4. Touch the button in the upper right-hand corner of the screen. The email is sent.

*Figure 4: Compose Screen*

# 4. Replying to and Forwarding Emails

After receiving an email in your Gmail inbox, a reply can be sent or the email can be forwarded. To reply to or forward an email:

1. Touch the ✉ icon. The Email application opens.
2. Touch the email to which you wish to reply or that you wish to forward. The email opens.
3. Touch **Respond** at the top of the screen, and then touch one of the following to reply to or forward an email, as outlined in **Figure 5**.

   - **Reply** - Creates a reply to the sender of the email.
   - **Reply All** - Creates a reply to the sender of the email, as well as anyone else who received the same email.
   - **Forward** - Creates a new email with the content of the original email copied into it. You will need to enter the recipient's email address.

4. Enter the message in the white space below 'Subject'.

5. Touch the ✈ button in the upper right-hand corner of the screen. The email is sent.

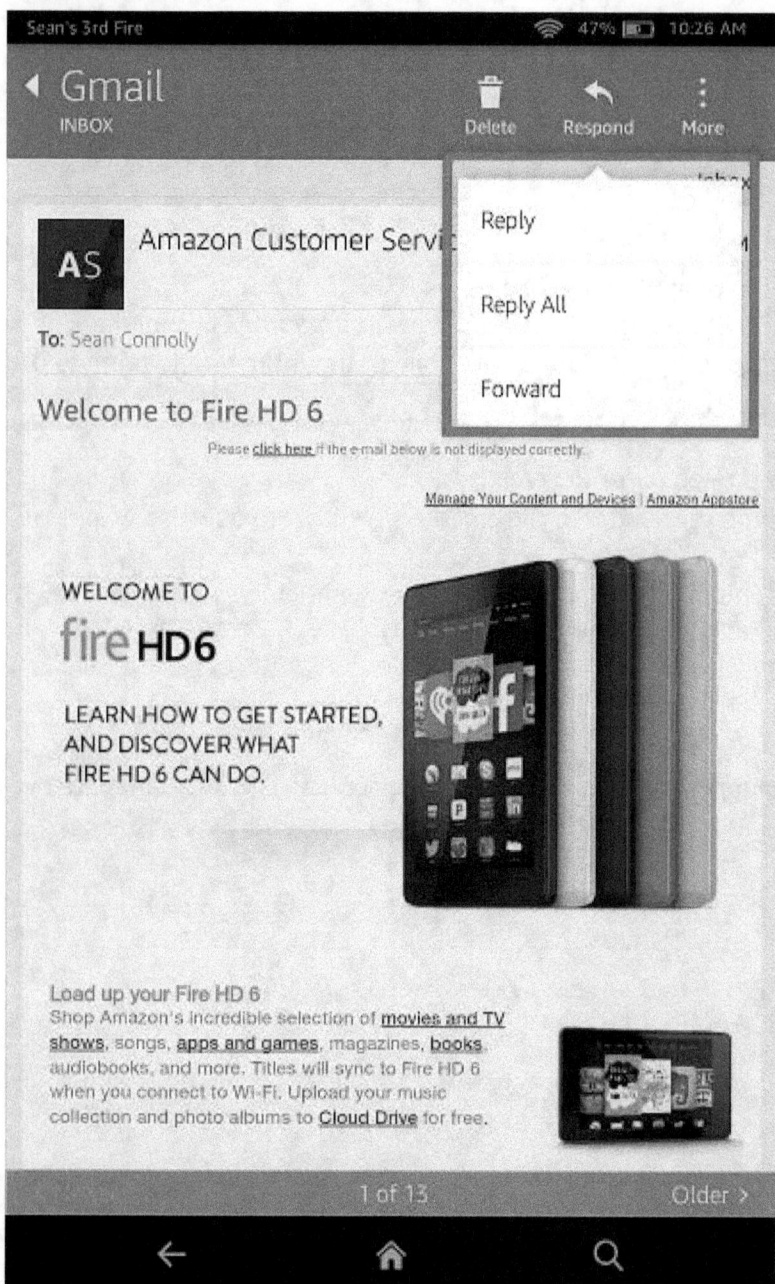

*Figure 5: Reply and Forward Icons Outlined*

# 5. Deleting Emails

Emails can be deleted to free up room in your Inbox. To delete an email:

1. Touch the  icon. The Email application opens.
2. Touch and hold the email that you want to delete. The email is selected.

3. Touch all other emails in the Inbox that you wish to delete. A ✓ box appears next to each selected email.

4. Touch the 🗑 icon at the top of the screen. The selected emails are deleted.

# 6. Moving an Email to a Different Folder

Moving emails between folders, such as 'Work' or 'Personal', can help you to organize your email. To move an email to a different folder:

1. Touch the ✉ icon. The Email application opens.
2. Touch and hold the email that you want to move. The email is selected.
3. Touch all other emails in the Inbox that you wish to move. A ✓ box appears next to each selected email.
4. Touch **Move** at the top of the screen. A list of available folders appears, as shown in **Figure 6**.
5. Touch the name of the folder to which you wish to move the emails. The selected emails are moved to the folder.

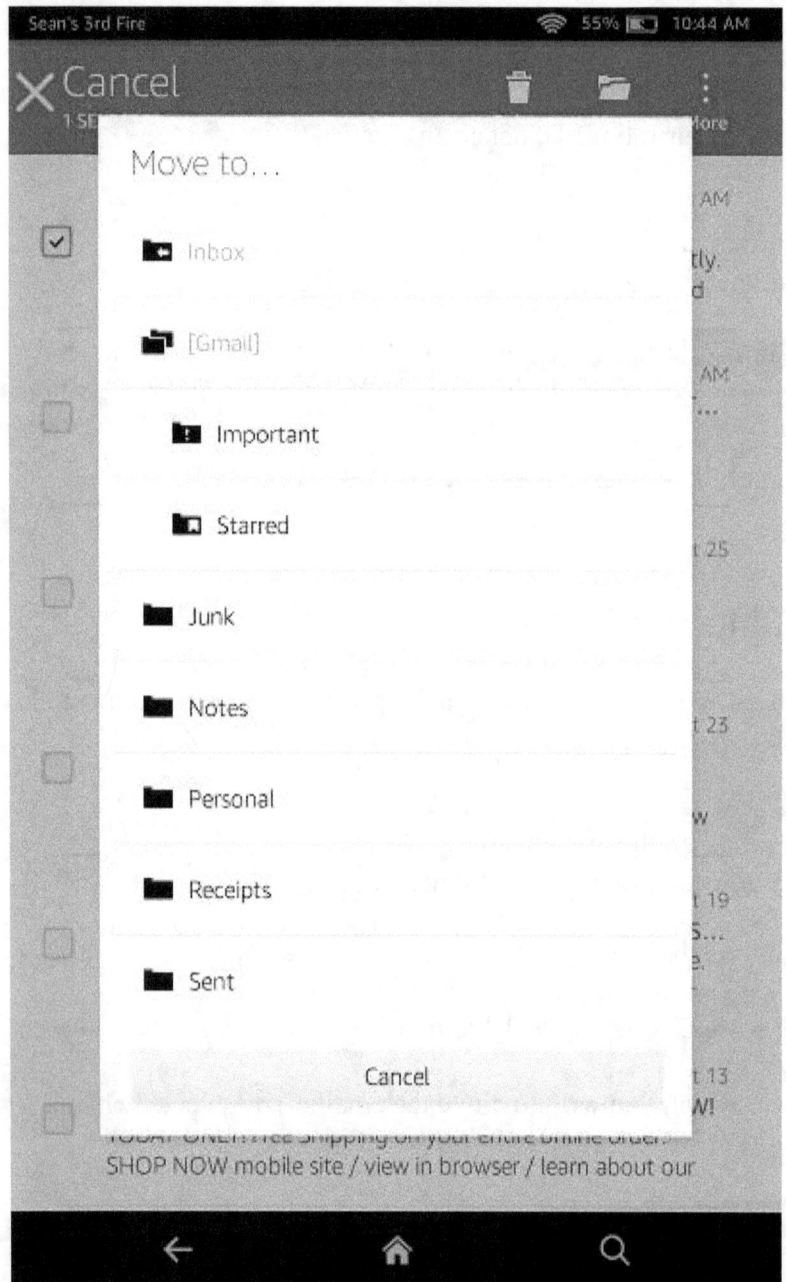

*Figure 6: List of Available Folders*

# 7. Searching the Inbox

To find a message in your Gmail inbox on the Kindle Fire HD 6, use the search function, which searches email addresses, message text, and subject lines. To search the Inbox:

1. Touch the ![icon] icon. The Email application opens.
2. Touch the ![search icon] icon at the bottom of the screen. The Search field appears at the top of the screen.
3. Touch **From** to the left of the Search field and select whether to search by the sender (From), recipient (To), subject of the email, or all text, including the content of the email. The search criteria is set.
4. Enter a search word or phrase, or the name or email address of a sender. The matching results appear as you type.

*Note: Searching using the 'All' criteria will disable instant search. In this case, touch* **Search** *to start the search.*

# 8. Managing Email Labels

Emails can be classified according to the nature of the message, such as 'work' or 'personal'. To add labels to emails:

1. Touch the ![icon] icon. The Email application opens.
2. Touch and hold the email that you want to label. The email is selected.
3. Touch all other emails in the Inbox that you wish to label. A ![checkmark box] box appears next to each selected email.
4. Touch the ![icon] icon in the upper right-hand corner of the screen. The Inbox menu appears, as shown in **Figure 7**.
5. Touch **Label**. A list of available labels appears, as shown in **Figure 8**.
6. Touch the ![box] boxes next to the labels that you wish to apply to the message. A ![checkmark] mark appears next to each selected label.
7. Touch **Apply** at the bottom of the screen. The selected labels are applied to the email.

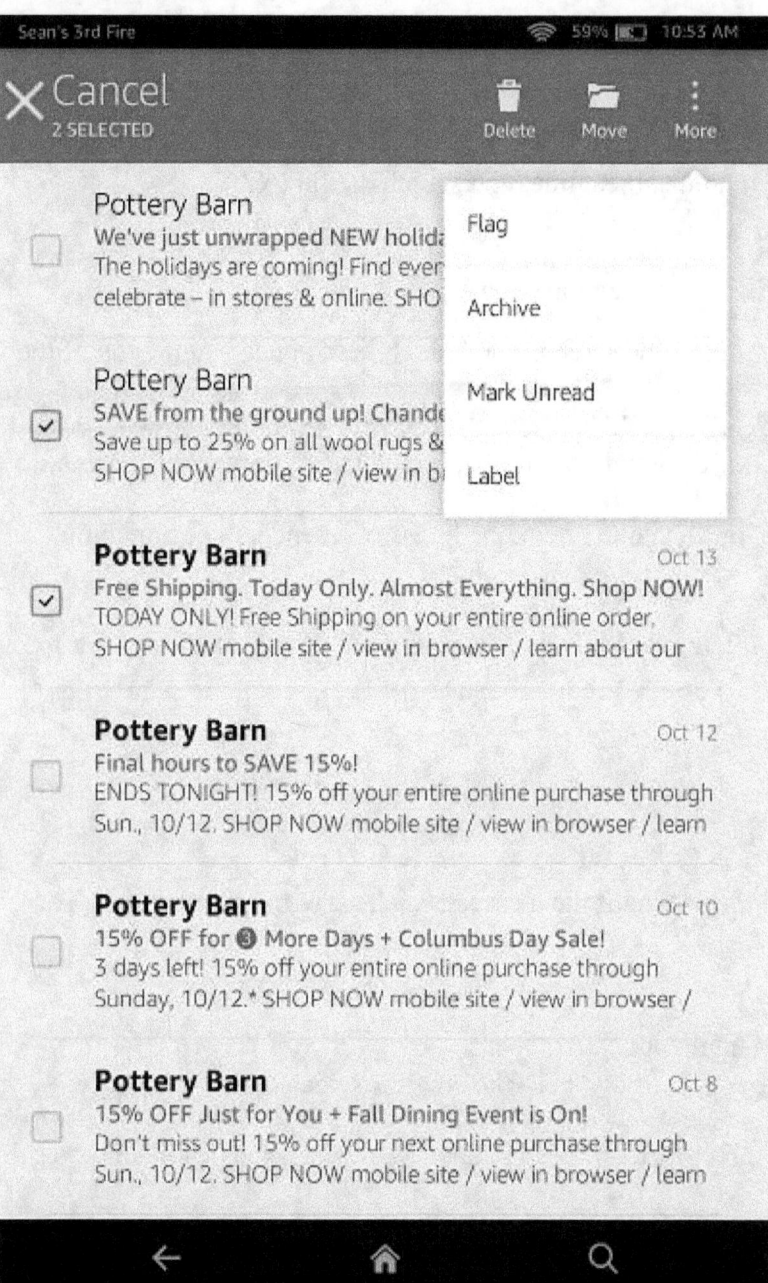

*Figure 7: Inbox Menu*

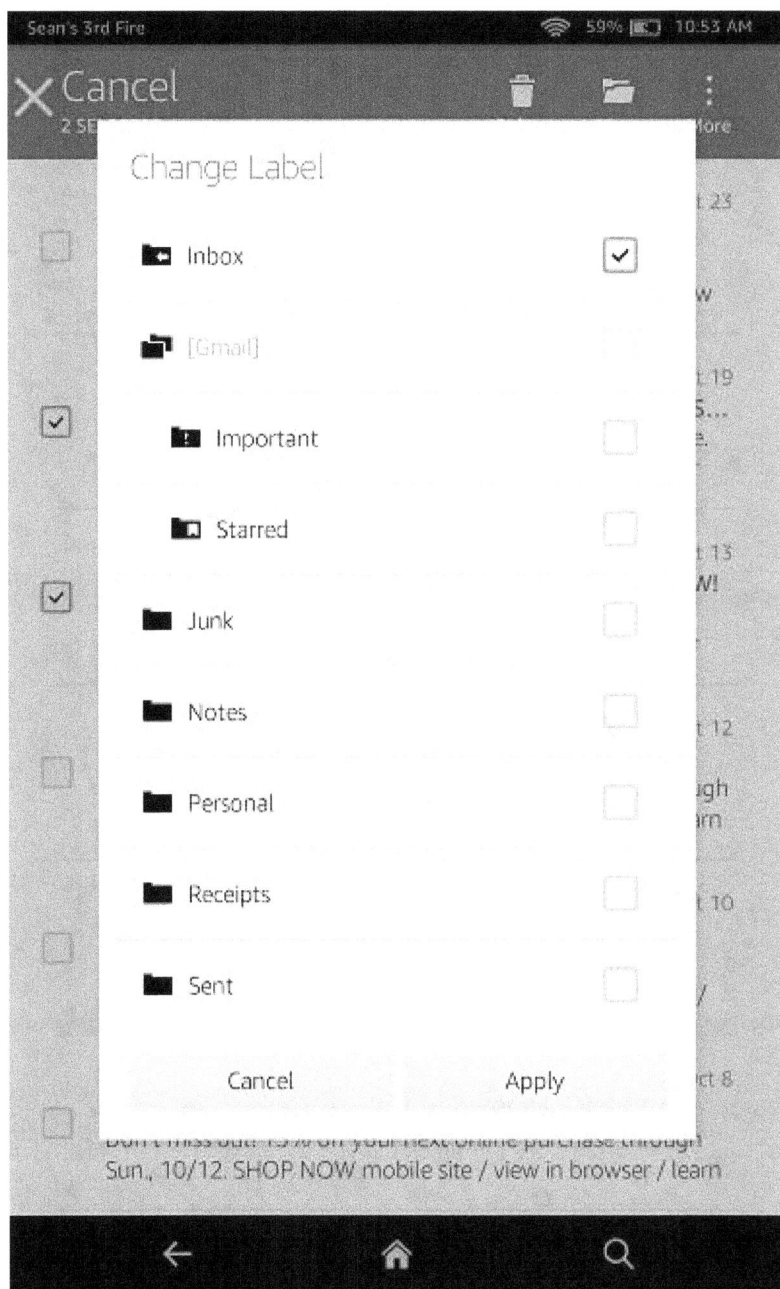

*Figure 8: List of Available Labels*

# Managing Photos and Videos

---

## Table of Contents

---

## 1. Taking a Picture

The Kindle Fire HD 6 has a built-in rear-facing 2 megapixel camera, and a 0.3 megapixel front-facing camera. To take a picture:

1. Touch **Apps** at the top of the Home screen. The Apps library appears, as shown in **Figure 1**.

2. Touch the icon. The camera turns on, as shown in **Figure 2**.

3. Touch the button. The picture is captured and stored in the 'Camera Roll' album. Refer to *"Browsing Pictures"* on page 139 to learn how to view your captured photos.

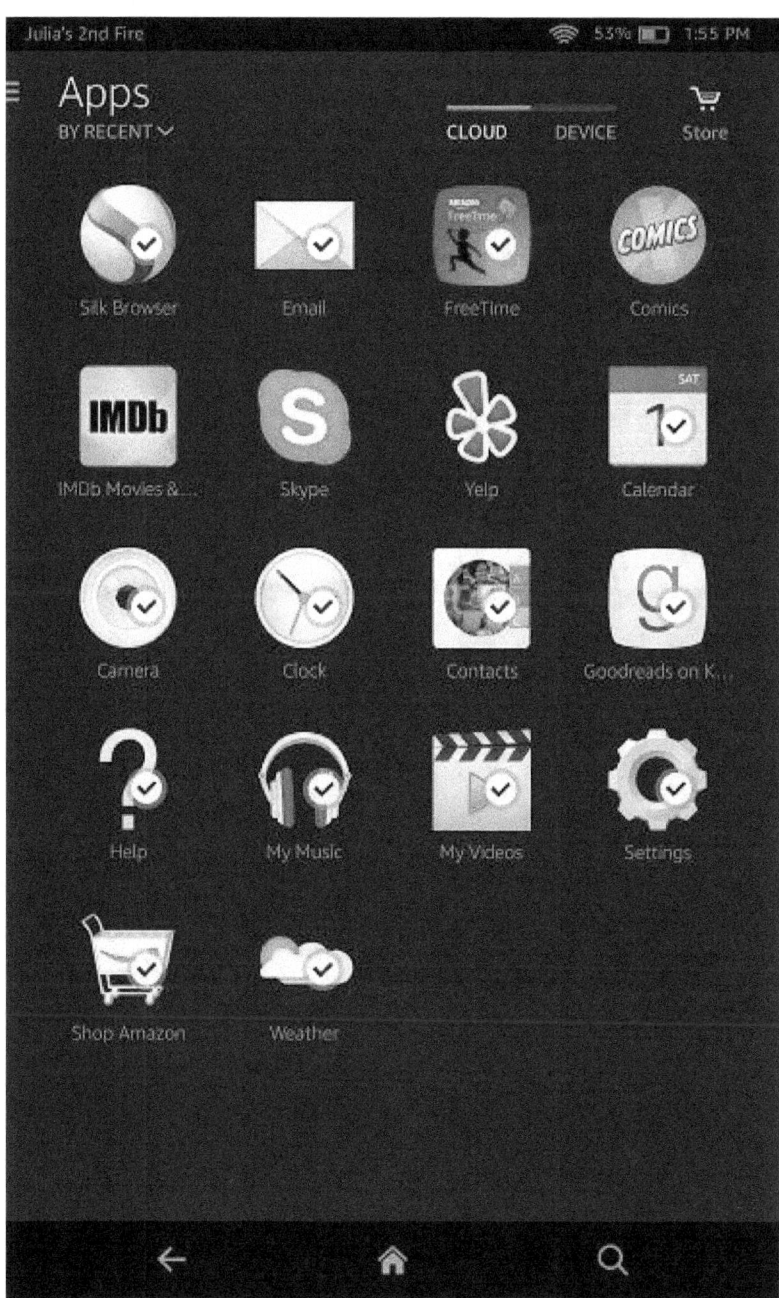

*Figure 1: Apps Library*

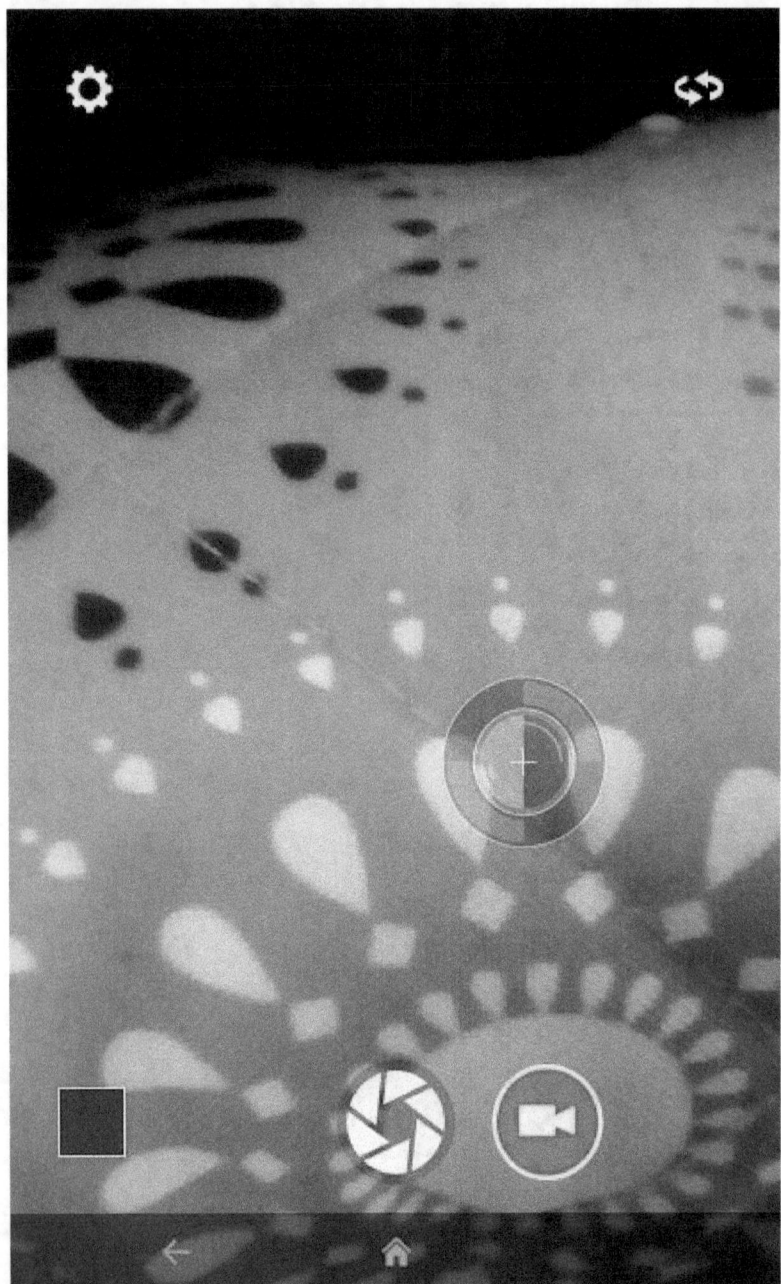

*Figure 2: Camera Turned On*

# 2. Capturing a Video

The Kindle Fire HD 6 has a built-in camcorder that can capture HD video. To capture a video:

1. Touch **Apps** at the top of the Home screen. The Apps library appears.

2. Touch the 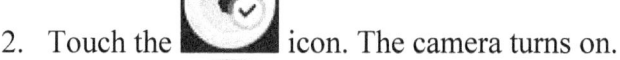 icon. The camera turns on.

3. Touch the 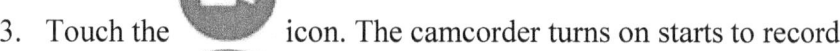 icon. The camcorder turns on starts to record.

4. Touch the button. The camcorder stops recording and the video is stored in the 'Camera Roll' album.

# 3. Browsing Pictures

You can browse captured or saved photos using the Photos application. To view the images stored on your device:

1. Touch **Photos** at the top of the Home screen. The first time that the Photos application opens, the device will offer various services that allow you to add pictures from other devices. You may skip this for now, if you like, by touching the X in the upper right-hand corner of the screen. The thumbnails of the pictures on your device appear, as shown in **Figure 3**.
2. Touch a photo. The photo appears in full-screen mode.
3. Touch the photo with two fingers spread apart and move them together. The photo thumbnails reappear.
4. Touch the edge of the screen and move your finger to the right. A list of available photo albums appears, as shown in **Figure 4**. Touch a photo album to open it.

*Figure 3: Picture Thumbnails*

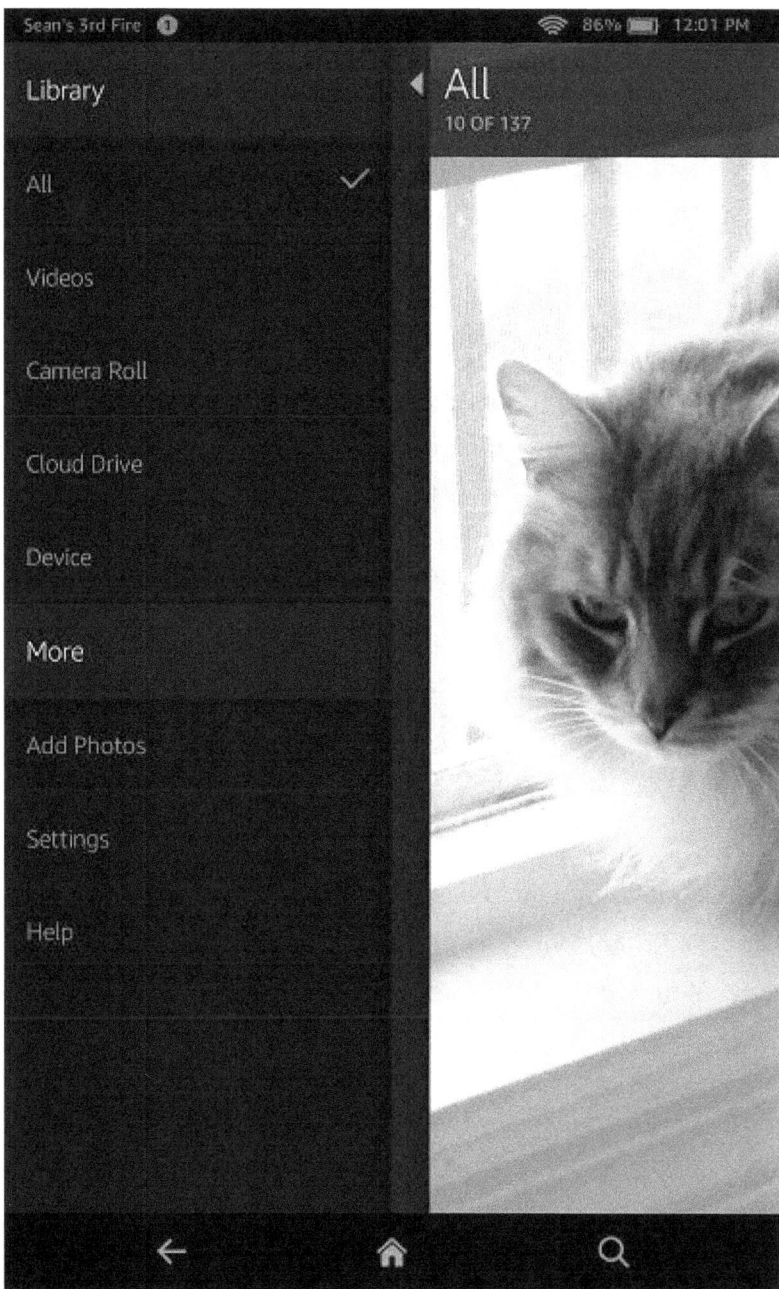

*Figure 4: Available Photo Albums*

# 4. Enhancing Pictures and Applying Special Effects

You may enhance a picture using various effects. To enhance a picture:

1. Touch **Photos** at the top of the Home screen. The thumbnails of the pictures on your device appear.
2. Touch and hold the picture that you wish to edit. The Picture options appear, as shown in **Figure 5**.
3. Touch **Edit**. The Picture Editing screen appears, as shown in **Figure 6**.
4. Touch one of the following icons at the bottom of the screen, and then touch **Apply** in the upper right-hand corner of the screen to apply the corresponding enhancement:

- Improve the quality of the photo. Touch **Hi-Def**, **Illuminate**, or **Color Fix** to apply the corresponding enhancement.

- Remove a red eye from the photo. Touch each red eye to correct it.

- Applies a color effect, similar to Sepia or Grayscale.

- Adds clip art stickers to the picture.

- Add text on top of the picture.

- Creates a meme for a social network, allowing you to edit pre-defined text boxes at the top and bottom of the picture.

- Allows you to draw on the picture. You will be able to select the color and thickness of the paintbrush.

- Adjust the brightness of the photo.

- Adjust the contrast of the picture.

- Adjust the color saturation. The higher the saturation, the more color there will be in the picture.

- Adjust the amount of reddish or bluish colors in the picture. Warm colors are associated with daylight or a sunset, whereas cool colors are associated with a gray or overcast day.

- Adjusts specific parts of the photo by adding more white color to it.

- Smoothens selected parts of the image, such as skin imperfections.

- Adjusts the sharpness of the picture. Increasing the sharpness will make the picture appear more detailed.

- Focuses on a specific area of a picture while making the rest of the picture out of focus.

- Converts the image into a grayscale picture, allowing you to add color to specific areas of the picture using a paintbrush.

5. Touch **Done** in the upper right-hand corner of the Picture Editing screen when you are finished. Your changes are saved.

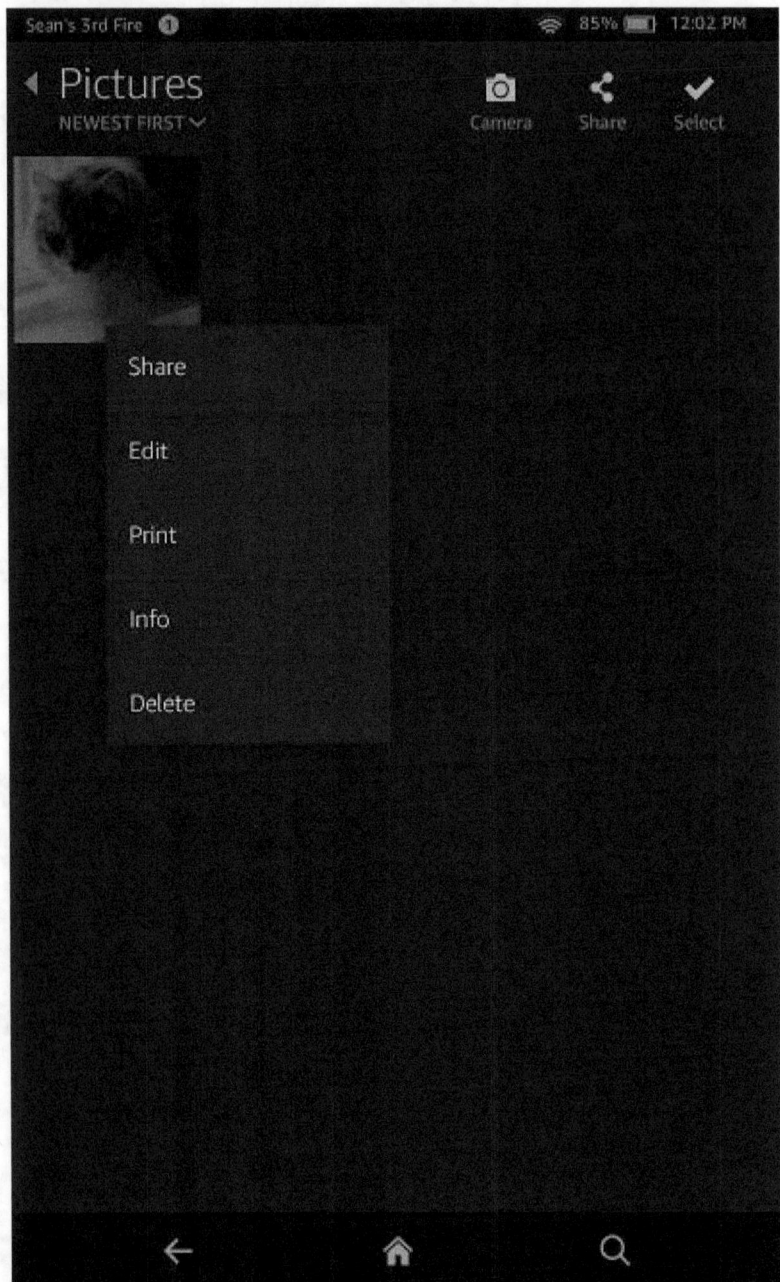

*Figure 5: Picture Options*

*Figure 6: Picture Editing Screen*

# 5. Cropping a Picture

You may crop a picture to use a specific piece of it. To crop a picture:

1.  Touch **Photos** at the top of the Home screen. The thumbnails of the pictures on your device appear.
2.  Touch and hold the picture that you wish to edit. The Picture options appear.
3.  Touch **Edit**. The Picture Editing screen appears.
4.  Touch the icon at the bottom of the screen. Crop marks appear on the picture, as shown in **Figure 7**.
5.  Touch one of the markers and drag it in any direction to change the size of the crop.
6.  Touch anywhere inside of the crop and drag it in any direction to adjust the area that is cropped. You can also touch one of the ratios at the bottom of the screen to change the dimensions of the crop.
7.  Touch **Apply** in the upper right-hand corner of the screen. The picture is cropped and the Editing screen appears.
8.  Touch **Done** in the upper right-hand corner of the screen. Your crop is saved.

*Figure 7: Crop Marks on a Picture*

# 6. Flipping or Rotating a Picture

You may rotate a photo in 90 degree increments, flip it to view it upside down or as a mirror image, or rotate it by a few degrees at a time. To flip or rotate a picture:

1. Touch **Photos** at the top of the Home screen. The thumbnails of the pictures on your device appear.
2. Touch and hold the picture that you wish to edit. The Picture options appear.
3. Touch **Edit**. The Picture Editing screen appears
4. Touch the  icon at the bottom of the screen. The Rotate screen appears, as shown in **Figure 8**.
5. Touch one of the following icons at the bottom of the screen to rotate or flip the picture accordingly:

    - Rotates the picture 90 degrees to the left.

    - Rotate the picture 90 degrees to the right.

    - Flips the picture horizontally, creating a horizontal mirror image.

    - Flips the picture vertical, creating a vertical mirror image.

6. You can also touch the 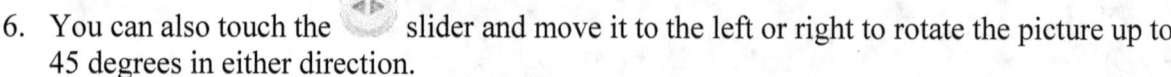 slider and move it to the left or right to rotate the picture up to 45 degrees in either direction.

*Figure 8: Rotate Screen*

# 7. Deleting Pictures or Videos

*Warning: Once a picture is deleted, there is no way to restore it.*

To free up some space in the device's memory, try deleting some pictures. To delete pictures:

1. Touch **Photos** at the top of the Home screen. The thumbnails of the pictures and videos on your device appear.
2. Touch **Select** in the upper right-hand corner of the screen. Then, touch all of the pictures or videos that you want to delete. A check mark appears on each selected item, as shown in **Figure 9**.
3. Touch **Delete** at the top of the screen. A confirmation dialog appears.
4. Touch **Delete** again. The selected pictures and videos are deleted.

*Note: To view the pictures and videos on your device, touch the left-hand side of the screen, and slide your finger to the right. Then, touch* **Device** *or* **Camera Roll**.

*Figure 9: Selected Media*

# 8. Importing and Exporting Pictures Using a PC or Mac

Pictures that you have taken or obtained elsewhere can be imported to the Kindle Fire HD 6. Refer to *"Connecting the Kindle Fire HD 6 to a PC or Mac"* on page 23 to learn how to import or export pictures. Double-click the 'Pictures' folder in step 4 to access the folder where all pictures are stored on your device.

# 9. Sharing a Picture or Video via Email

You may share up to 10 pictures or one video by attaching it to an email. To share a picture or video:

1. Touch **Photos** at the top of the Home screen. The thumbnails of the pictures on your device appear.
2. Touch the ![icon] icon in the upper right-hand corner of the screen. Then, touch each picture that you want to share. A check mark appears on each selected picture.
3. Touch **E-mail** at the top of the screen. The Compose screen appears with the selected photos attached, as shown in **Figure 10**.
4. Enter the email address of the recipient, and an optional subject. You can also enter optional text by touching the white space beneath the attached pictures.
5. Touch the ![button] button in the upper right-hand corner of the screen. The email is sent with the attached pictures.

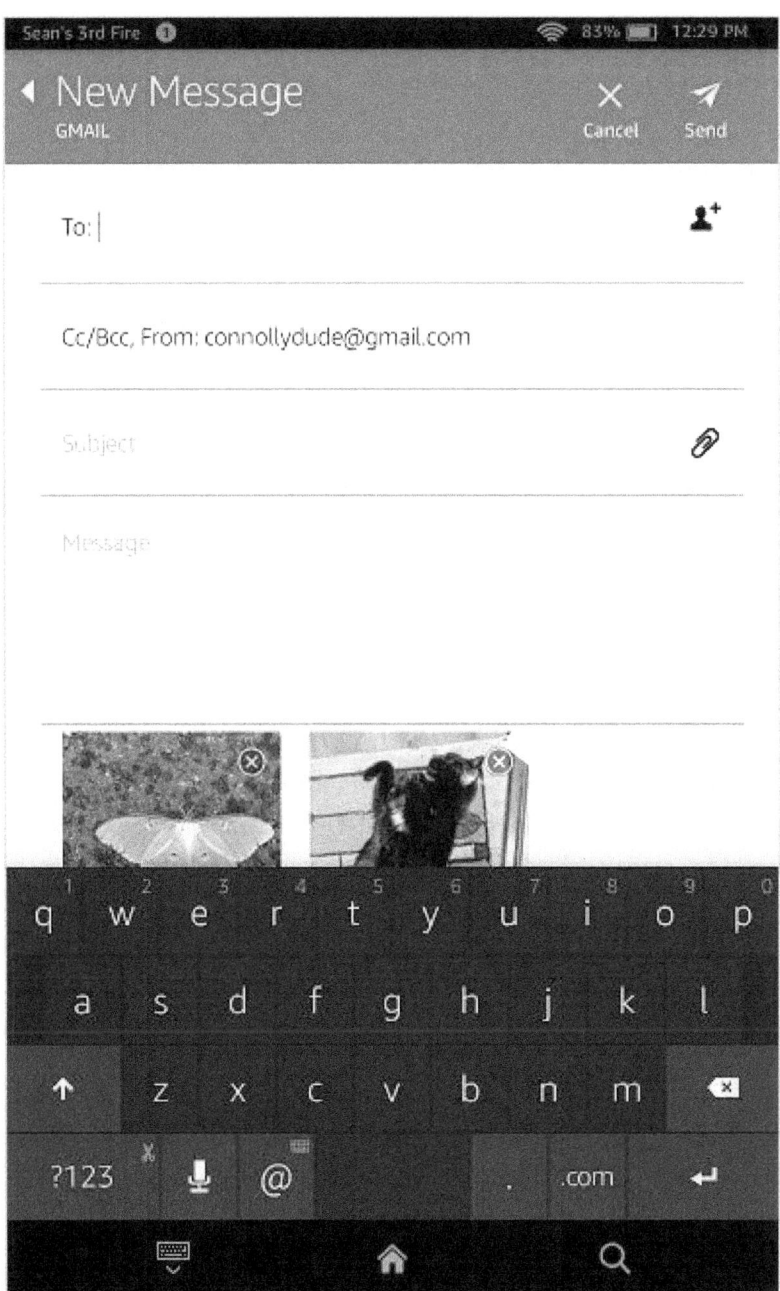

*Figure 10: Compose Screen with Attached Pictures*

# Managing Contacts

## Table of Contents

## 1. Adding a New Contact

The Kindle Fire HD 6 allows you to manage your contacts using the Contacts application. To add a new contact:

1. Touch **Apps** at the top of the Library. The Apps Library appears, as shown in **Figure 1**.

2. Touch the icon. The Address Book opens, as shown in **Figure 2**.

3. Touch the icon in the upper right-hand corner of the screen. The Synchronization menu appears, as shown in **Figure 3**. The appearance of this menu will vary based on the accounts that you have added to your device.

4. Touch the account with which you would like to sync the new contact. The contact will appear in address books on all devices registered with the selected account. The New Contact screen appears, as shown in **Figure 4**.

5. Touch each field and enter the desired information. Touch **Save** in the upper right-hand corner of the screen. The contact is added to your address book.

*Figure 1: Apps Library*

*Figure 2: Address Book*

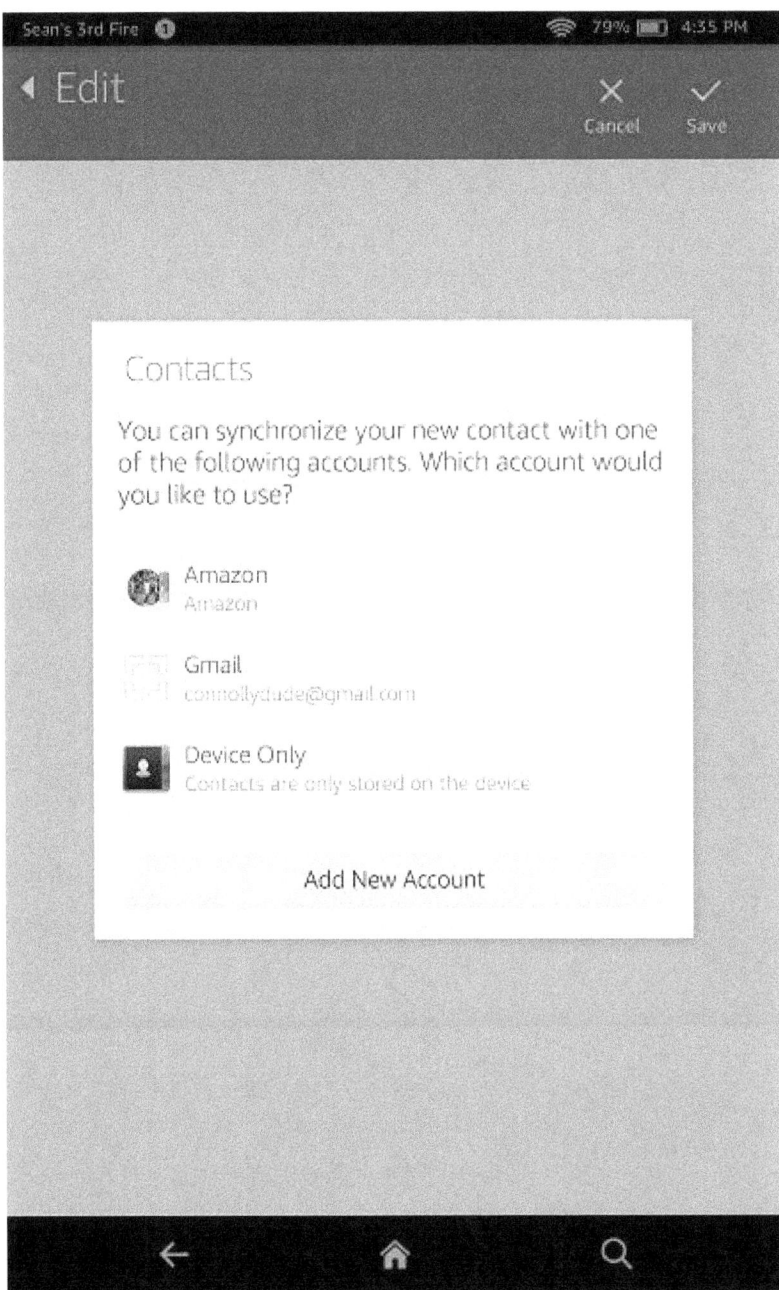

*Figure 3: Synchronization Menu*

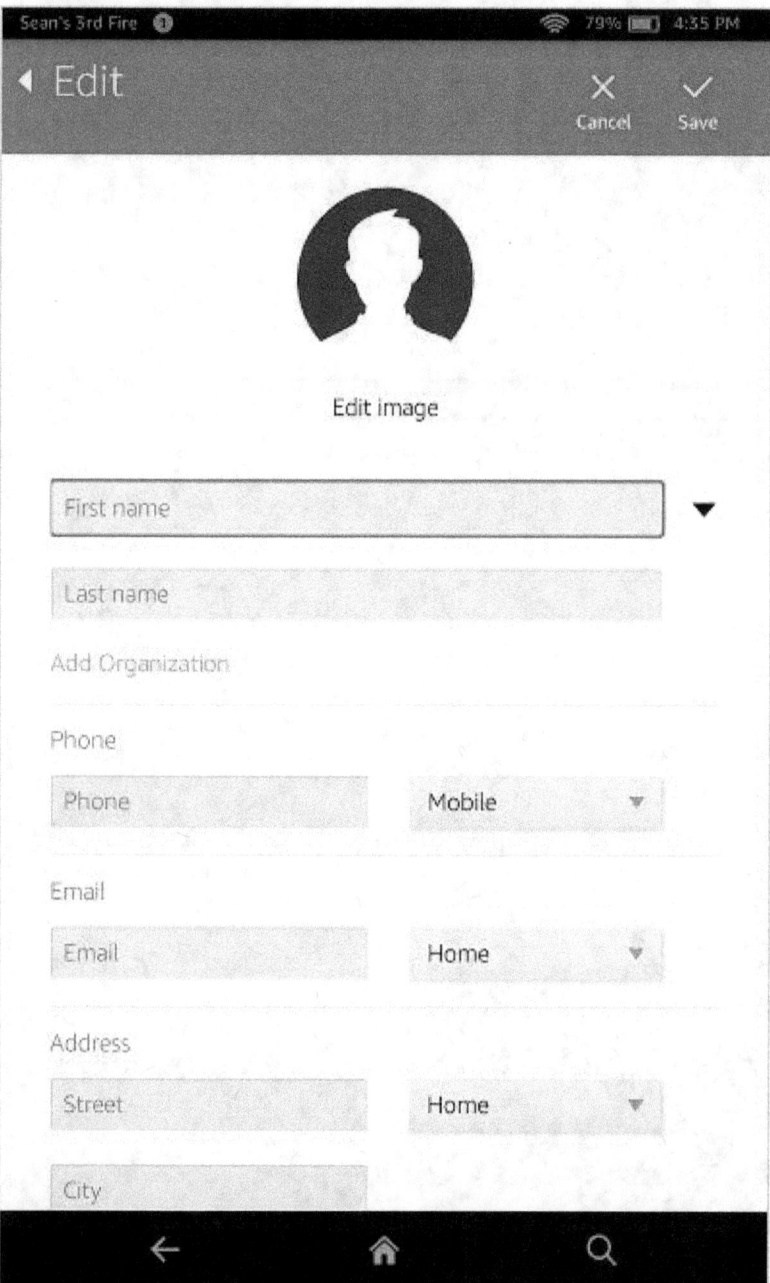

*Figure 4: New Contact Screen*

## 2. Editing a Contact's Information

Edit a contact's information to add additional data, such as an email address or additional phone number. To edit an existing contact's information:

1. Touch **Apps** at the top of the Library. The Apps screen appears.

2. Touch the icon. The Address Book opens.
3. Touch and hold a contact's name. The Contact Info menu appears, as outlined in **Figure 5**.
4. Touch **Edit**. The contact's information appears.
5. Touch each field to edit the contact's information. Touch **Save** in the upper right-hand corner of the screen. The contact's information is saved.

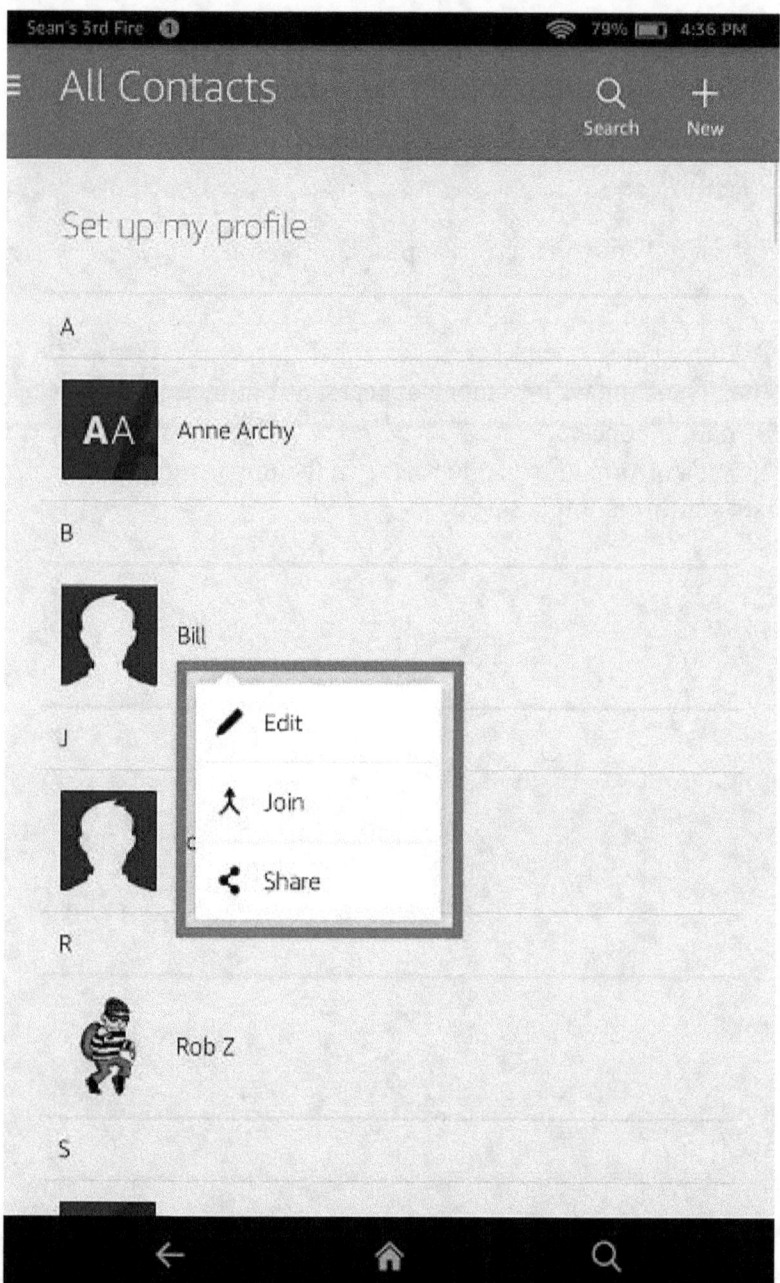

*Figure 5: Contact Info Menu*

# 3. Deleting a Contact

Free up memory by deleting contacts from the Kindle Fire HD 6. To delete an unwanted contact:

1. Touch **Apps** at the top of the Library. The Apps screen appears.

2. Touch the icon. The Address Book application opens.
3. Touch the name of the contact that you wish to delete. The Contact Info screen appears.
4. Touch **More** in the upper-right hand corner of the screen. The Contact Options appear, as outlined in **Figure 6**.
5. Touch **Delete**. A confirmation dialog appears.
6. Touch **OK**. The contact is deleted.

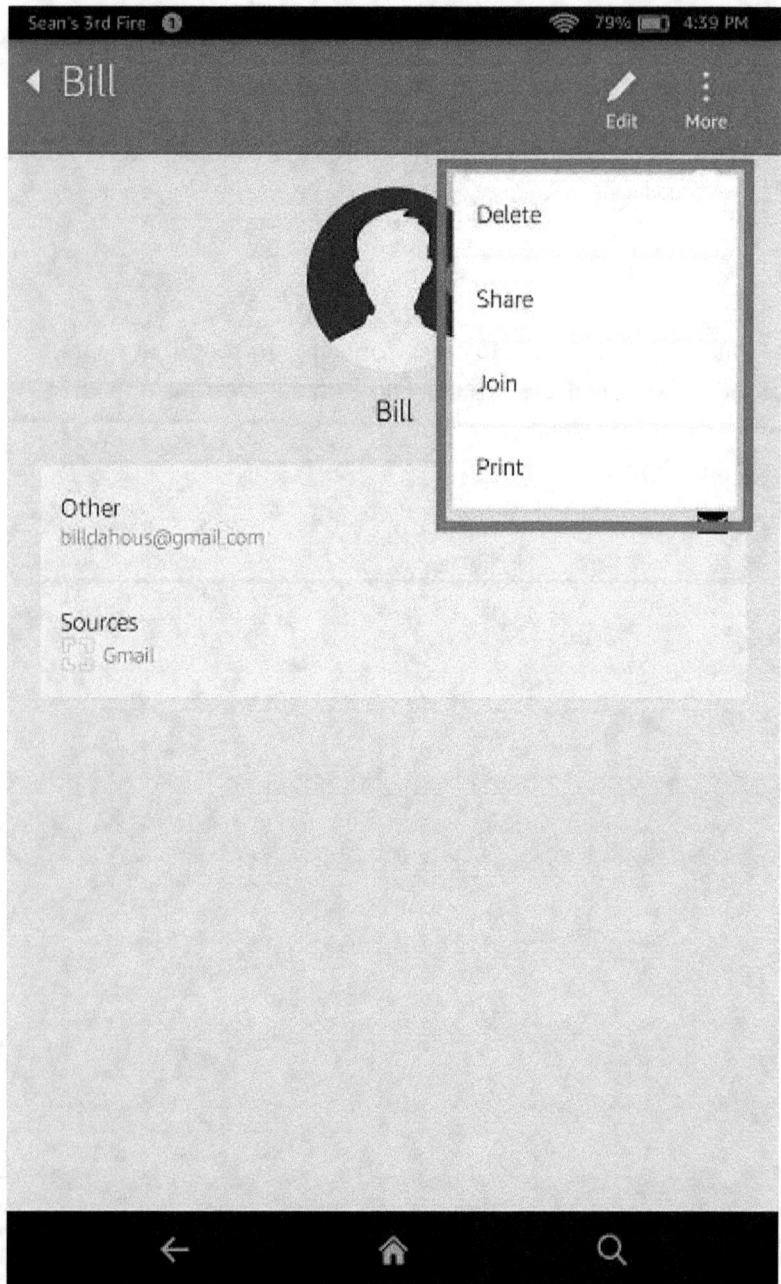

*Figure 6: Contact Options*

# 4. Sharing a Contact's Information

You can share a contact's information with others via email. To share a contact's information:

1. Touch **Apps** at the top of the Library. The Apps screen appears.

2. Touch the ![icon] icon. The Address Book opens.

3. Touch and hold a contact's name. The Contact Info menu appears.

4. Touch **Share**. The New Email screen appears with the contact's information attached, as shown in **Figure 7**.

5. Enter the recipient's email address and an optional subject. You can also enter an optional message in the white space beneath the attached contact.

6. Touch the ![button] button in the upper right-hand corner of the screen. The contact's information is shared.

*Figure 7: New Email Screen with Contact's Information Attached*

# Using the Silk Web Browser

## Table of Contents

## 1. Navigating to a Web Page

The Kindle Fire HD 6 has a built-in Web browser called Silk. To navigate to a web page using its web address:

1. Touch **Web** at the top of the Home screen, or touch **Silk Browser** at the bottom of the Home screen. The Silk browser opens, as shown in **Figure 1**.
2. Touch **Enter search term of URL** at the top of the screen. The virtual keyboard appears.
3. Enter a web address and touch **Go**. The Silk browser navigates to the web page.

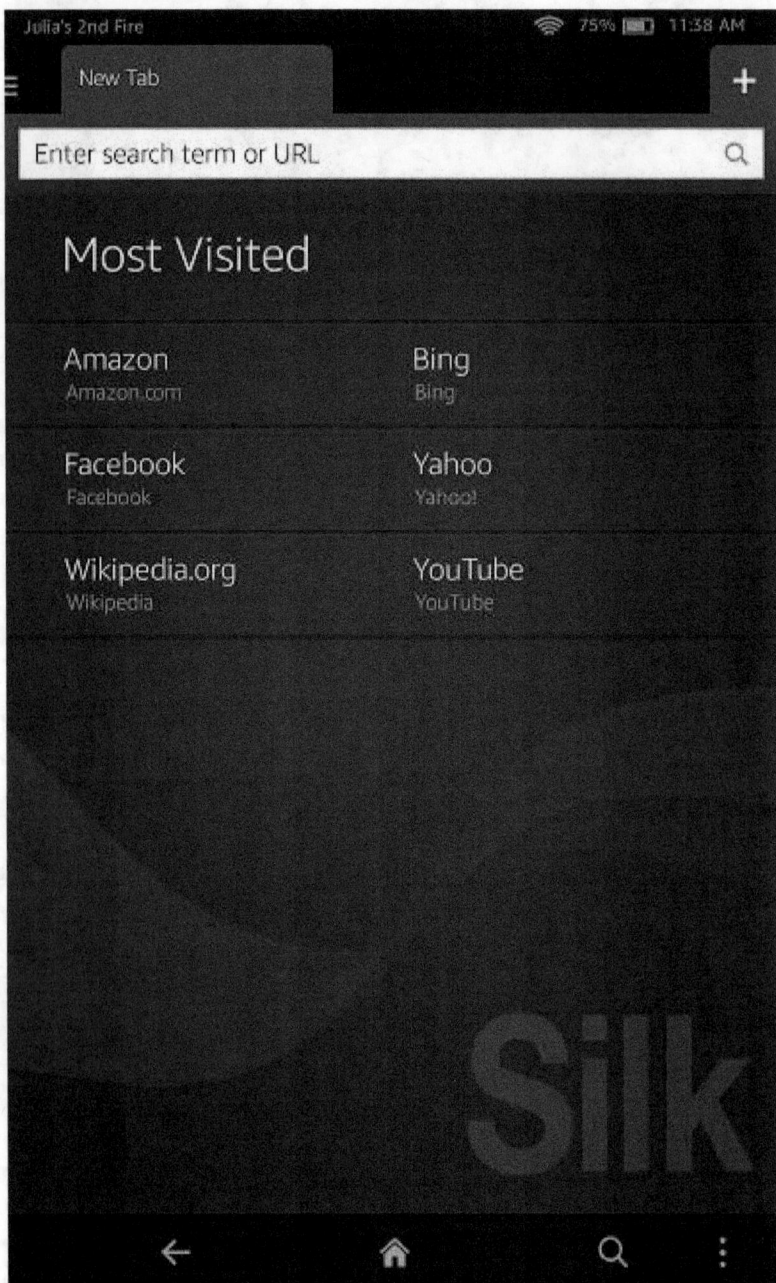

*Figure 1: Silk Browser*

## 2. Adding Bookmarks

Web pages can be stored as bookmarks for faster access. To add a web page to your bookmarks:

1. Navigate to a web page. Refer to *"Navigating to a Web Page"* on page 165 to learn how.

2. Touch the ▓ icon at the bottom of the screen. The Silk menu appears, as shown in **Figure 2**.

3. Touch **Add Bookmark**. The Add Bookmark dialog appears, as shown in **Figure 3**.

4. Touch the 'Name' field and enter a custom name for the bookmark, if desired. Touch **OK**. The web page is saved to bookmarks.

*Note: Touch the left edge of the screen while using the Silk browser, slide your finger to the right, and touch **Bookmarks** to view a list of your bookmarks.*

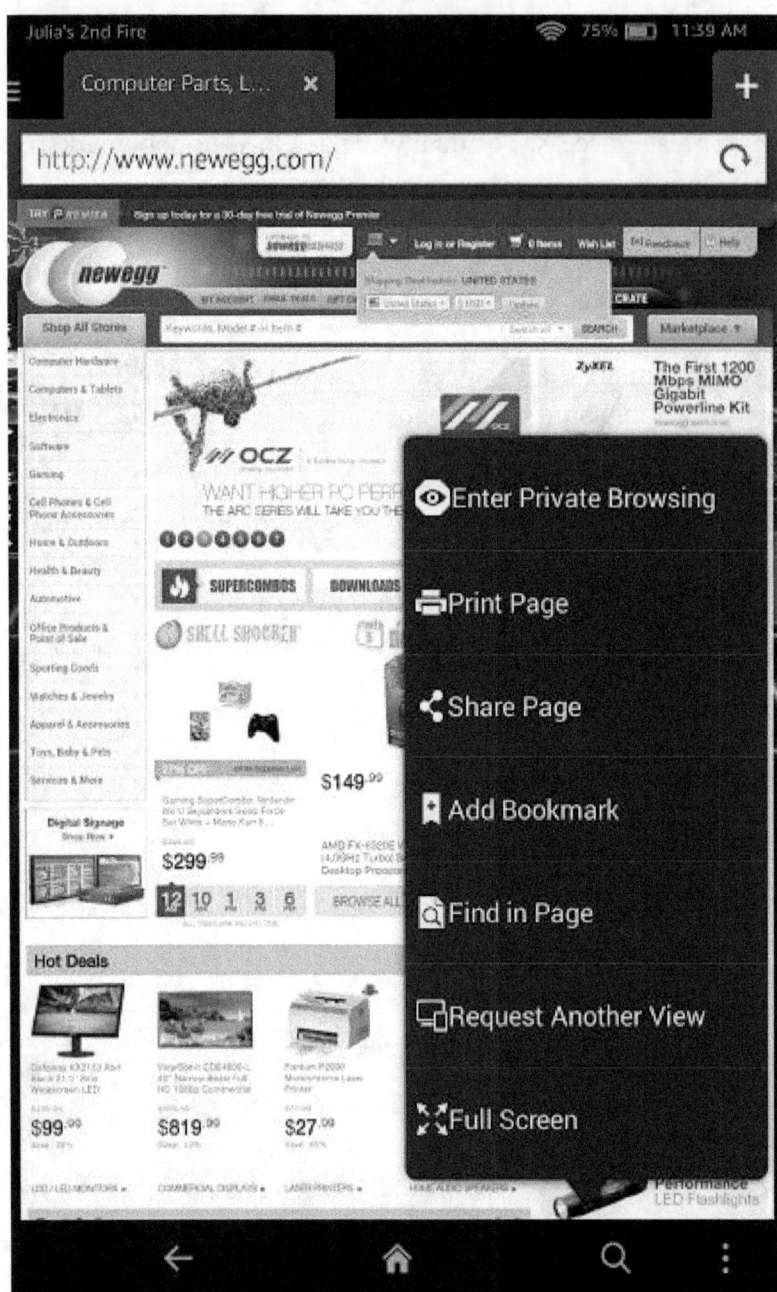

*Figure 2: Silk Menu*

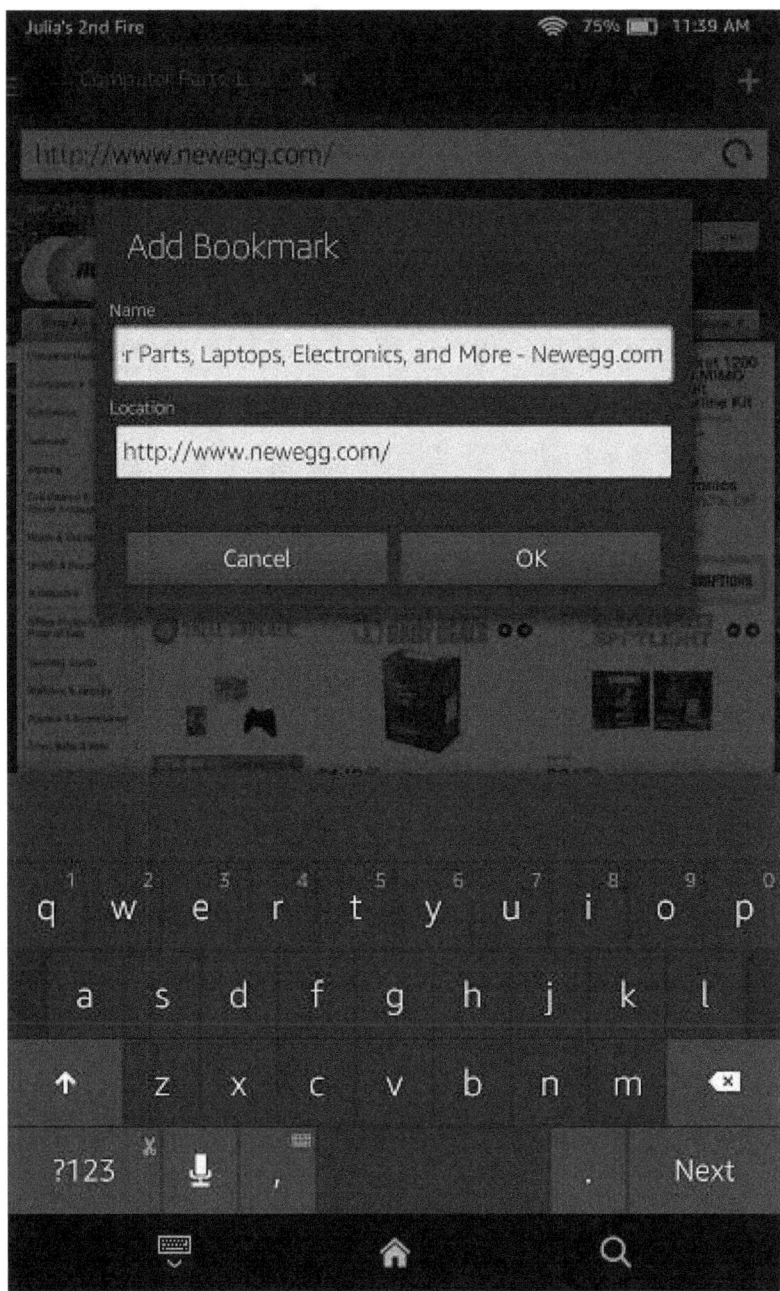

*Figure 3: Add Bookmark Dialog*

# 3. Managing Tabs

Up to ten tabs can be opened at once and displayed at the top of the Silk browser. Use the following tips to manage tabs:

- Touch the ➕ icon in the upper right-hand corner of the Silk browser to open a new tab.
- Touch the ✖ icon on a tab to close it.
- Touch a tab and drag your finger to the left or right to view more open tabs when more than three tabs are open.

*Note: Refer to "Tips and Tricks" on page 252 to learn how to close all tabs at once.*

# 4. Using Links

In addition to touching a link to navigate to its destination, there are other link options. Touch and hold a link to see all of the link options, as follows:

- **Open in new tab** - Opens the link in a new tab without closing the existing one.
- **Open in private tab** - Opens the link in a new tab, which will not keep track of the currently opened link, or any other web pages that you visit in the browsing history.
- **Open in Background Tab** - Opens the link in a new tab without switching to it. The current tab remains open.
- **Bookmark Link** - Adds the link to the bookmarks.
- **Share Link** - Copies the link into an email or a friend's Facebook wall, depending on your selection.
- **Copy link URL** - Copies the link to the clipboard, allowing it to be pasted in any text field.
- **Save Link -** Saves the current web page to your device where it can be viewed even if you are not connected to the internet. You will not be able to access any links on the web page when viewing it offline. Touch the left edge of the screen, slide your finger to the right, and touch **Downloads** to view a list of downloaded web pages.

# 5. Searching a Web Page for a Word or Phrase

While surfing the web, any web page can be searched for a word or phrase. To search a web page:

1. Touch the ▪ button at the bottom of the screen. The Silk menu appears.
2. Touch **Find in Page**. The Search field and virtual keyboard appear.
3. Enter a search word or phrase. The search results are highlighted as you type, as shown in **Figure 4**. Touch the ⋀ and ⋁ buttons to the left of the search field to scroll through the results on the web page.

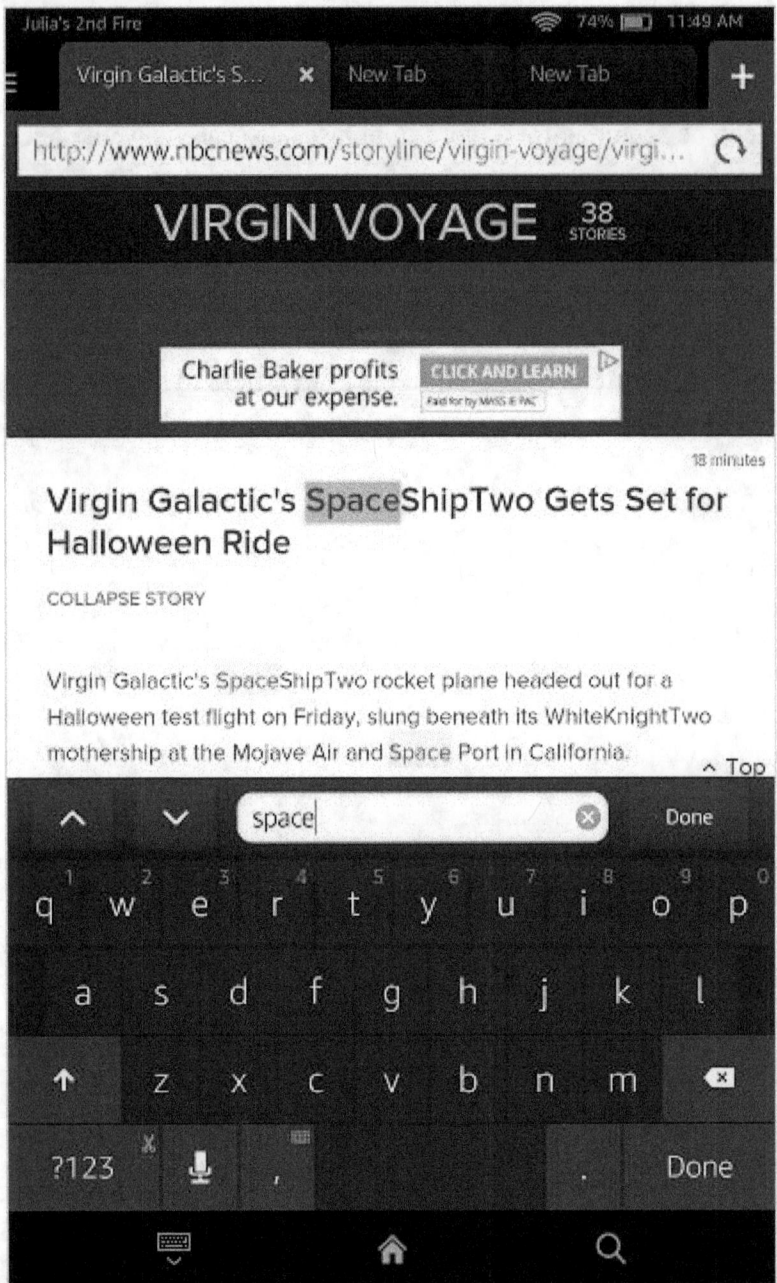

*Figure 4: Matching Results Highlighted*

# 6. Viewing Recently Visited Websites

The Kindle Fire HD 6 stores all recently visited websites in its Browsing History. To view the History, touch the left edge of the screen and slide your finger to the right. The Silk options appear, as shown in **Figure 5**. Touch **History**. The Browsing History screen appears, as shown in **Figure 6**.

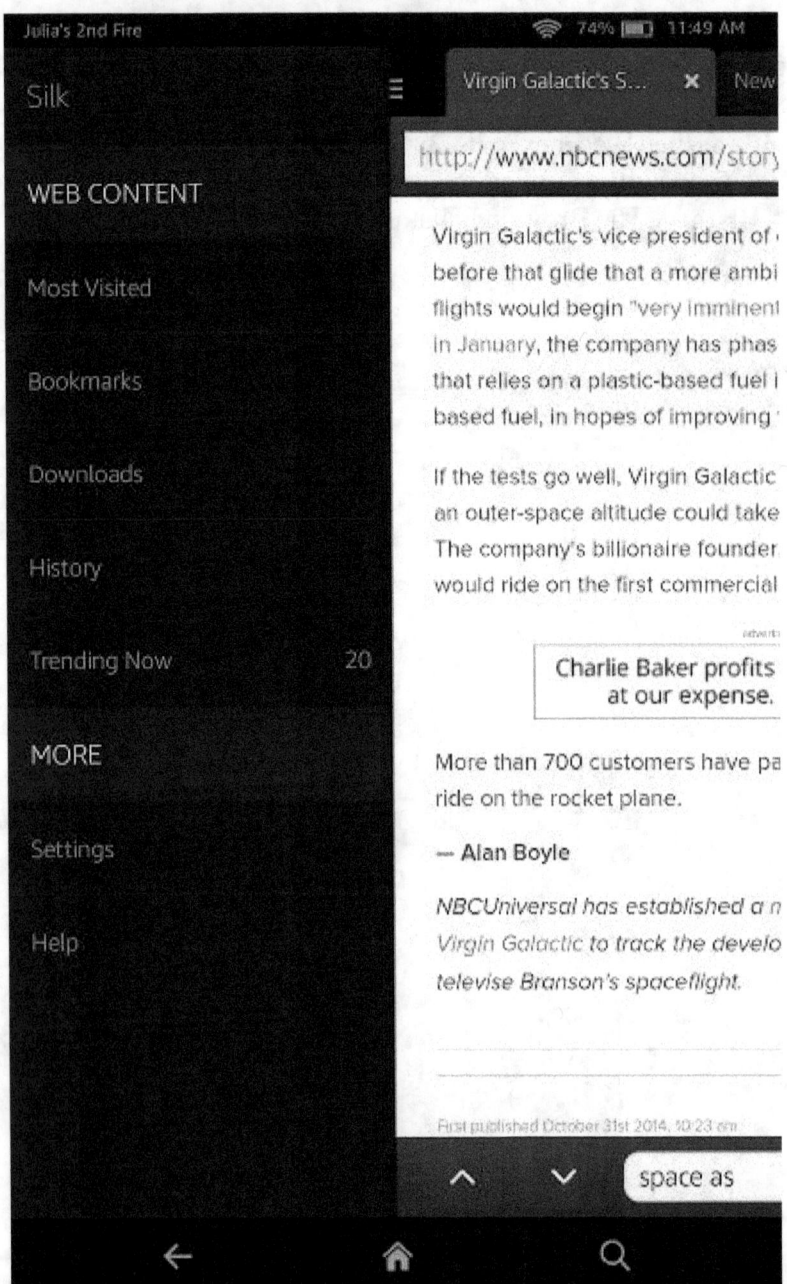

*Figure 5: Silk Options*

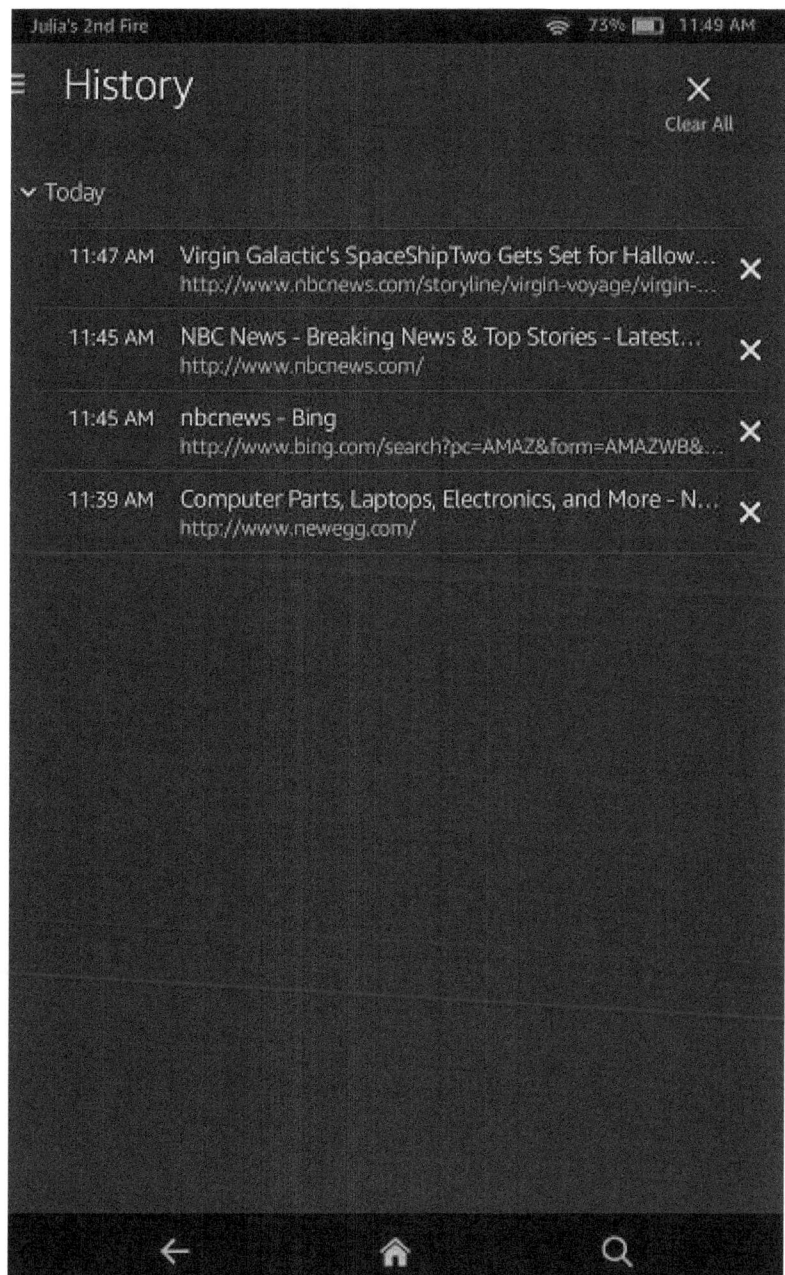

*Figure 6: Browsing History*

# 7. Blocking Pop-Up Windows

Some websites may have pop-up windows that will interfere with web browsing. To block pop-ups:

1. Touch the left edge of the screen and slide your finger to the right. The Silk options appear.
2. Touch **Settings**. The Silk Settings screen appears, as shown in **Figure 7**.
3. Touch **Block pop-up windows**. The Block Pop-Up Windows menu appears.
4. Touch **Always**. Pop-up windows will now be blocked.

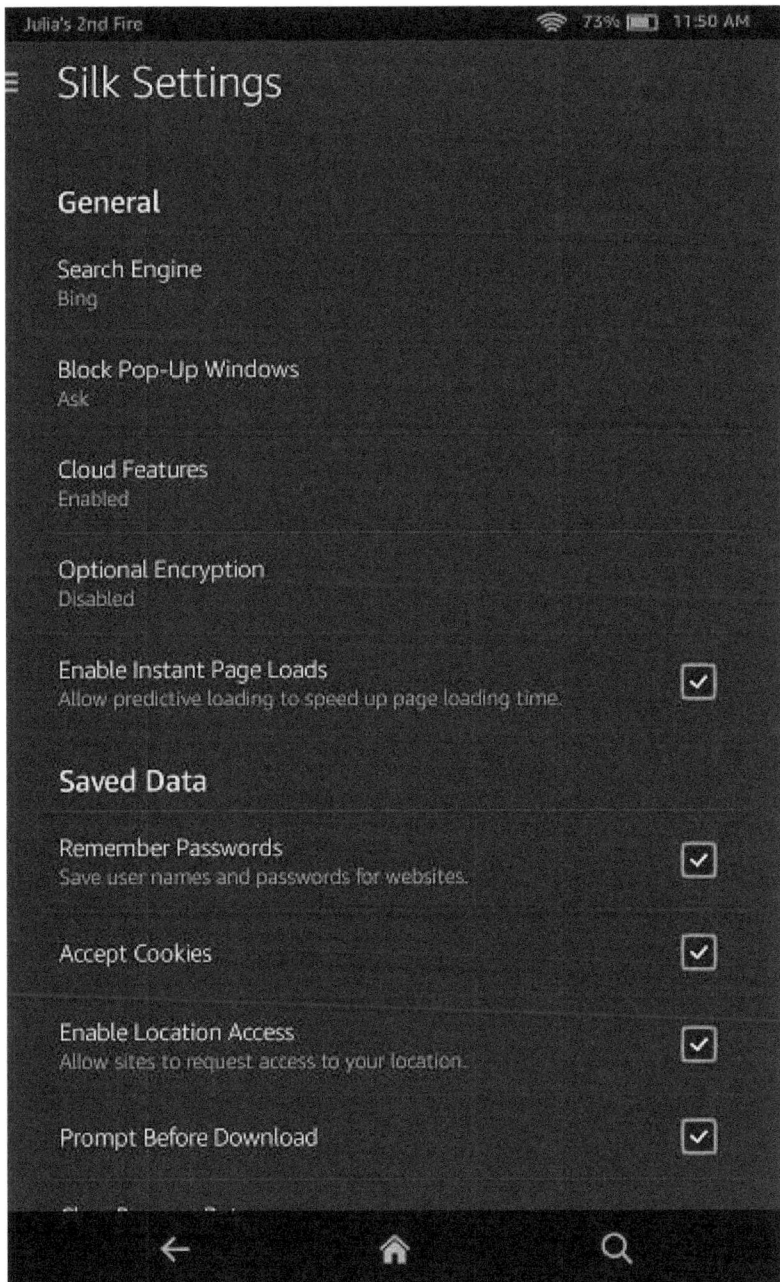

*Figure 7: Silk Settings Screen*

# 8. Changing the Default Search Engine

When you type a search term in the web address field, the default search engine is used to perform the search. The default search engine is Google. To change the default search engine:

1. Touch the left edge of the screen and slide your finger to the right. The Silk options appear.
2. Touch **Settings**. The Silk Settings screen appears.
3. Touch **Search engine**. A list of available search engines appears, as shown in **Figure 8**.
4. Touch your preferred search engine. The new default search engine is set and will be used for all searches.

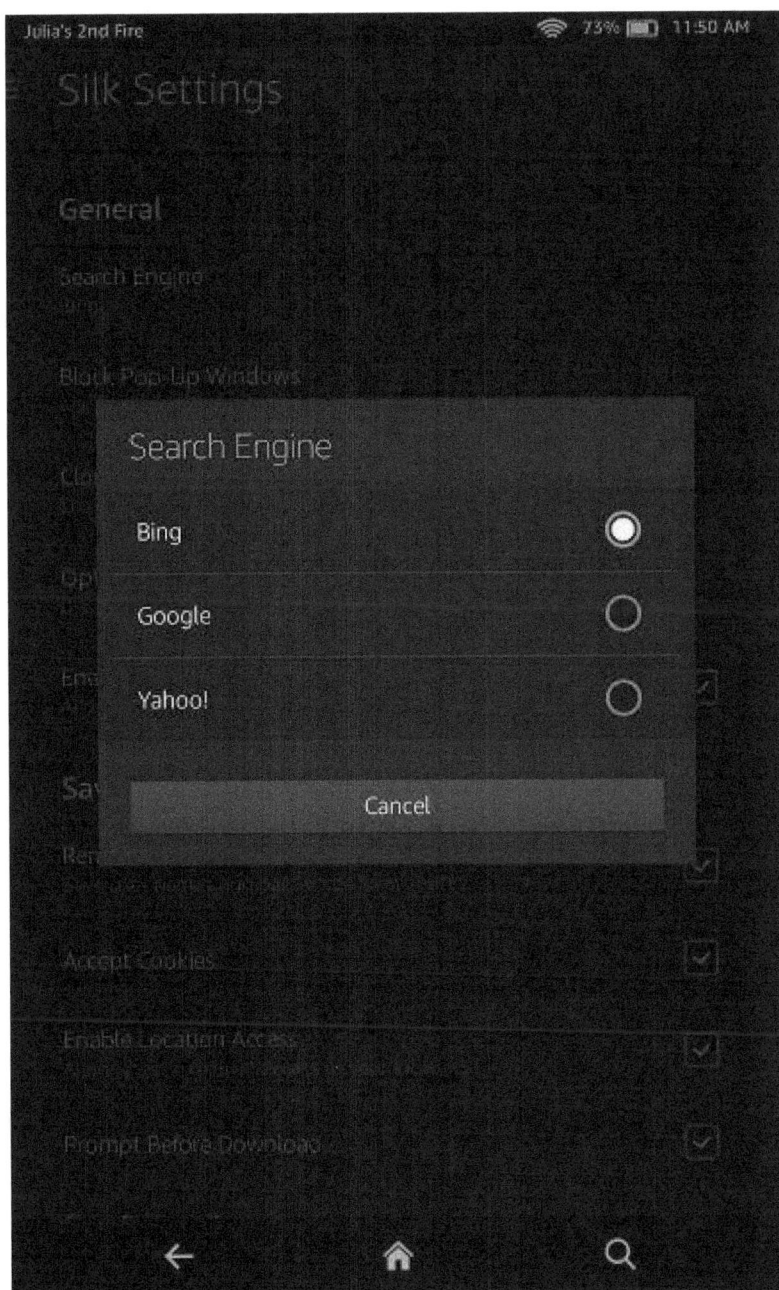

*Figure 8: List of Available Search Engines*

# 9. Saving Passwords in Forms

The Silk browser can automatically save the passwords that you enter in forms. To save passwords in forms:

1.  Touch the left edge of the screen and slide your finger to the right. The Silk options appear.
2.  Touch **Settings**. The Browser Settings screen appears.

3.  Touch **Remember passwords**. The ✓ appears to the right of 'Remember passwords' and the feature is turned on.

4.  Touch **Remember passwords** again. The ☐ disappears and the feature is turned off.

# 10. Turning Private Browsing On or Off

To protect your privacy, you can browse the web without having your activity recorded in the browsing or search histories. To turn on private browsing:

1.  Touch the ⁞ button at the bottom of the screen. The Silk menu appears.
2.  Touch **Enter Private Browsing**. Private Browsing is turned on, as shown in **Figure 9**. Your currently opened tabs are hidden while you are in Private Browsing mode.

3.  Touch the ⁞ button at the bottom of the screen, and then touch **Exit Private Browsing** to turn off Private Browsing. All of the tabs that you opened in Private Browsing mode are closed. You can also choose to delete any files that you downloaded to the Kindle Fire HD 6.

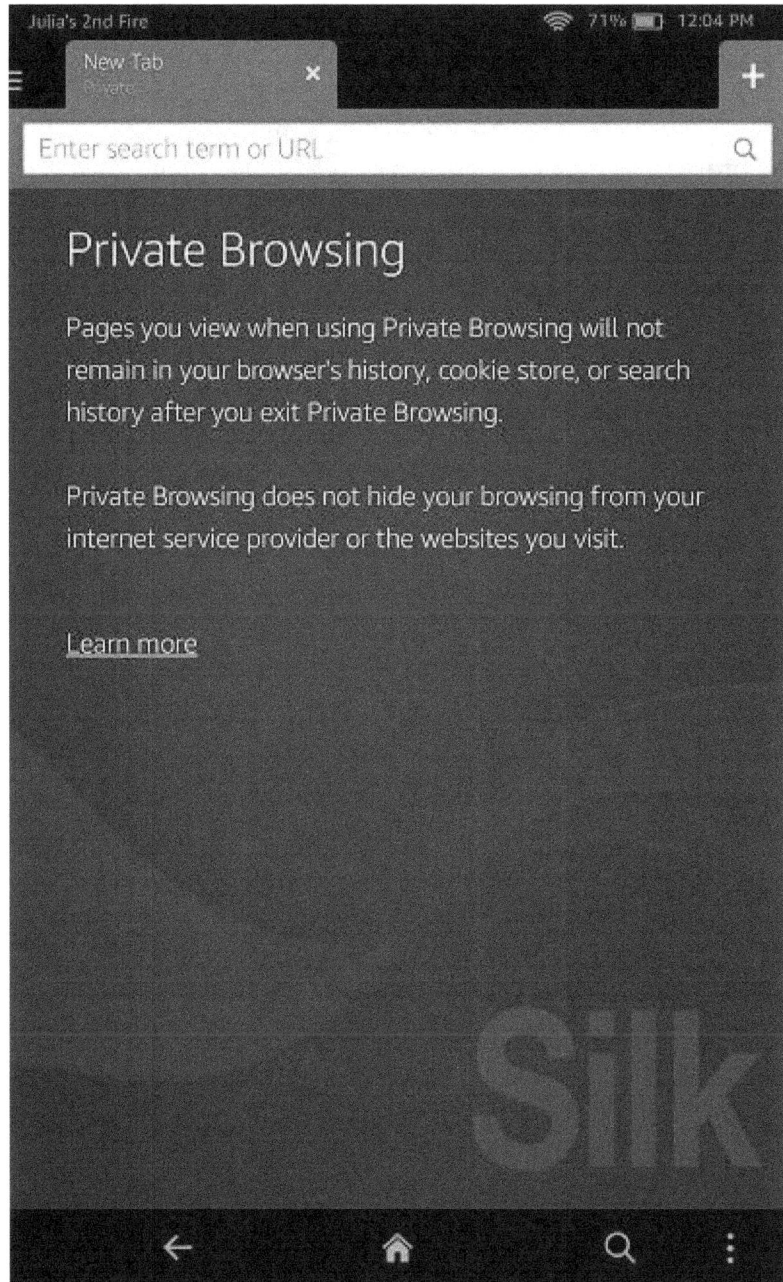

*Figure 9: Private Browsing*

# 11. Turning Reading View On or Off

The Silk browser can display certain news articles in Reading View, which allows you to read them like a book with no images or advertisements. To view an article in Reading View, touch the ▭▭ Reading View button in the address bar at any time (when available), as outlined in red in **Figure 10**. Reader View turns on, as shown in **Figure 11**. Touch **Aa** at the top of the screen to adjust the font, margins, and line spacing. To exit Reading View, touch the ✕ button at the top of the screen.

*Figure 10: Reading View Button Outlined*

Arctic Halloween Weather: Snow, Re...    Aa |

www.nbcnews.com

# Arctic Halloween Weather: Snow, Record Lows for Eastern U.S.

collapse story

advertisement

  Presented by

An arctic blast is giving millions of people a real reason to shiver on Halloween.

Trick-or-treaters from the Midwest to the Mississippi Valley to the East Coast face a deep chill Friday, and strong, freezing winds are taking hold across the Great Lakes region, which is expecting the season's first lake-effect snow. The southern Appalachians are expected to get up to 8 inches of snow by Saturday morning, forecasters say. Record low temperatures are expected as far south as Miami.

*Figure 11: Reading View*

# Managing Applications

## Table of Contents

## 1. Searching for an Application in the Amazon App Store

There are two ways to search for applications in the App Store on the Kindle Fire HD 6:

**Manual Search**

To search for an application manually:

1. Touch **Apps** at the top of the library. The Apps Library appears, as shown in **Figure 1**.
2. Touch **Store** in the upper right-hand corner of the screen. The Appstore opens, as shown in **Figure 2**.
3. Touch the ⌕ icon at the top of the screen. The virtual keyboard appears.
4. Enter the name of an application and touch the ⌕ key. All matching applications appear, as shown in **Figure 3**.

**Browse by Category**

To browse applications by category:
1. Touch **Apps** at the top of the library. The Apps Library appears.
2. Touch **Store** in the upper right-hand corner of the screen. The Appstore opens.
3. Touch the left edge of the screen and slide your finger to the right. The App Store menu appears, as shown in **Figure 4**.
4. Touch **Browse Categories**. A list of categories appears, as shown in **Figure 5**.

5. Touch a category, such as **Games**, **Entertainment**, or **Music**. All of the applications available for that category appear.

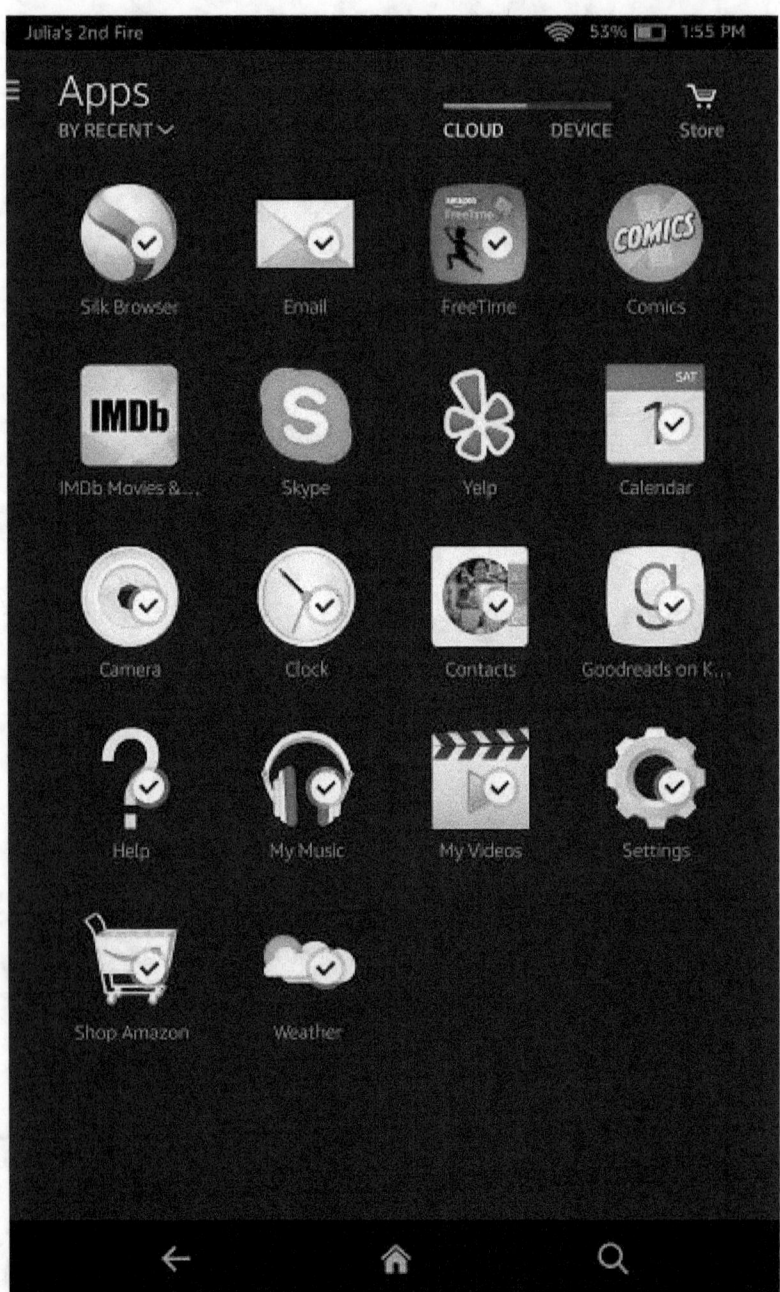

*Figure 1: Apps Library*

*Figure 2: Appstore*

*Figure 3: Matching Applications*

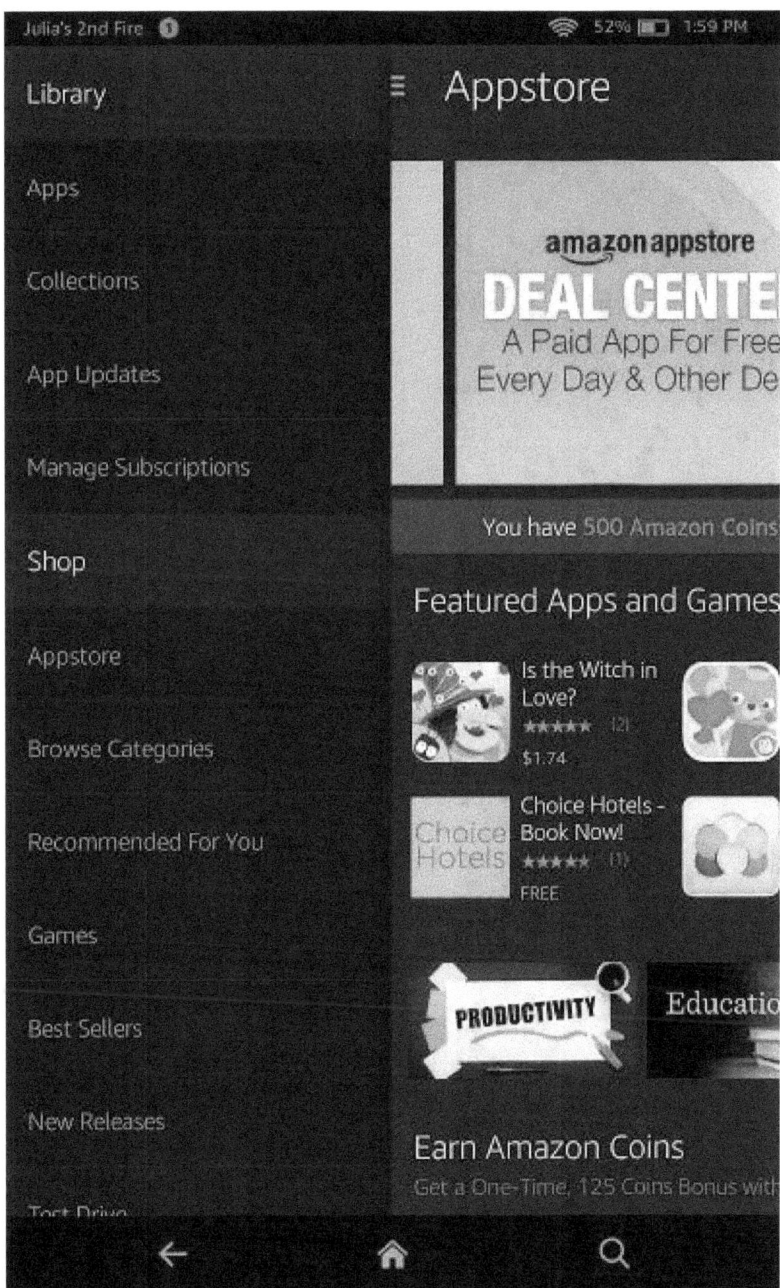

*Figure 4: App Store Menu*

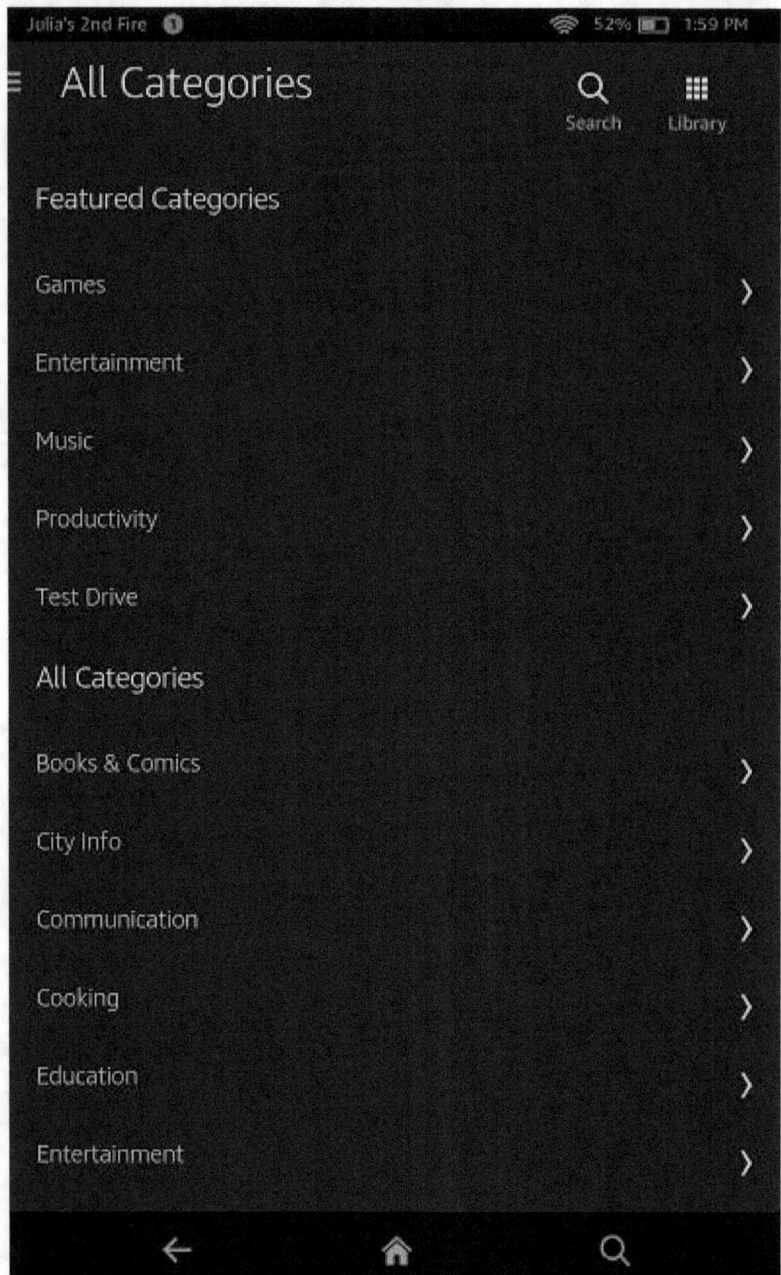

*Figure 5: List of Categories*

# 2. Buying an Application

Applications can be purchased directly from the Kindle Fire HD 6 using the Amazon App Store. To buy an application:

***Warning: Before purchasing an application, make sure that you want it. There are no refunds for applications in the Amazon App Store.***

1. Find the application that you wish to purchase. Refer to *"Searching for an Application in the Amazon App Store"* on page 185 to learn how.
2. Touch the name of the application. The Application description appears, as shown in **Figure 6**.

3. Touch the price of the application or touch the **FREE** button.

The **Get App** button appears, if the application is free.

4. Touch the **Get App** button, if the application is free, or touch **Buy Now** if the application is paid. The application is purchased and downloaded to your Apps library.

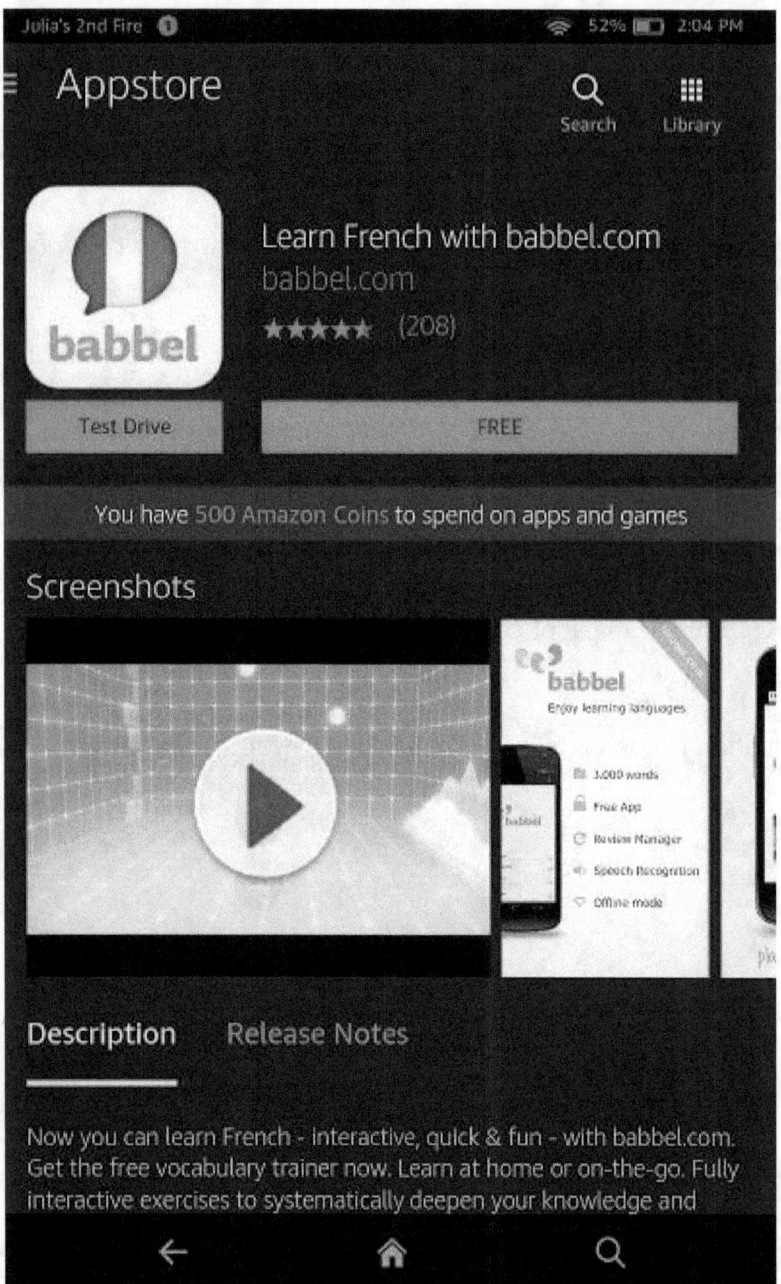

*Figure 6: Application Description*

# 3. Archiving an Application

In order to free up memory on the device, you can remove applications from the Kindle Fire HD 6 and store them in the Amazon cloud. Any application that is removed can always be downloaded for free later using a Wi-Fi connection. To remove an application:

1. Touch **Apps** at the top of the library. The Apps Library appears.
2. Touch and hold an application icon. The Application options appear above the icon, as shown in **Figure 7**.
3. Touch **Remove from Device**. A confirmation dialog appears.
4. Touch **OK**. The application is removed from the Kindle Fire HD 6.

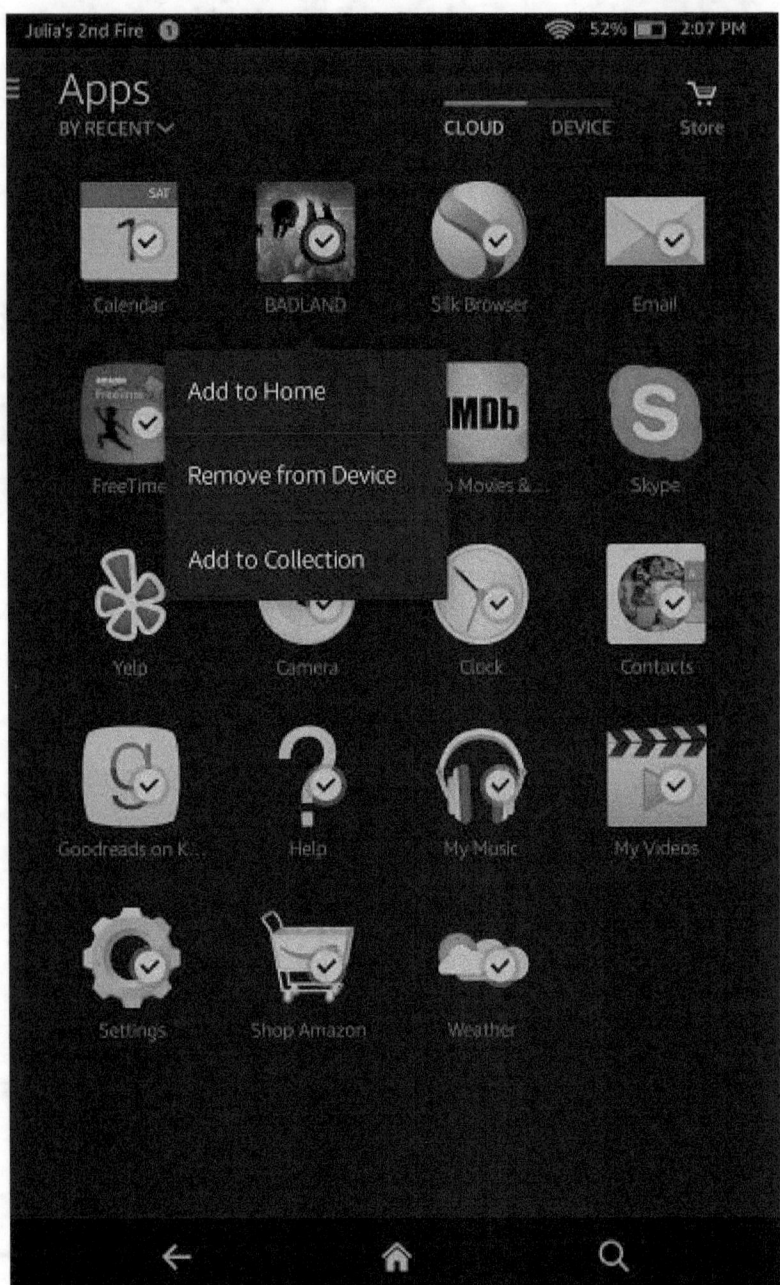

*Figure 7: Application Options*

# 4. Managing Applications on the Home Screen

Any application can be added to the Home screen for easy access. You can view the Home screen by touching the Library and moving your finger up.

To add an application to the Home screen:

- Touch **Apps** at the top of the library. The Apps Library appears.
- Touch and hold an application icon. The Application options appear above the icon.
- Touch **Add to Home**. The application is added to the Home screen.

To remove applications from the Home screen:

1. Touch and hold an application on the Home screen. 'Remove' appears at the top of the screen.
2. Touch each application that you wish to remove from the Home screen. A check mark appears on the icon of each selected application, as shown in **Figure 8**.
3. Touch **Remove**. The selected applications are removed from the Home screen.

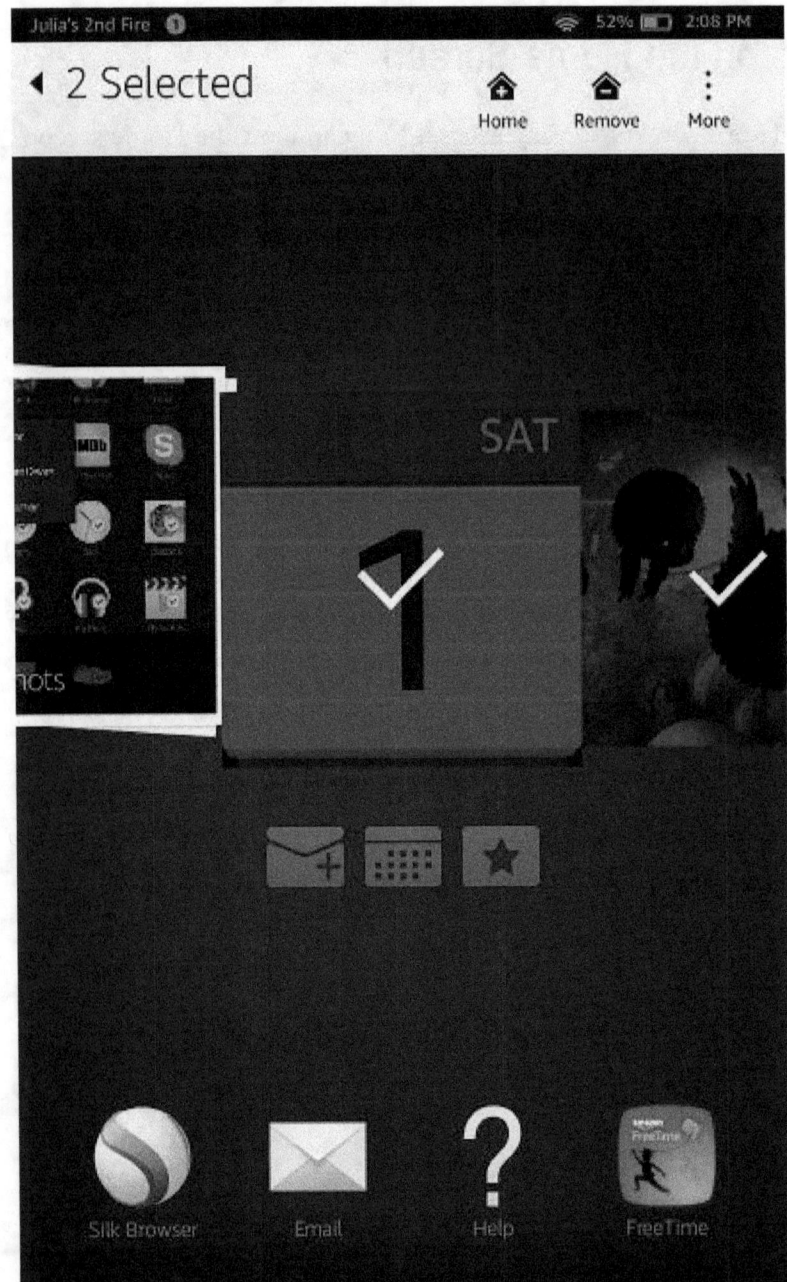

*Figure 8: Selected Applications*

# 5. Switching to Another Application while Using an App

While using an application, you can view a list of the currently open applications, and switch to one. To switch to another application, touch the bottom edge of the screen and slide your finger up. A list of open applications appears, as shown in **Figure 9**. Touch an application in the list. The application is opened. You can also touch the list and slide your finger to the left or right to view more open applications.

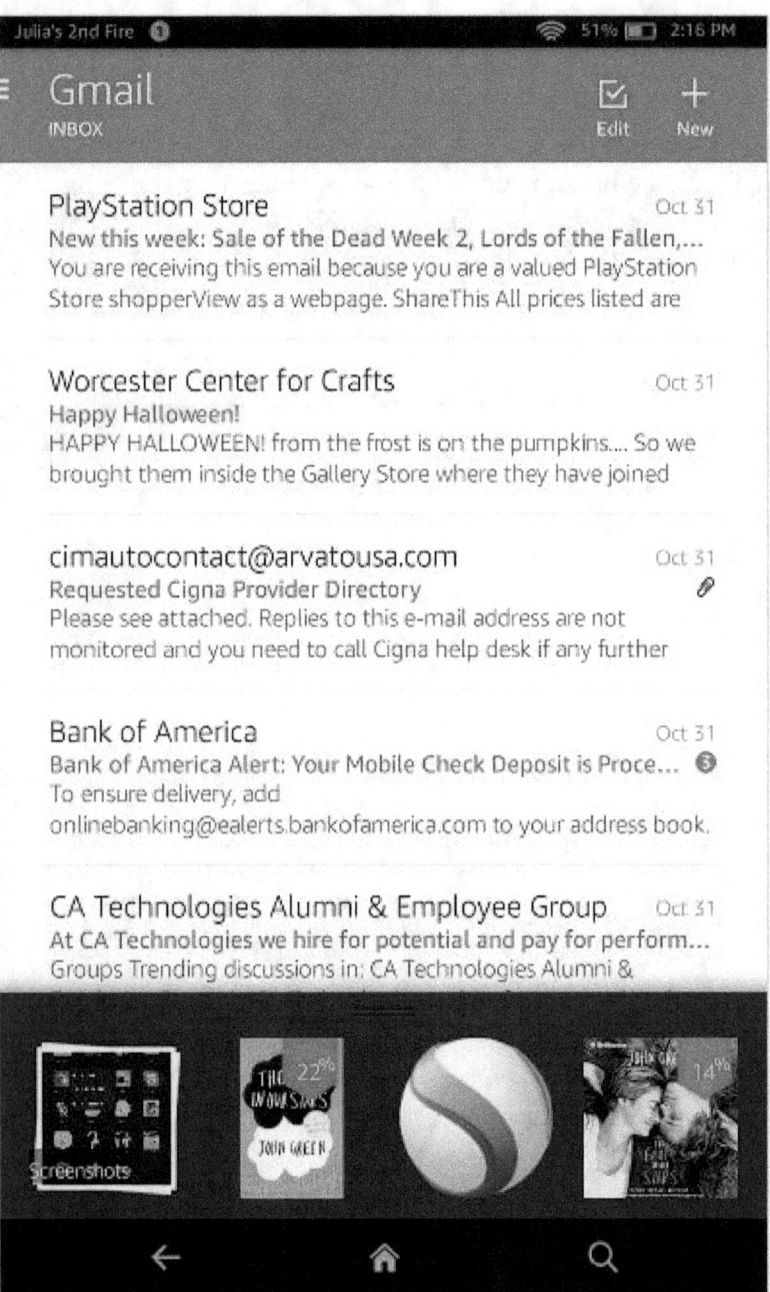

*Figure 9: List of Open Applications*

# 6. Reporting an Issue with an Application

If an application malfunctions or is offensive in any way, you can report the issue to Amazon, who will get in touch with the developer to address your concern. To report an issue with an application:

1. Touch **Apps** at the top of the library. The Apps Library appears.
2. Touch **Store** in the upper right-hand corner of the screen. The Apps Store opens.
3. Find the application that you wish to report. Refer to *"Searching for an Application in the Amazon App Store"* on page 185 to learn how.
4. Touch the title of the application. The Application description appears.
5. Scroll down to the bottom of the description. Touch **Report an Issue**. The Issue Type menu appears, as shown in **Figure 10**.
6. Touch the type of issue that you wish to report. The appropriate reporting screen appears. Follow the instructions on the screen, which vary depending on your issue.

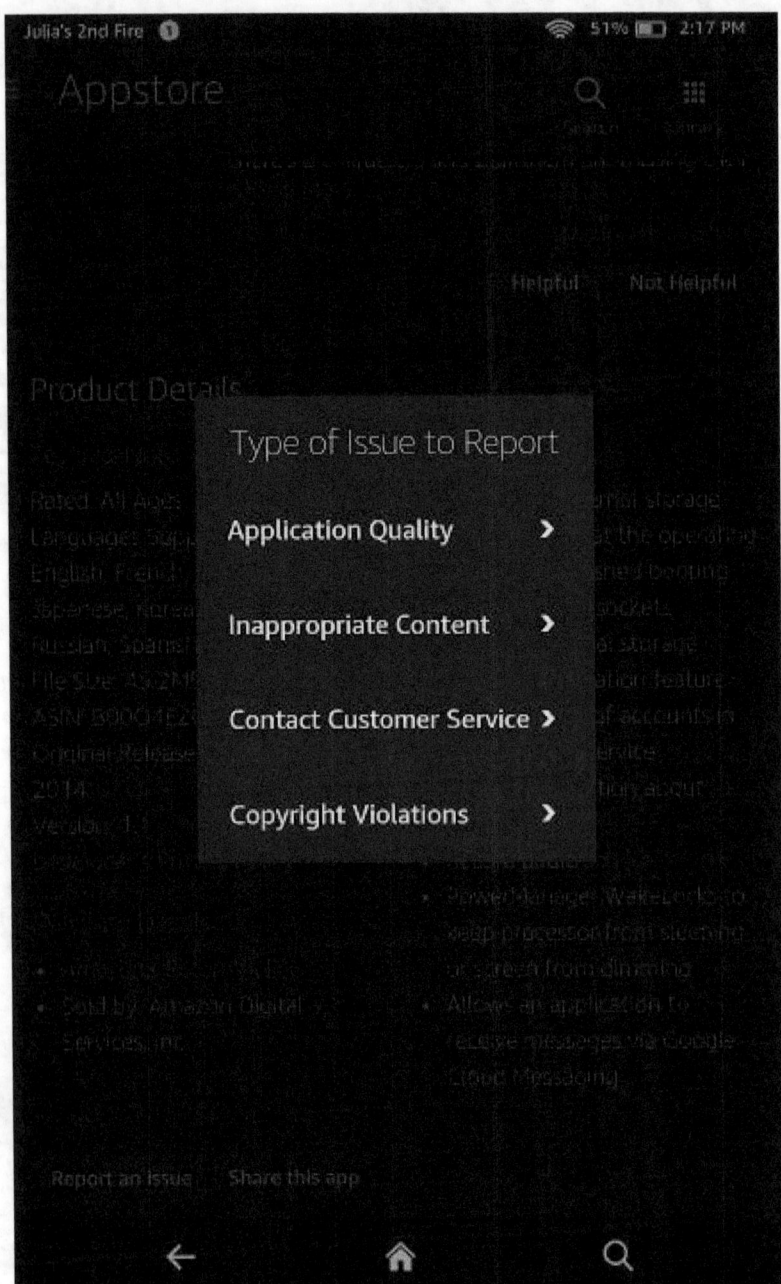

*Figure 10: Issue Type Menu*

# 7. Test Driving an Application

The Amazon application store allows you to test an application for ten minutes before downloading it. To test drive an application:

1. Touch **Apps** at the top of the library. The Apps Library appears.
2. Touch the left edge of the screen and slide your finger to the right. The Application Library menu appears, as shown in **Figure 11**.
3. Touch **Test Drive**. A list of applications that are available for Test Drive, as shown in **Figure 12**.
4. Touch an application in the list. The application description appears.
5. Touch **Test Drive**. The application opens in Test Drive, as shown in **Figure 13**.
   Touch **Quit** in the upper left-hand corner of the screen at any time to close Test Drive.

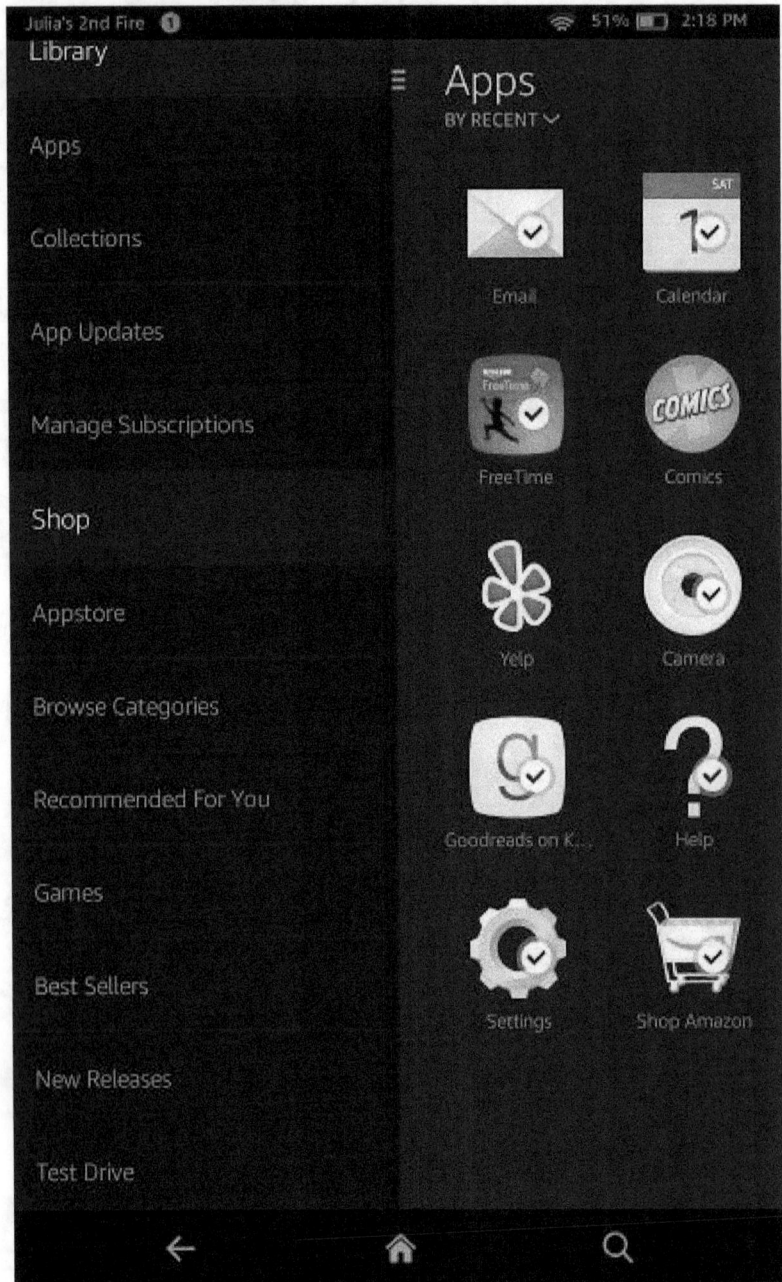

*Figure 11: Application Library Menu*

*Figure 12: List of Applications Available for Test Drive*

*Figure 13: Application in Test Drive*

# 8. Checking for Application Updates

To find out whether a developer has fixed a bug in an application, or has added new levels or features, check for application updates. To check for updates, touch the left edge of the screen in the Apps library. The Application library menu appears. Touch **App Updates**. A list of applications that have available updates appears. Touch an application name to update it.

# Adjusting the Settings

## Table of Contents

## 1. Adjusting the Brightness

The brightness of the screen can be changed. You can also have the device set the brightness automatically, depending on the current lighting conditions. To adjust the brightness:

1. Touch the time at the top of the screen and slide your finger down. The Quick Settings Banner appears, as shown in **Figure 1**.
2. Touch **Brightness**. The Brightness bar appears.
3. Touch the white slider on the brightness bar and drag it to the left to decrease the brightness or to the right to increase it. The brightness is adjusted accordingly.

*Figure 1: Quick Settings Banner*

# 2. Setting Up Parental Controls

You can set up parental controls to restrict the ways in which your children use the Kindle Fire HD 6. To set up parental controls:

1. Touch the time at the top of the screen and slide your finger down. The Quick Settings Banner appears.
2. Touch the [icon] icon. The Settings screen appears, as shown in **Figure 2**.
3. Touch **Household Profiles**. The Household Profiles screen appears, as shown in **Figure 3**.
4. Touch **Add Child** to set up an account with parental controls enabled. The Lock Screen password screen appears, as shown in **Figure 4**.
5. Enter your preferred password twice and touch **Finish**. The Parental Controls password is set and the Add Child Profile screen appears, as shown in **Figure 5**.
6. Enter the child's name, select a gender, and enter the birth date of the child. You can also select whether to use Amazon Freetime, a feature created for children eight and younger, or Teen Profiles, for kids nine and older.
7. Touch **Add Profile** when you are finished. The profile is created and the content management screen appears, as shown in **Figure 6**. A list of children's eBooks that are already on your device appears.
8. Touch the title of an eBook to allow the child to view it while using his or her profile. You can also touch **For Kids** to select other content types, such as Videos and Apps, or touch **All** to view all content.
9. Touch **Done** at the top of the screen. The child profile setup is complete. To access the child's profile, touch the [icon] icon (or your profile picture) in the upper left-hand corner of the screen, and then touch the child's name. To access your Adult account, unlock the Kindle Fire HD 6 normally, and then enter the password that you set in step 5.

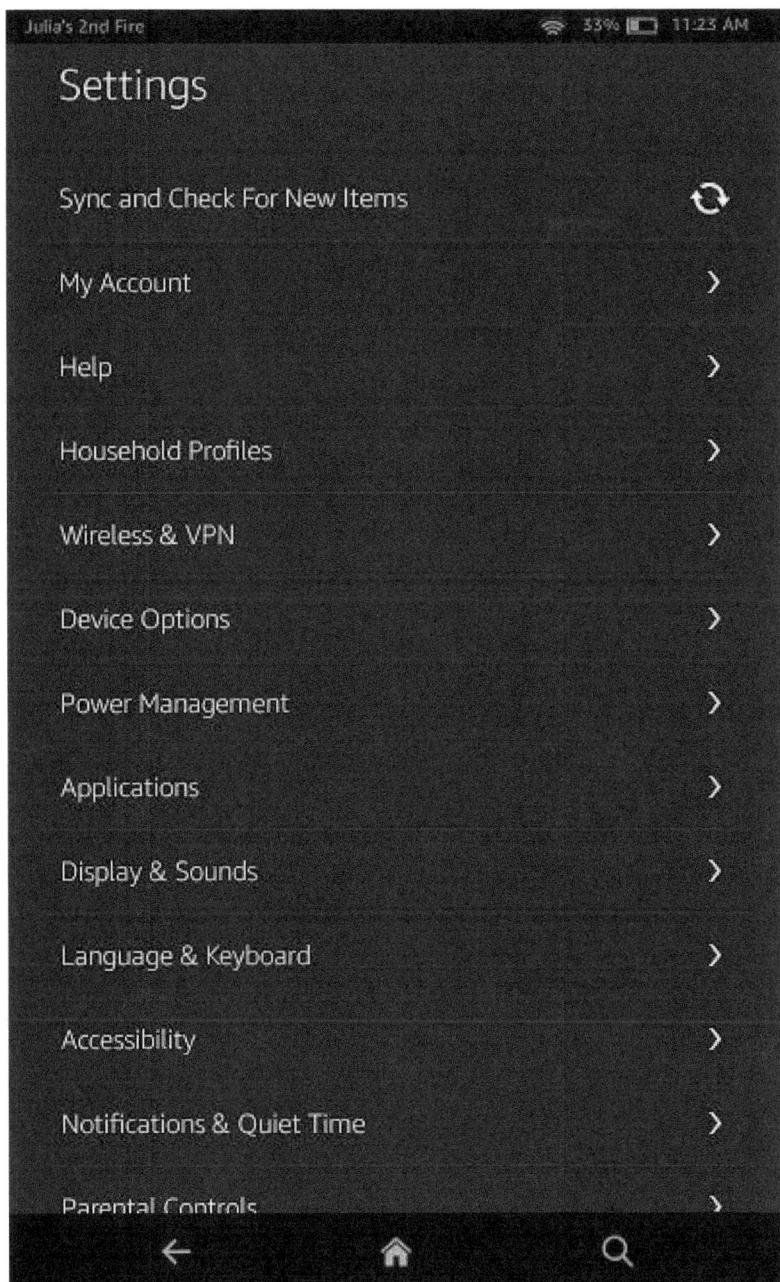

*Figure 2: Settings Screen*

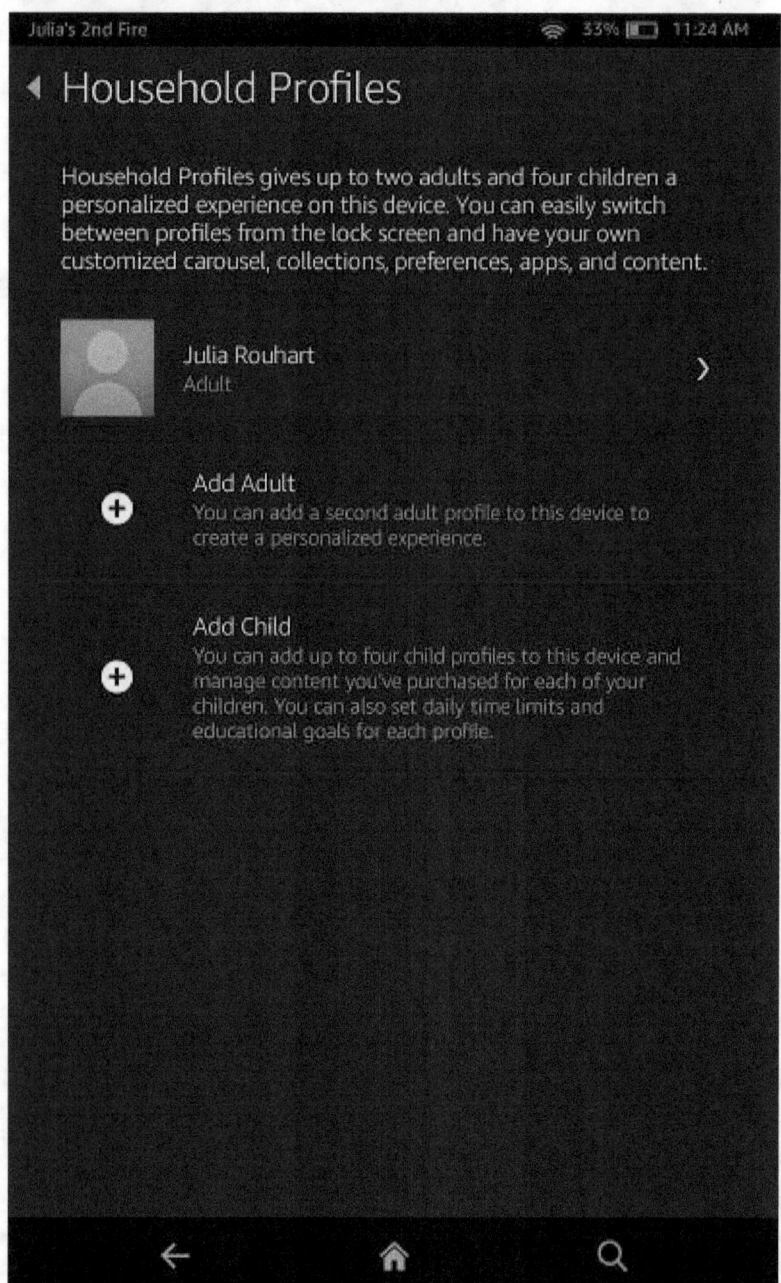

*Figure 3: Household Profiles Screen*

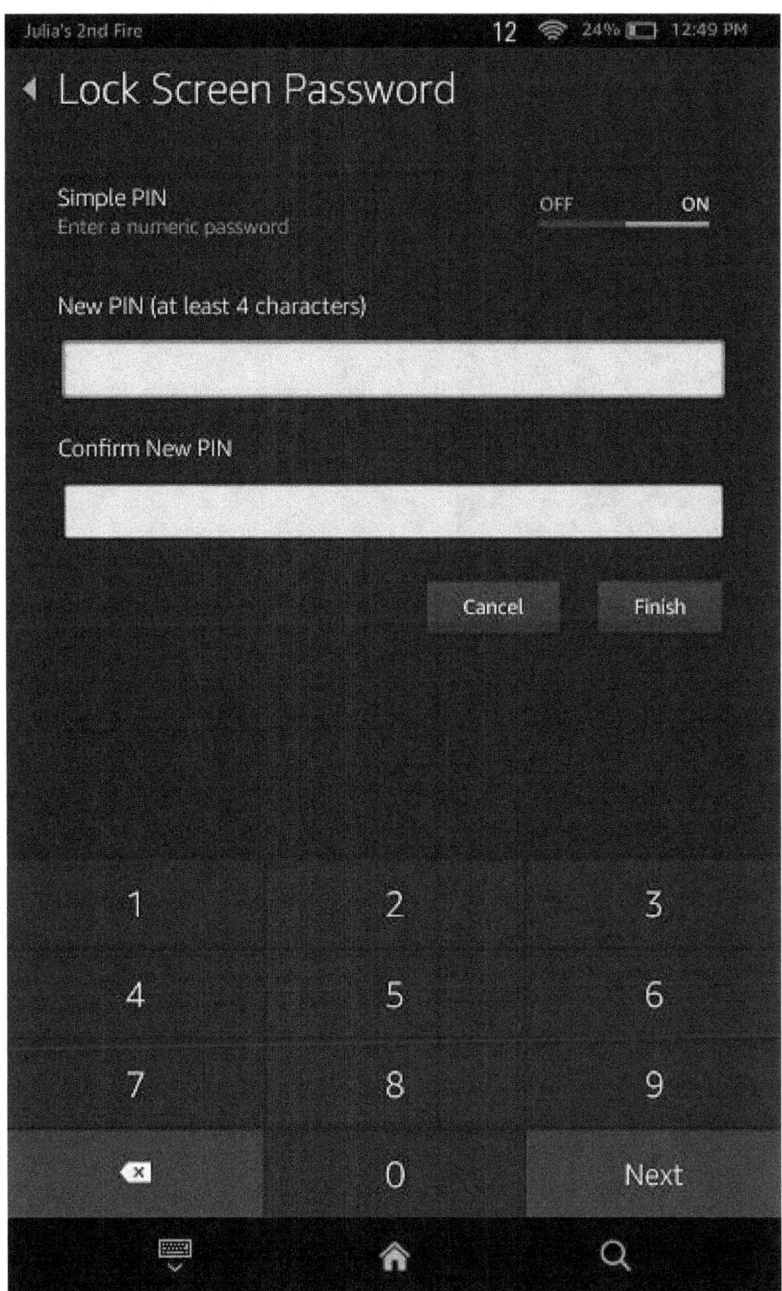

*Figure 4: Lock Screen Password Screen*

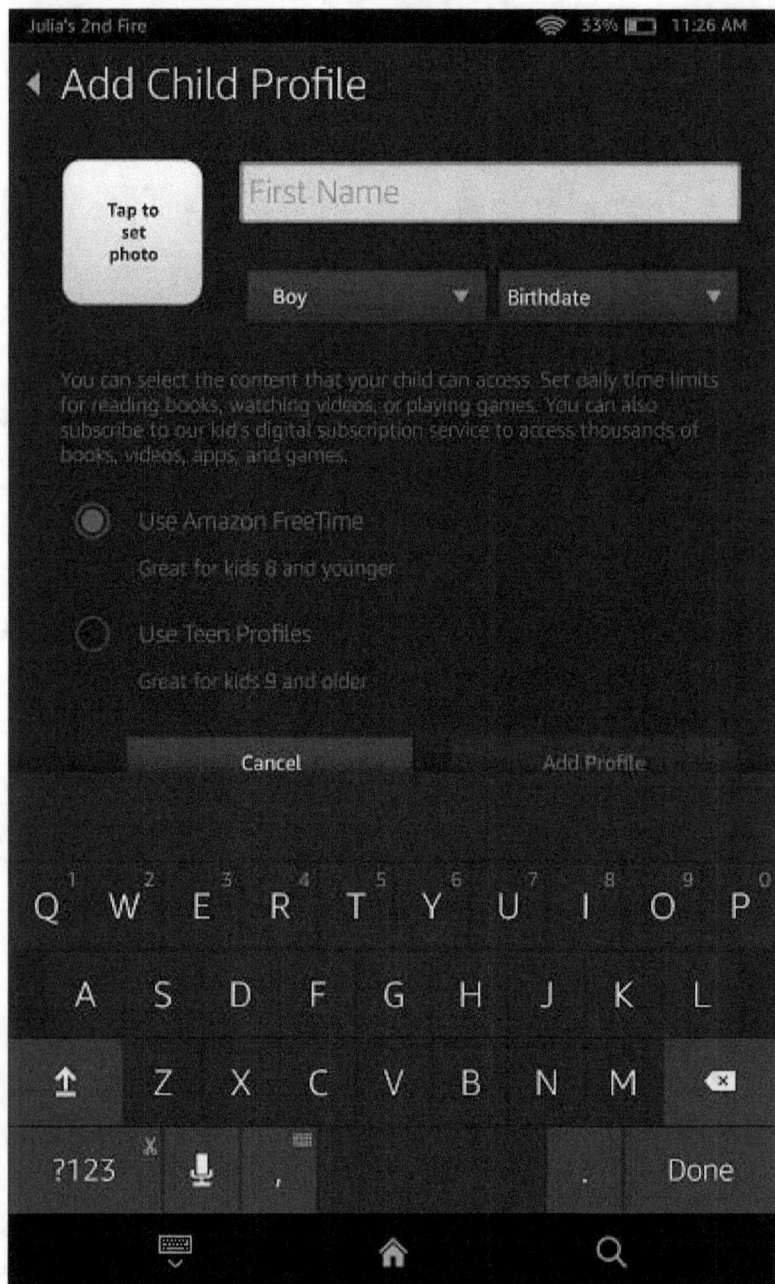

*Figure 5: Add Child Profiles Screen*

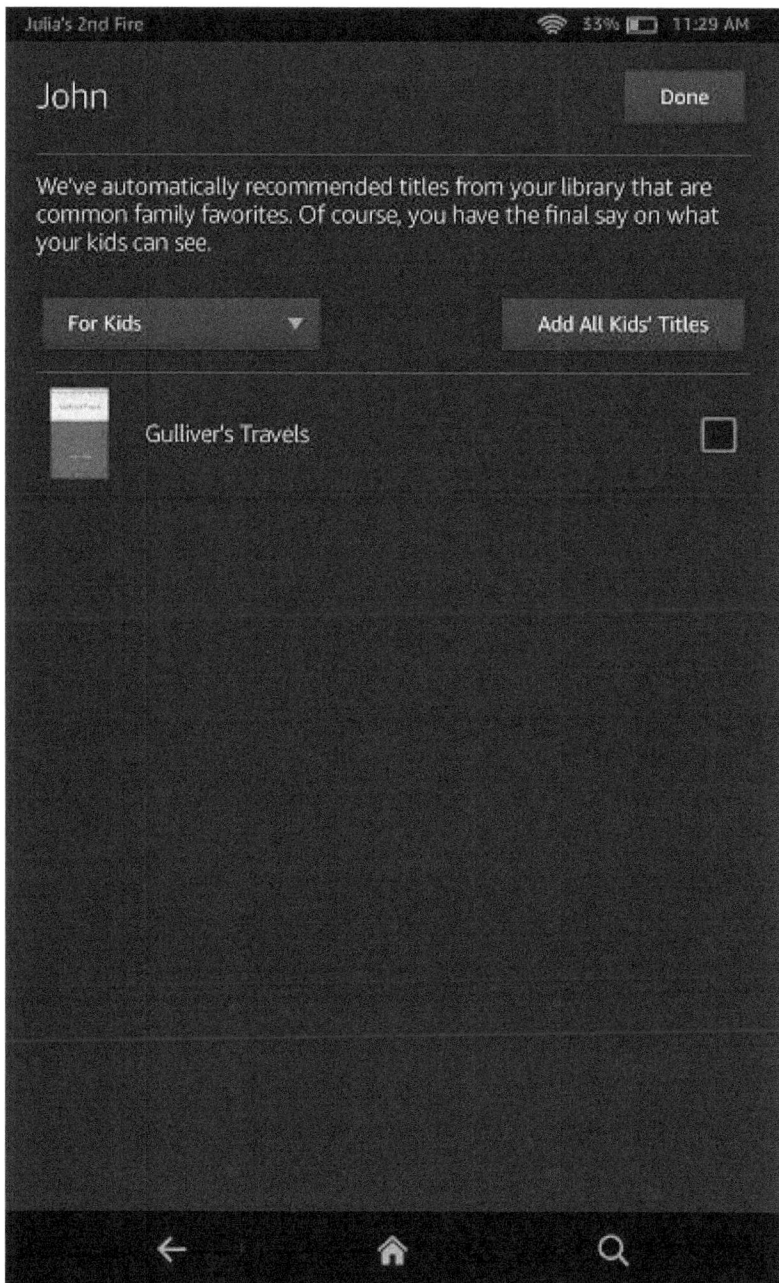

*Figure 6: Content Management Screen*

# 3. Setting the System Language

The language that is used to display menus and options on the Kindle Fire HD 6 can be changed. To set the system language:

1. Touch the time at the top of the screen and slide your finger down. The Quick Settings Banner appears.
2. Touch the ⚙ icon. The Settings screen appears.
3. Touch **Language & Keyboard**. The Language & Keyboard screen appears, as shown in **Figure 7**.
4. Touch **Language**. A list of available languages appears, as shown in **Figure 8**.
5. Touch a language in the list. The selected language is applied to all menus and options.

*Note: All web content and downloaded media will not be translated to the system language.*

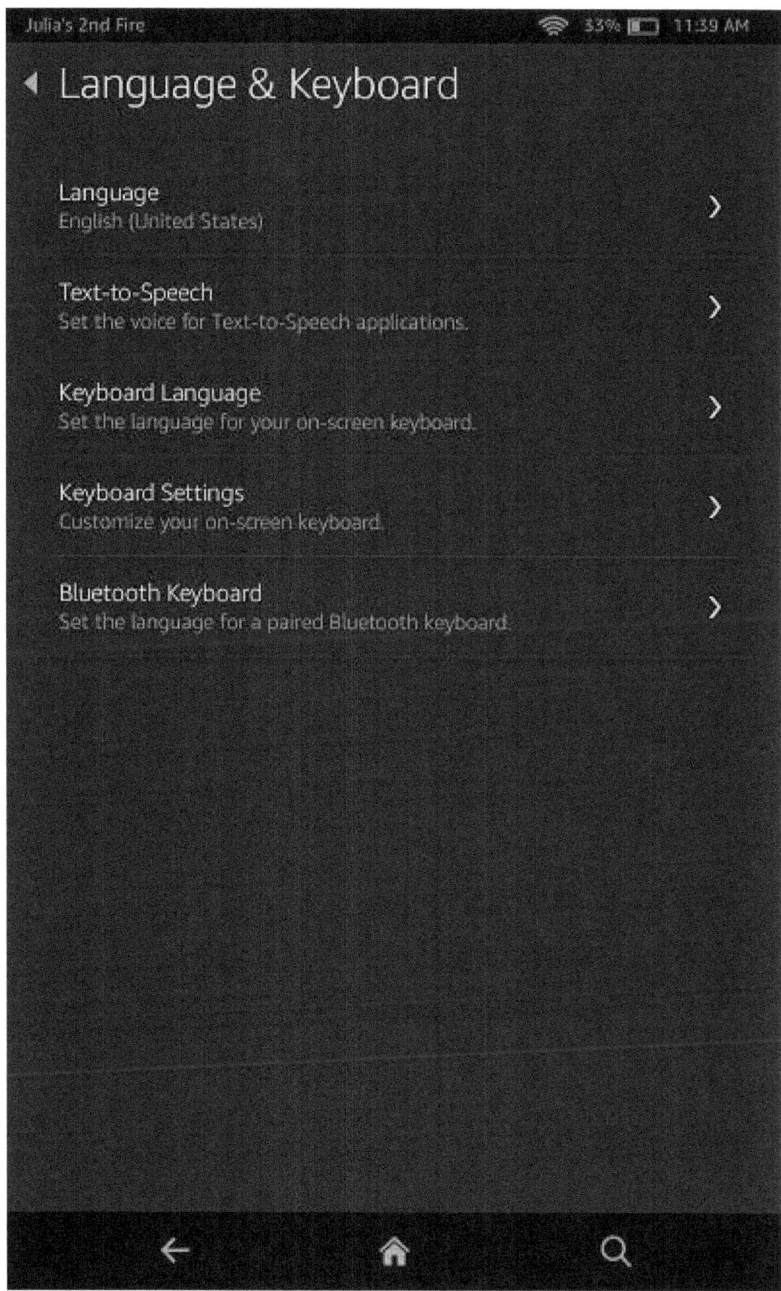

*Figure 7: Language & Keyboard Screen*

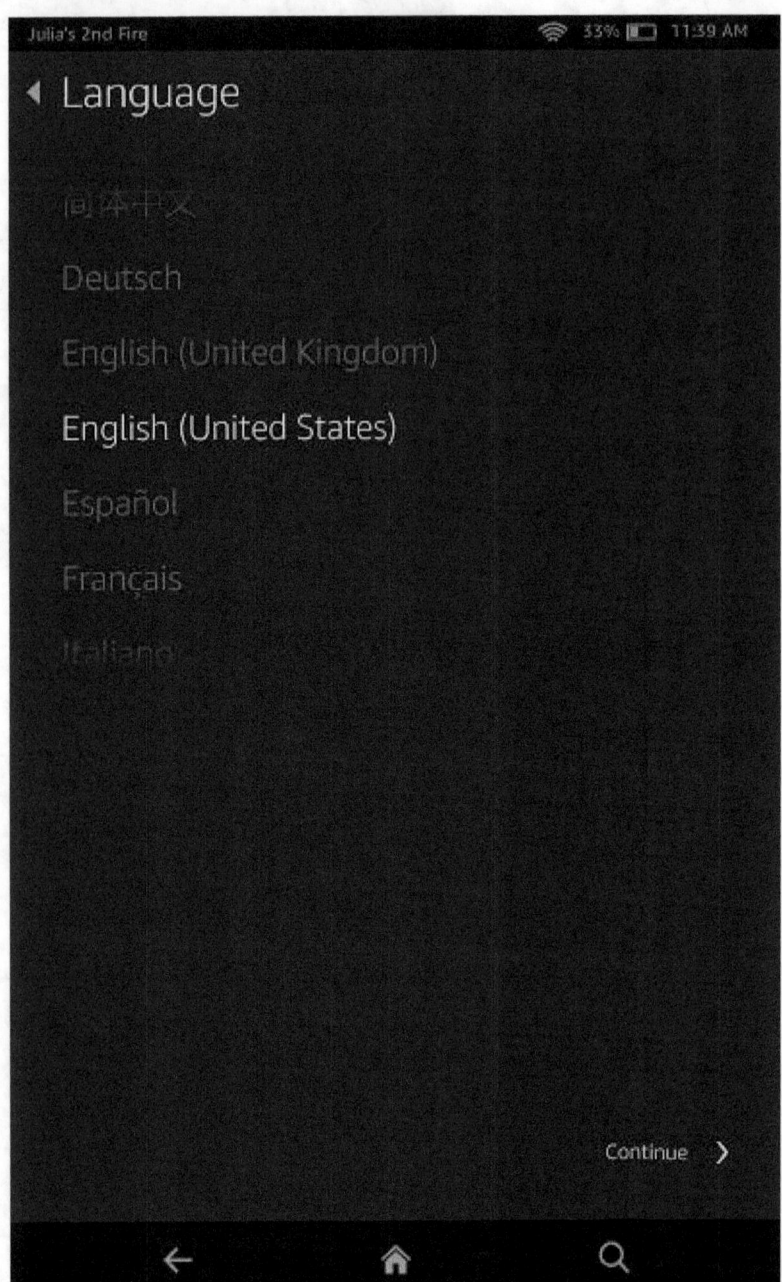

*Figure 8: List of Available Languages*

# 4. Setting the Text-to-Speech Language

The device allows you to select the voice and language that is used when using applications that support text-to-speech. To set the text-to-speech language:

1. Touch the time at the top of the screen and slide your finger down. The Quick Settings Banner appears.
2. Touch the ⚙ icon. The Settings screen appears.
3. Touch **Language & Keyboard**. The Language & Keyboard screen appears.
4. Touch **Text-to-Speech**. The Text-to-Speech Settings screen appears, as shown in **Figure 9**. By default, there is only one voice installed on your device.
5. Touch **Download Additional Voices**. A list of downloadable voices appears, as shown in **Figure 10**.
6. Touch the language that you would like to download. The selected language is downloaded. When the download is finished, the language will appear in the Default Voice list, accessible from the Text-to-Speech Settings screen.

*Note: Downloaded media will not be translated to the system language.*

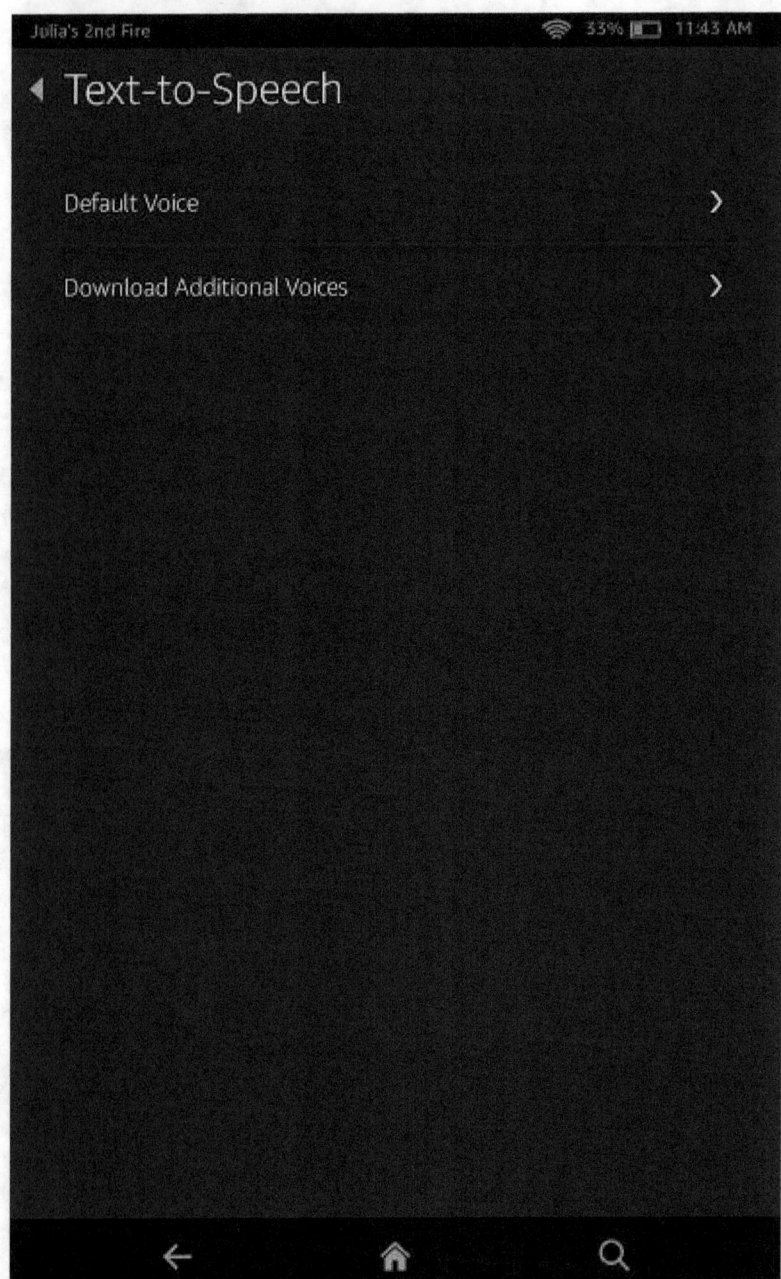

*Figure 9: Text-to-Speech Settings Screen*

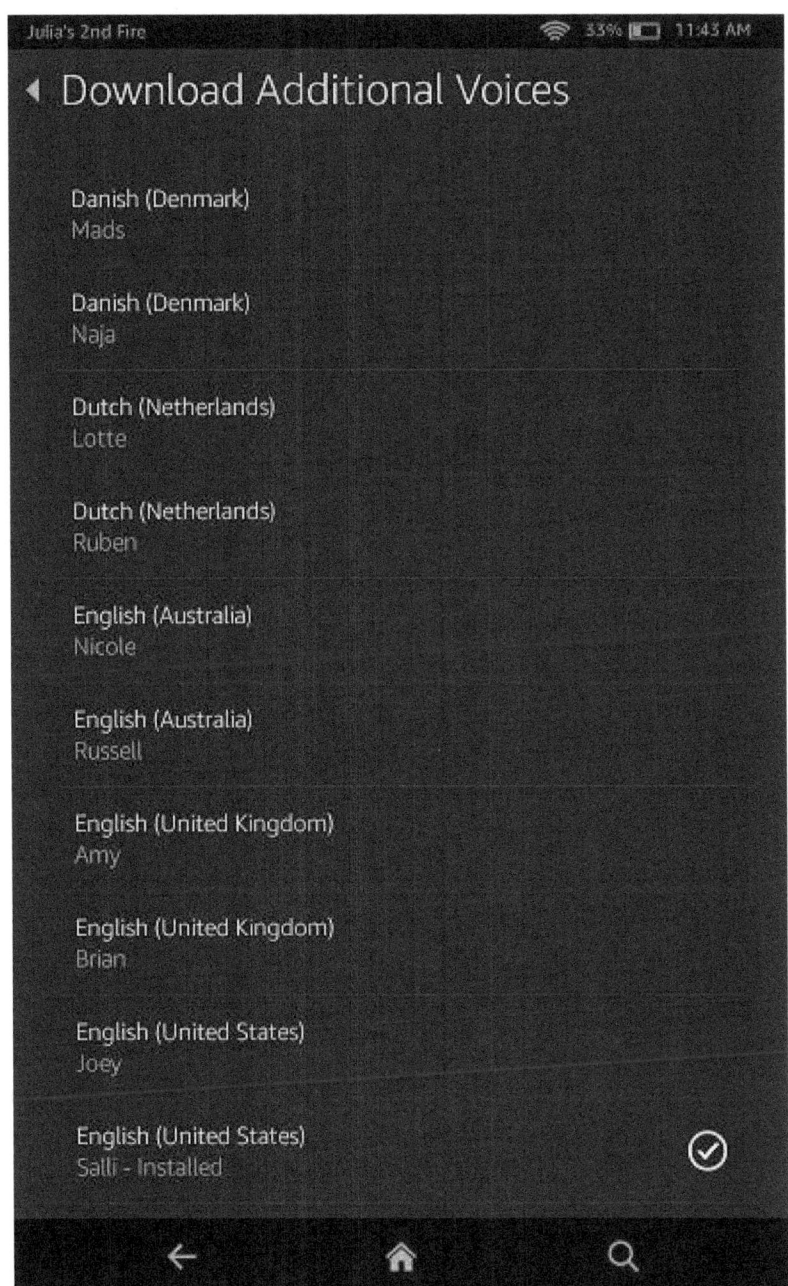

*Figure 10: List of Downloadable Voices*

# 5. Setting the Time Zone

The Kindle Fire HD 6 will automatically set the time according to the time zone, even when you are traveling. If you have a To set the time zone:

1. Touch the time at the top of the screen and slide your finger down. The Quick Settings Banner appears.
2. Touch the icon. The Settings screen appears.
3. Touch **Device Options**. The Device Settings screen appears, as shown in **Figure 11**.
4. Touch **Date & Time**. The Date & Time Settings screen appears, as shown in **Figure 12**.
5. Touch **Automatic Time Zone**. Automatic time zone setting is turned off.
6. Touch **Select Time Zone**. The Time Zone Selection screen appears, as shown in **Figure 13**.
7. Select your current time zone from the time zone drop-down menu. The time zone is set and the time is automatically adjusted. Remember to change the time zone if you travel outside of the current one.

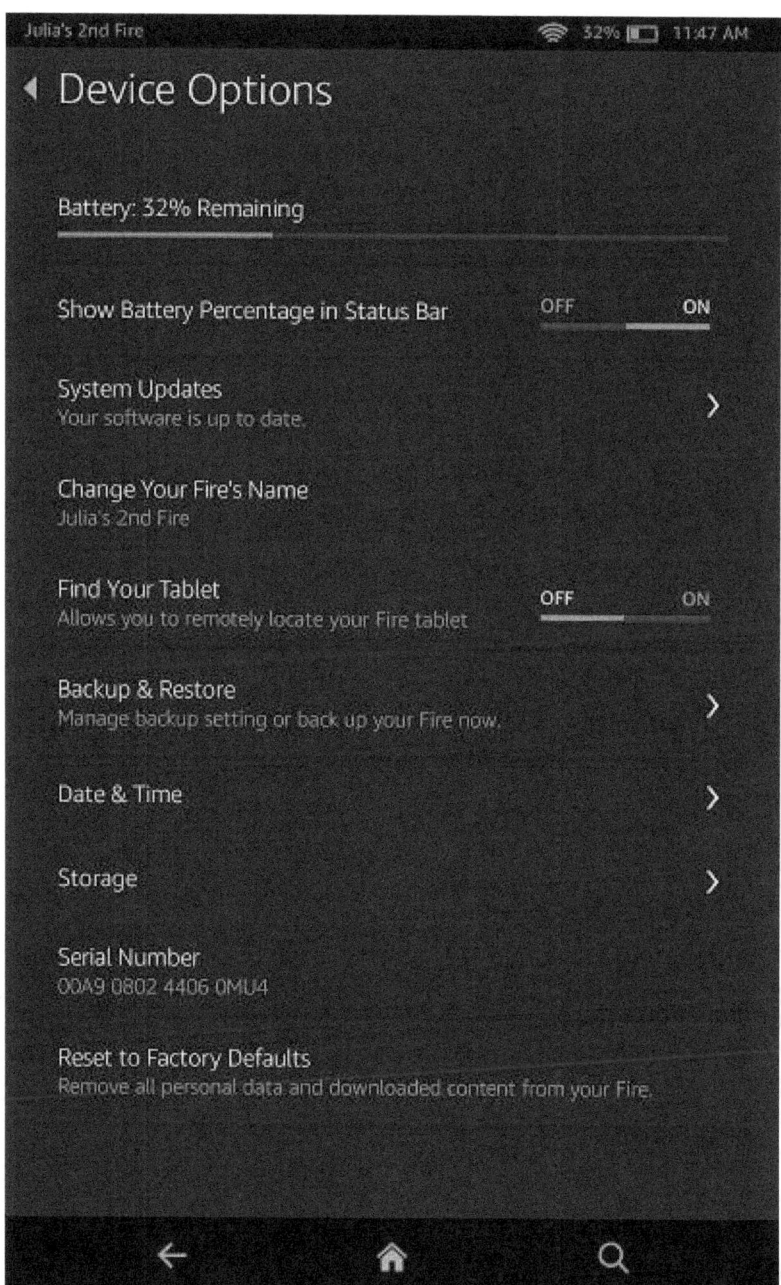

*Figure 11: Device Settings Screen*

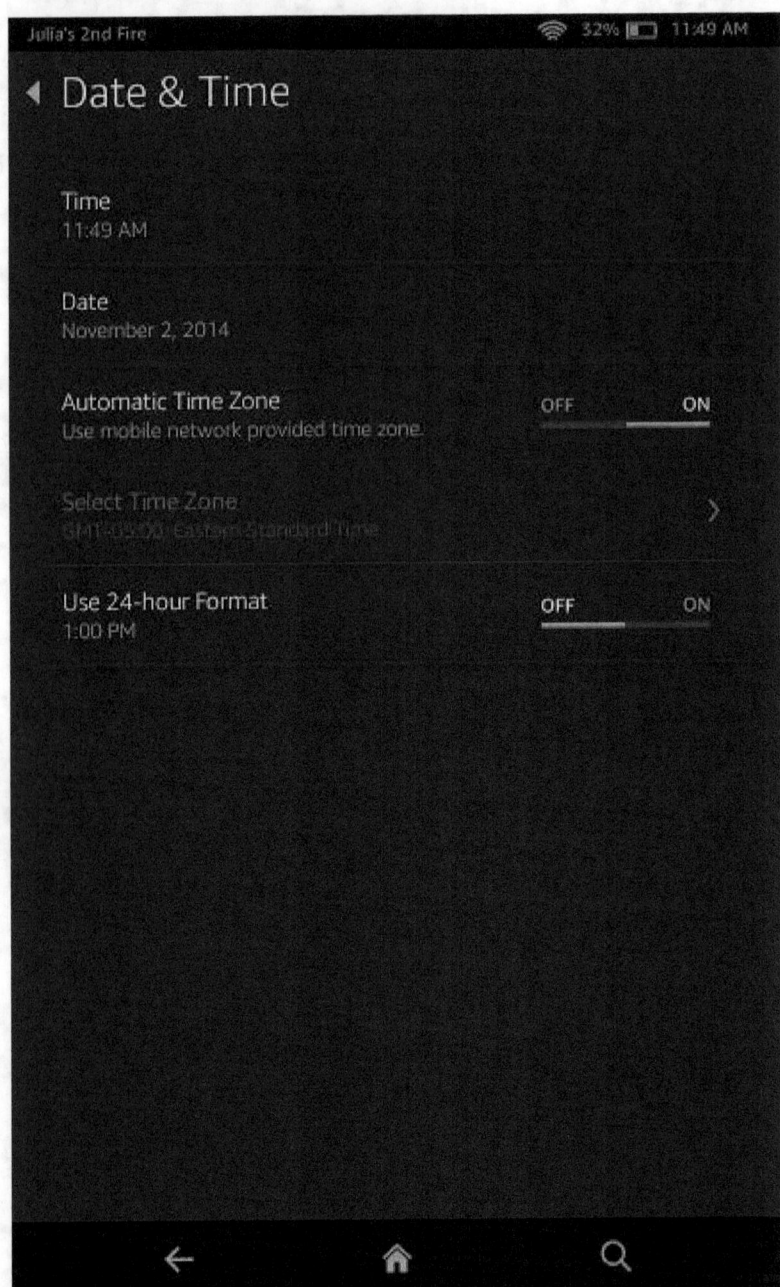

*Figure 12: Date & Time Settings Screen*

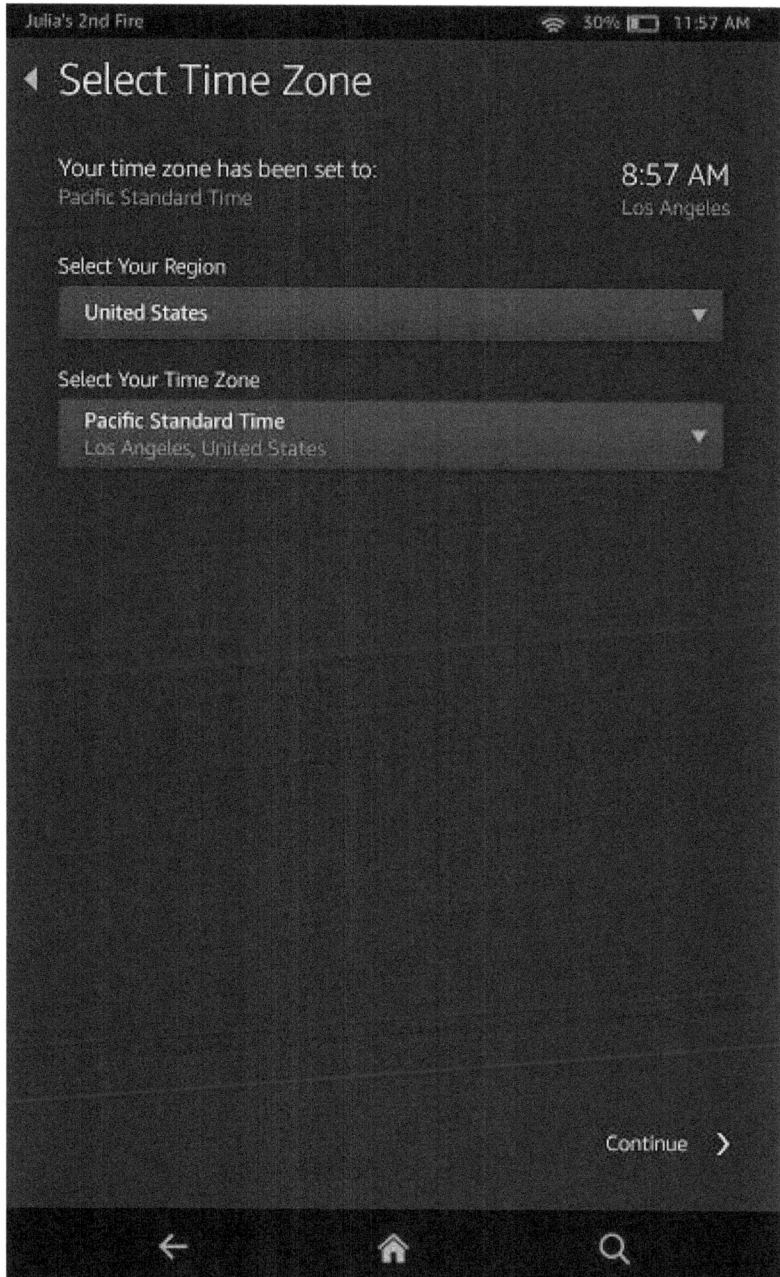

*Figure 13: Time Zone Selection Screen*

# 6. Turning Airplane Mode On or Off

Airplane Mode is used to turn off all wireless communications and, in certain instances, it is easier to turn it on rather than turn off the device entirely. To turn Airplane Mode on or off:

1. Touch the time at the top of the screen and slide your finger down. The Quick Settings Banner appears.
2. Touch the ⚙ icon. The Settings screen appears.
3. Touch **Wireless & VPN**. The Wireless & VPN screen appears, as shown in **Figure 14**.
4. Touch the OFF/ON switch next to Airplane Mode. The OFF/ON switch appears and Airplane Mode is turned on.
5. Touch the OFF/ON switch next to Airplane Mode. The OFF/ON switch appears and Airplane Mode is turned off.

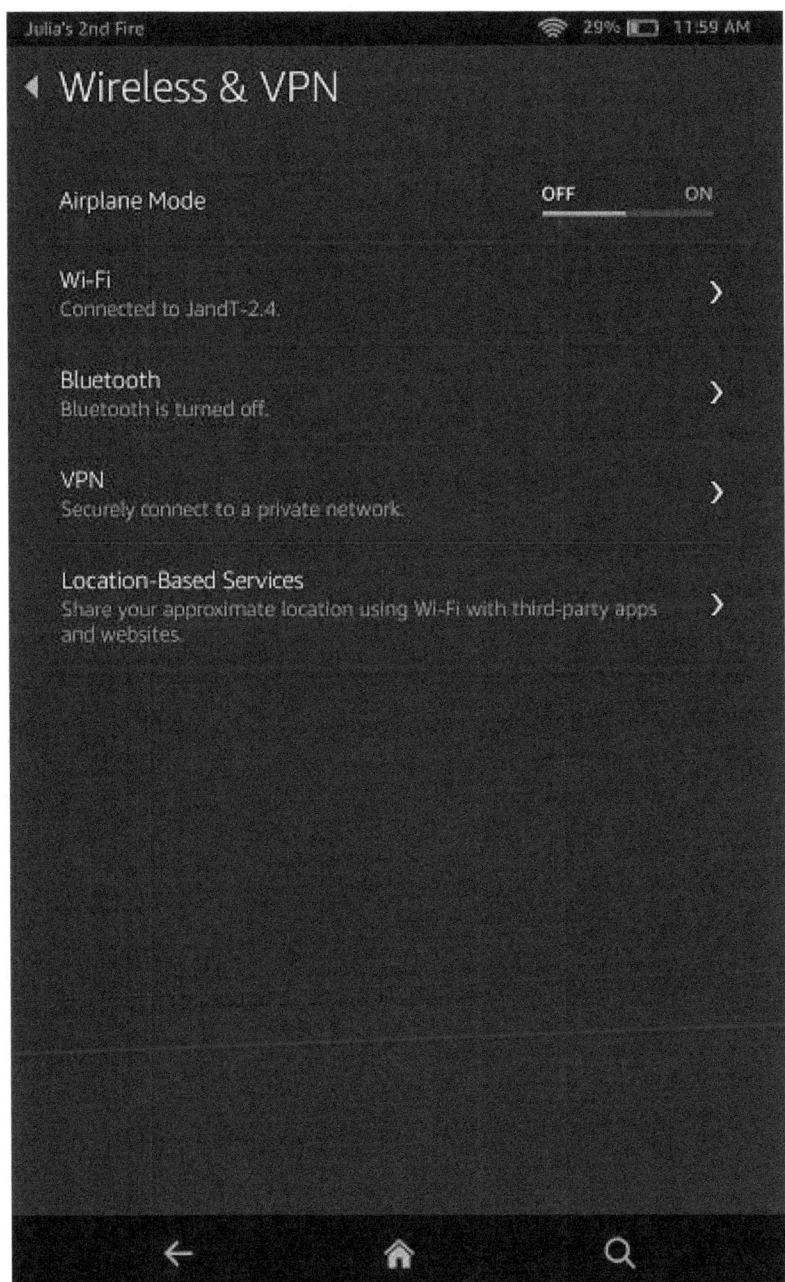

*Figure 14: Wireless & VPN Screen*

# 7. Setting Up Wi-Fi

Connect to a Wi-Fi network to access the internet, which is required to stream and download media, surf the web, and use certain applications. To set up Wi-Fi:

1. Touch the time at the top of the screen and slide your finger down. The Quick Settings Banner appears.
2. Touch the ⚙ icon. The Settings screen appears.
3. Touch **Wireless & VPN**. The Wireless & VPN screen appears.
4. Touch **Wi-Fi**. The Wi-Fi Settings screen appears.
5. Touch the [OFF ─── ON] switch next to Wi-Fi. A list of Wi-Fi networks that are in range of your device appears, as shown in **Figure 15**.
6. Touch the network to which you would like to connect. The Network Password prompt appears, as shown in **Figure 16**. If you do not have a password protected network, the device immediately connects to the selected network.
7. Enter your network password (usually found on your wireless router), and touch **Connect**. The device connects to the selected Wi-Fi network.

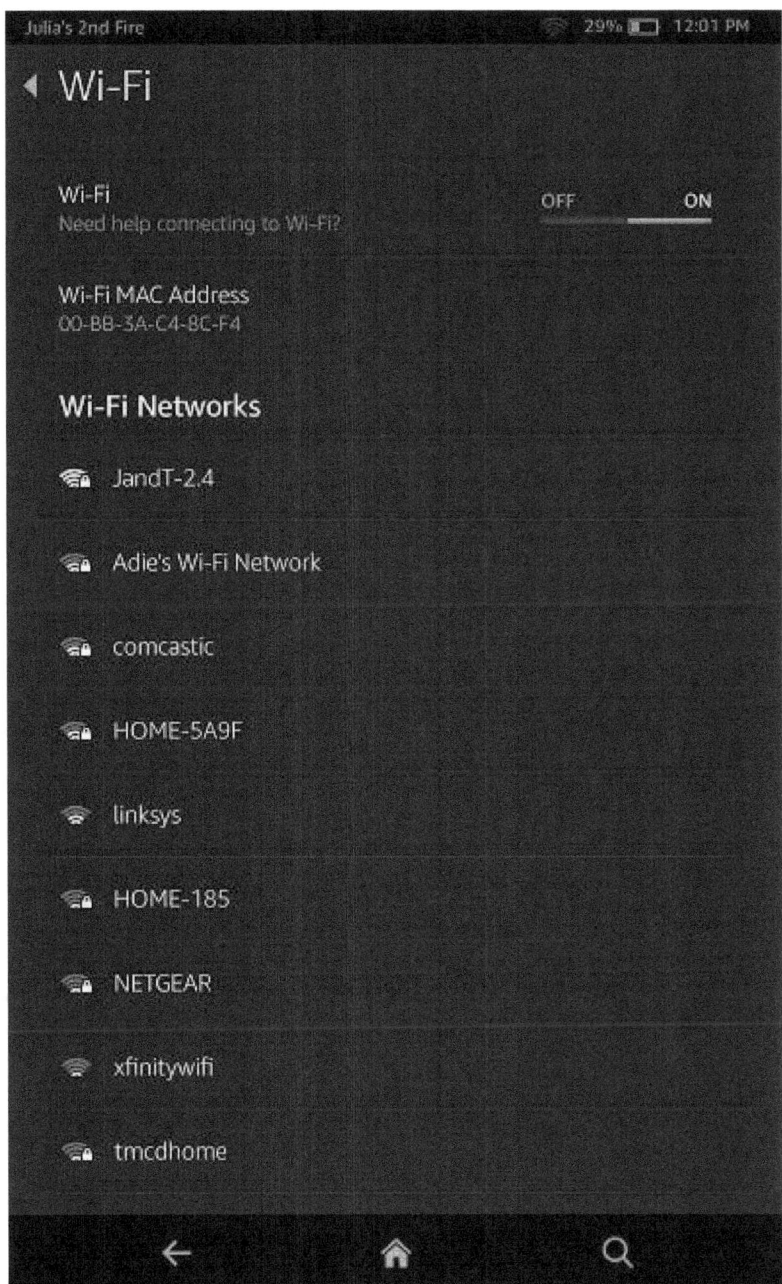

*Figure 15: List of Wi-Fi Networks*

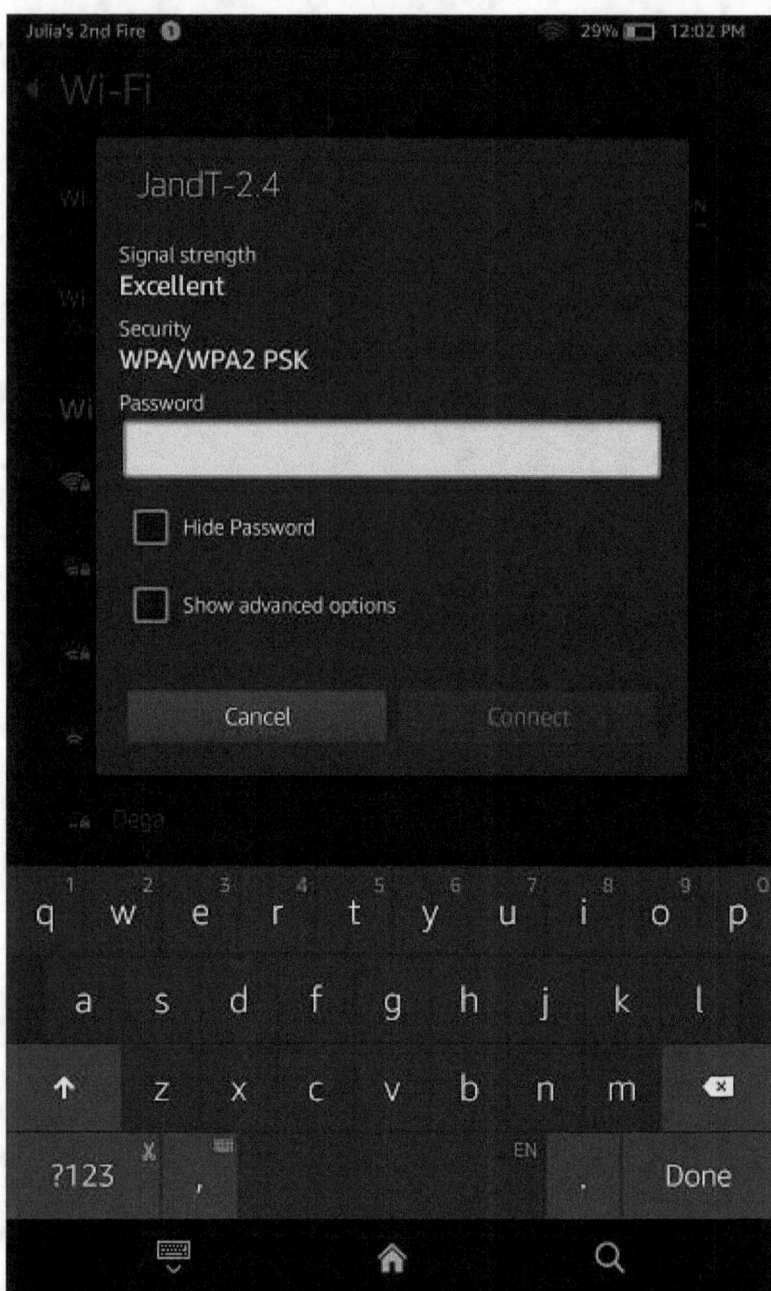

*Figure 16: Network Password Prompt*

# 8. Setting Up Bluetooth

Bluetooth allows you to connect to other devices to transfer media, or to wireless control devices, such as a keyboard. To set up Bluetooth:

1. Touch the time at the top of the screen and slide your finger down. The Quick Settings Banner appears.

2. Touch the icon. The Settings screen appears.

3. Touch **Wireless & VPN**. The Wireless & VPN screen appears.

4. Touch **Bluetooth**. The Bluetooth Settings screen appears.

5. Touch the switch next to 'Bluetooth'. Bluetooth is turned on.

6. Touch **Pair a Bluetooth Device**. A list of discoverable devices appears, as shown in **Figure 17**. Make sure that Bluetooth is turned on on your secondary device or keyboard.

7. Touch the name of a device in the list. The Kindle Fire HD 6 pairs with the selected device. You may need to enter a code on the secondary device before it can be paired.

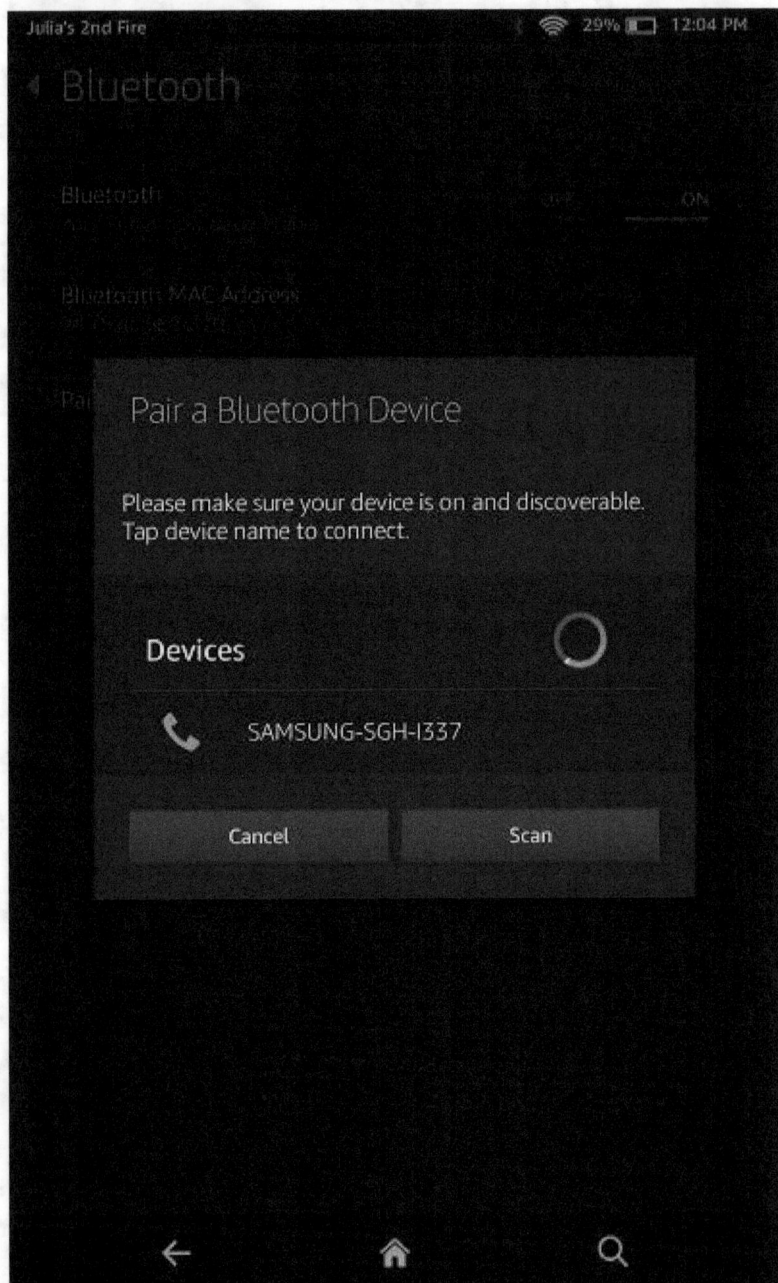

*Figure 17: List of Discoverable Devices*

# 9. Turning Location Services On or Off

Certain applications, such as navigation apps, need to determine your location. However, leaving Location Services turned on may drain your battery slightly more quickly. To turn Location Services on or off:

1. Touch the time at the top of the screen and slide your finger down. The Quick Settings Banner appears.
2. Touch the ⚙ icon. The Settings screen appears.
3. Touch **Wireless & VPN**. The Wireless & VPN screen appears.
4. Touch **Location-Based Services**. The Location-Based Services screen appears, as shown in **Figure 18**.
5. Touch the [OFF ON] switch next to 'Location-Based Services'. The feature is turned on.
6. Touch the [OFF ON] switch next to any specific application for which you want to turn off Location Services. The [OFF ON] switch appears and Location Services are turned off for the selected application.
7. Touch the [OFF ON] switch next to 'Location-Based Services'. The [OFF ON] switch appears and Location Services are turned off.

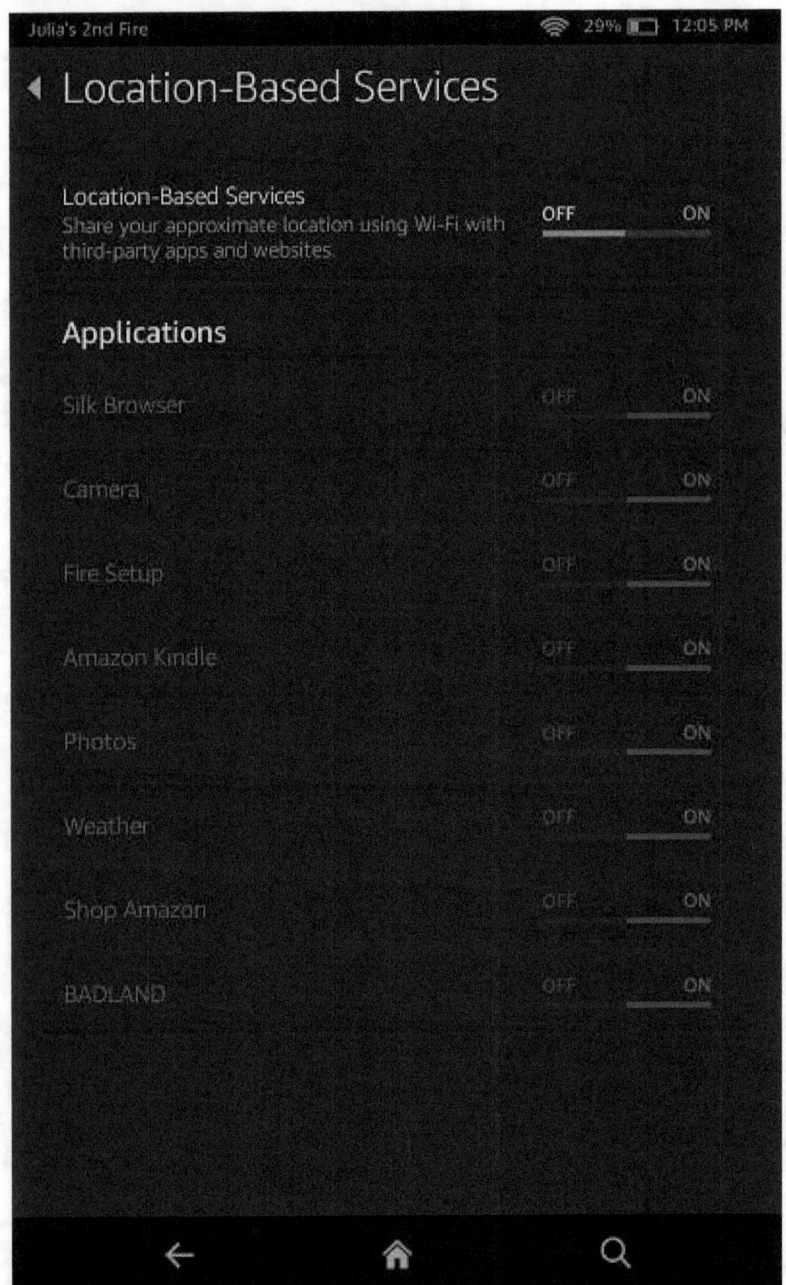

*Figure 18: Location-Based Services Screen*

# 10. Managing Application Settings

Many applications, such the Amazon App Store, have customizable settings. For instance, you may turn Automatic Application Updates on or off for the Amazon App Store. To manage application settings:

1. Touch the time at the top of the screen and slide your finger down. The Quick Settings Banner appears.

2. Touch the [icon] icon. The Settings screen appears.

3. Touch **Applications**. The Application Settings screen appears, as shown in **Figure 19**. Touch an application to edit its settings.

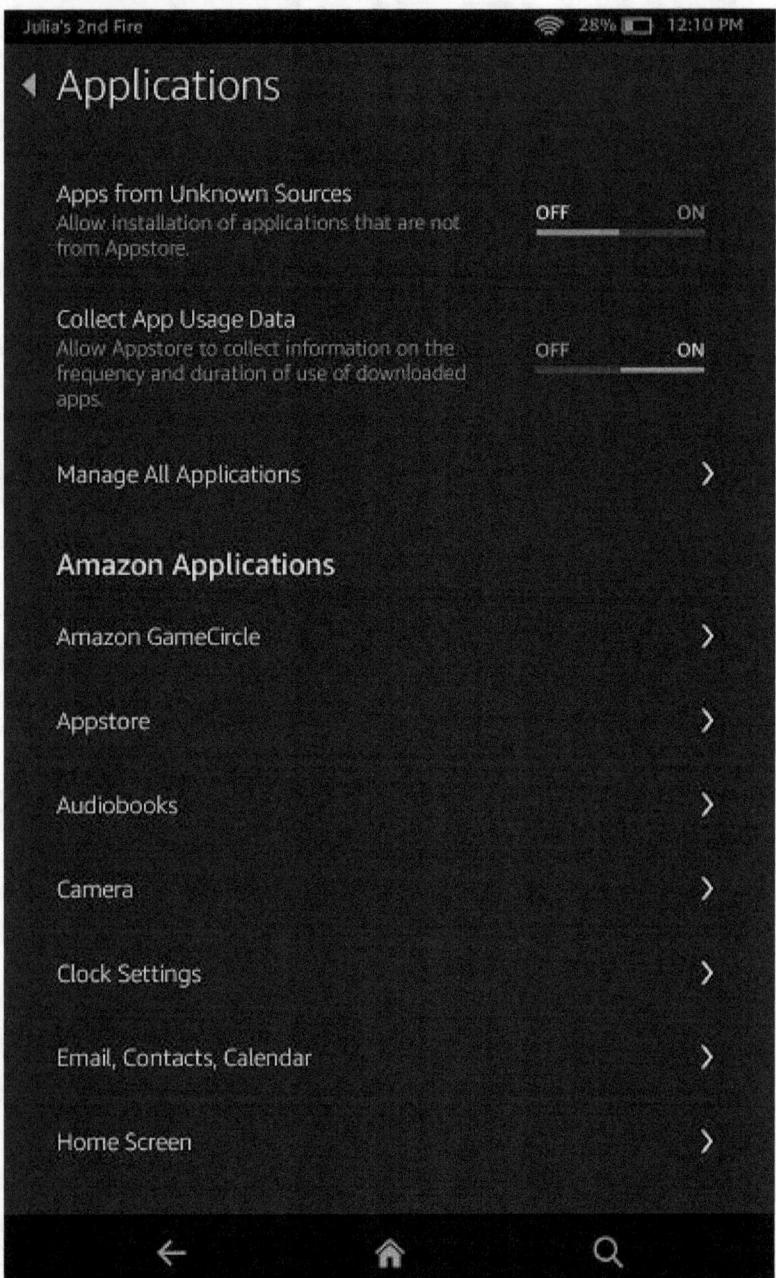

*Figure 19: Application Settings Screen*

# 11. Setting Up Quiet Time

The Quiet Time feature allows you to disable notifications while you are performing specific activities or during certain times of day. To set up Quiet Time:

1. Touch the time at the top of the screen and slide your finger down. The Quick Settings Banner appears.
2. Touch the ⚙ icon. The Settings screen appears.
3. Touch **Notifications & Quiet Time**. The Notifications & Quiet Time screen appears, as shown in **Figure 20**.
4. Touch **Quiet Time**. The Quiet Time Settings screen appears, as shown in **Figure 21**.
5. Touch the OFF ON switch next to Schedule Quiet Time. Scheduled Quiet Time is turned on, and a time range appears, as shown in **Figure 22**.
6. Select the time range for Quiet Time, and touch **Set Time**. Quiet Time turns on during the indicated time range.
7. You can also touch any options under 'TURN ON QUIET TIME WHENEVER I AM:'. A check mark appears next to each selected option, and you will not be bothered by notifications while you are performing the selected actions.

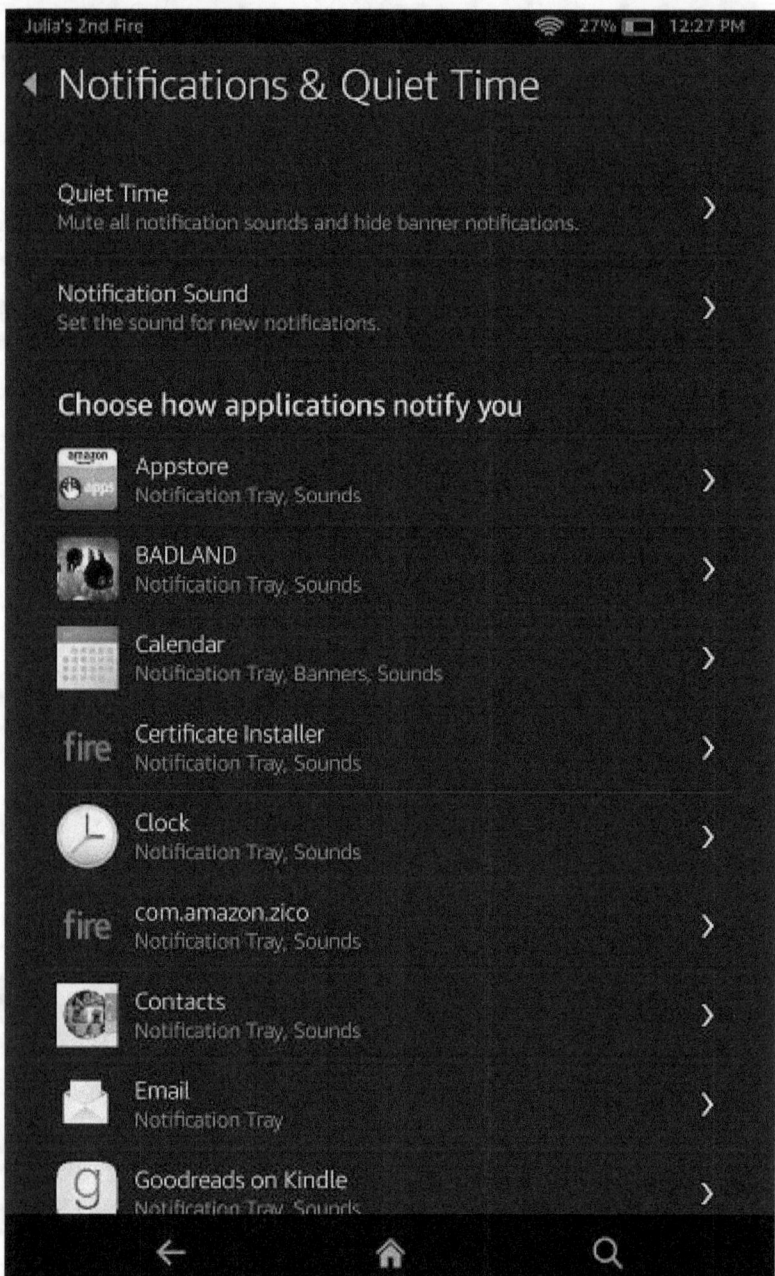

*Figure 20: Notifications & Quiet Time Screen*

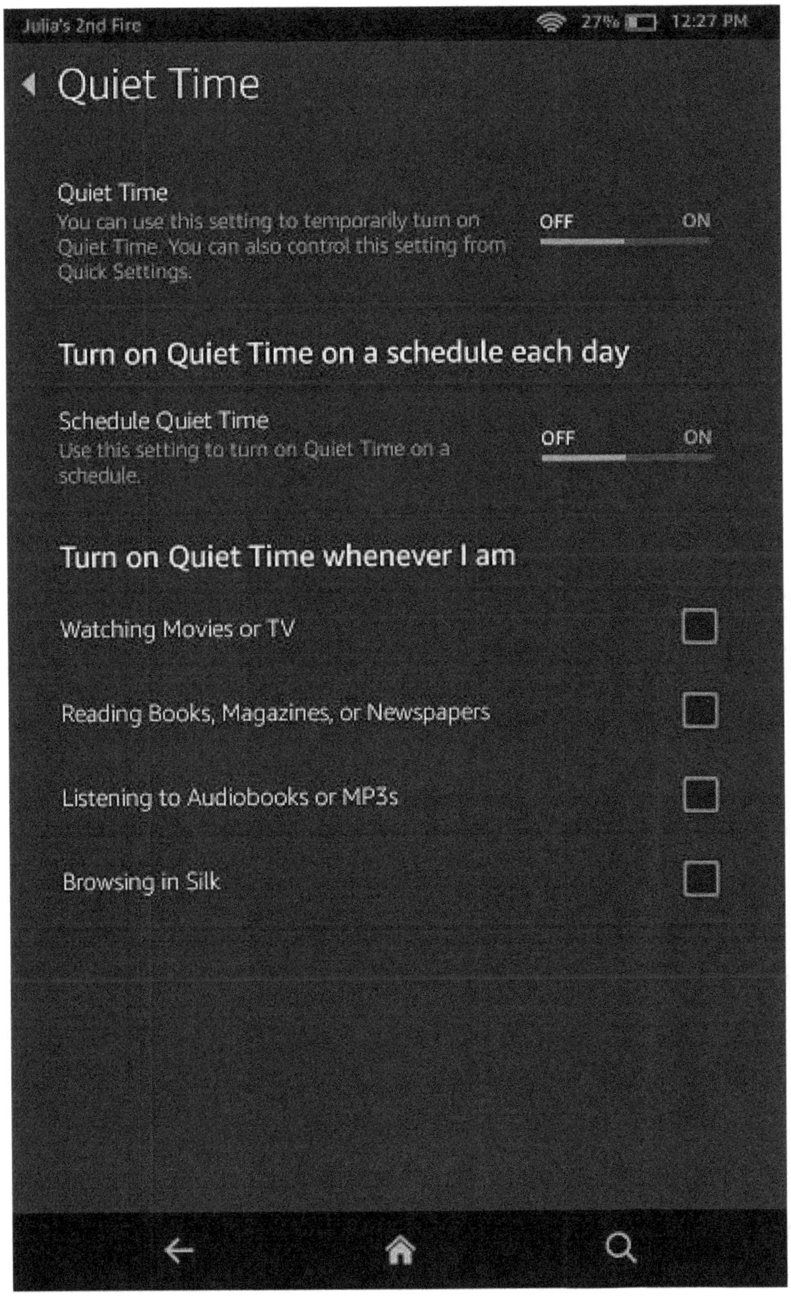

*Figure 21: Quiet Time Settings Screen*

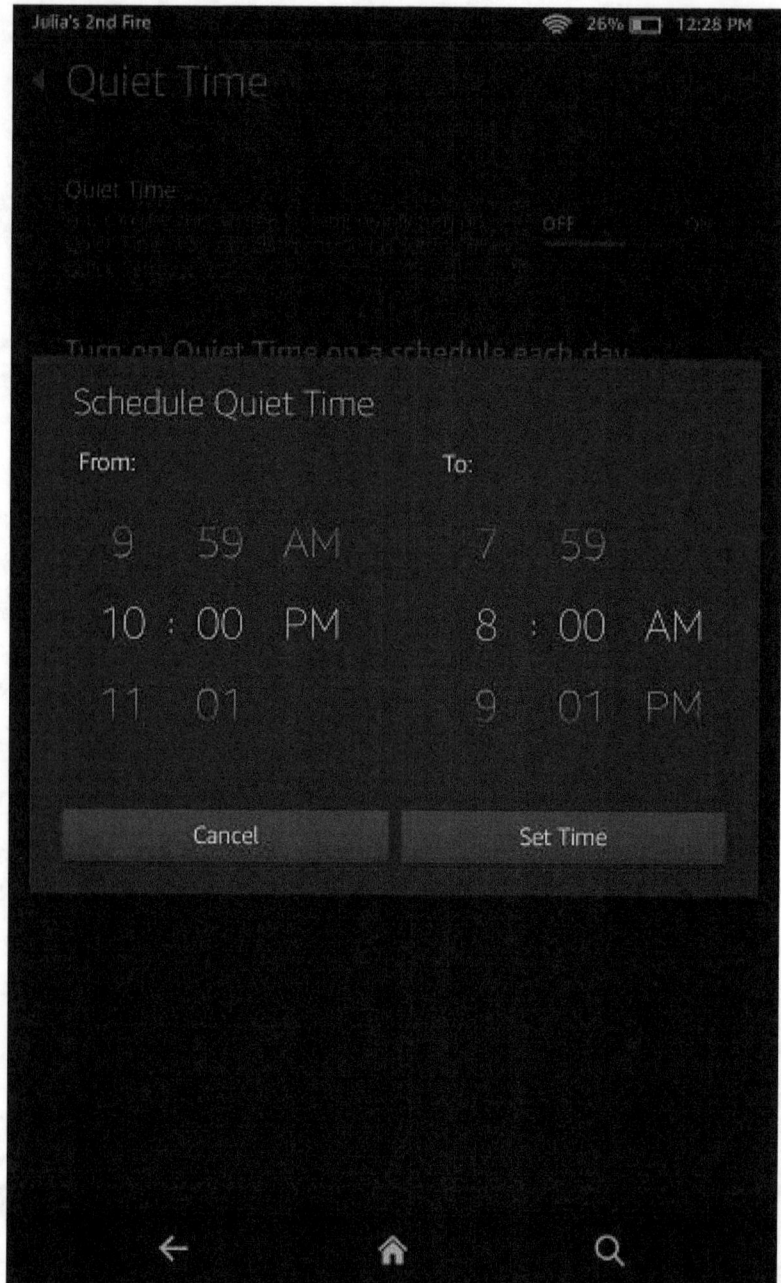

*Figure 22: Time Range Screen*

# 12. Setting the Notification Sound

Whenever an application sends you a notification, the Kindle Fire HD 6 can play a sound. To set the notification sound:

1. Touch the time at the top of the screen and slide your finger down. The Quick Settings Banner appears.
2. Touch the ⚙ icon. The Settings screen appears.
3. Touch **Notifications & Quiet Time**. The Notifications & Quiet Time screen appears.
4. Touch **Notification Sound**. A list of available notification sounds appears, as shown in **Figure 23**.
5. Touch an option in the list. The selected notification sound is set.

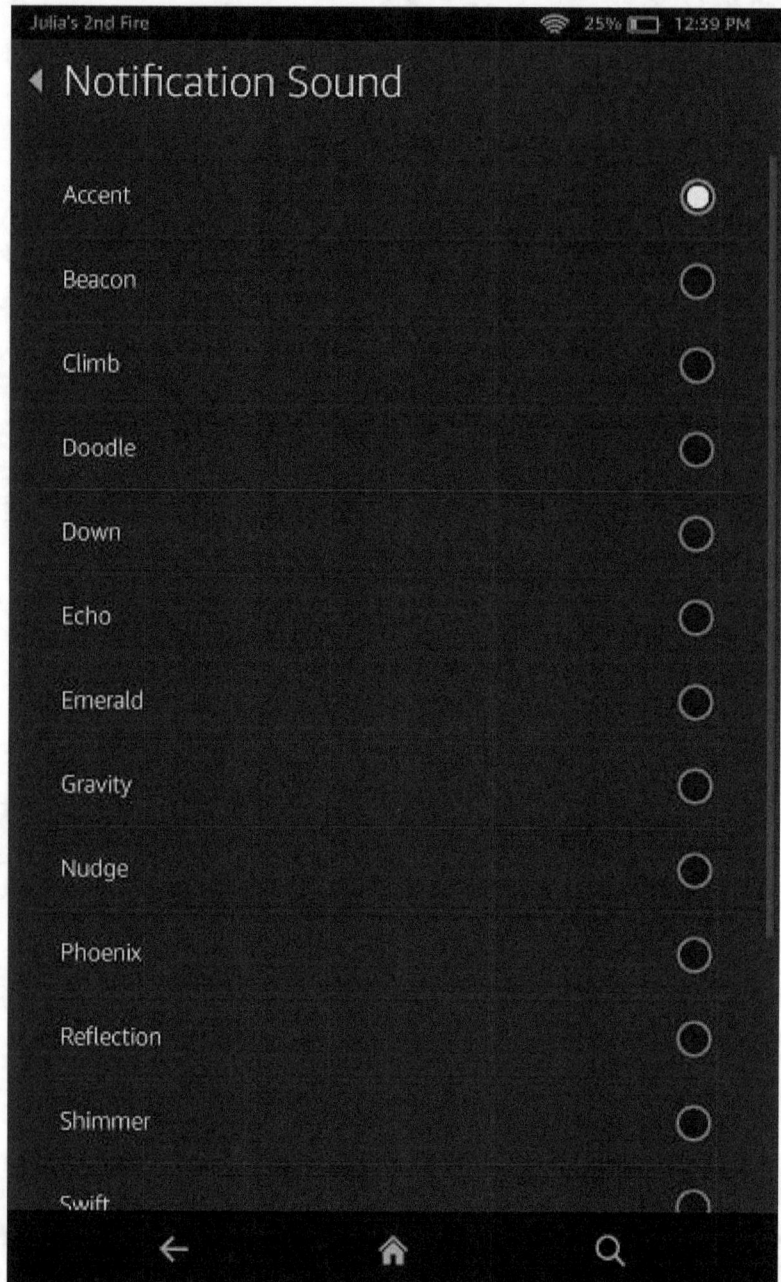

*Figure 23: List of Available Notification Sounds*

# 13. Setting the Screen Timeout

The display on your device can automatically turn off after a preset amount of time in order to preserve battery life. To set the screen timeout:

1. Touch the time at the top of the screen and slide your finger down. The Quick Settings Banner appears.
2. Touch the icon. The Settings screen appears.
3. Touch **Display & Sounds**. The Display & Sounds Settings screen appears, as shown in **Figure 24**.
4. Touch **Display Sleep**. A list of screen timeout options appears, as shown in **Figure 25**.
5. Touch an option in the list. The screen timeout is set.

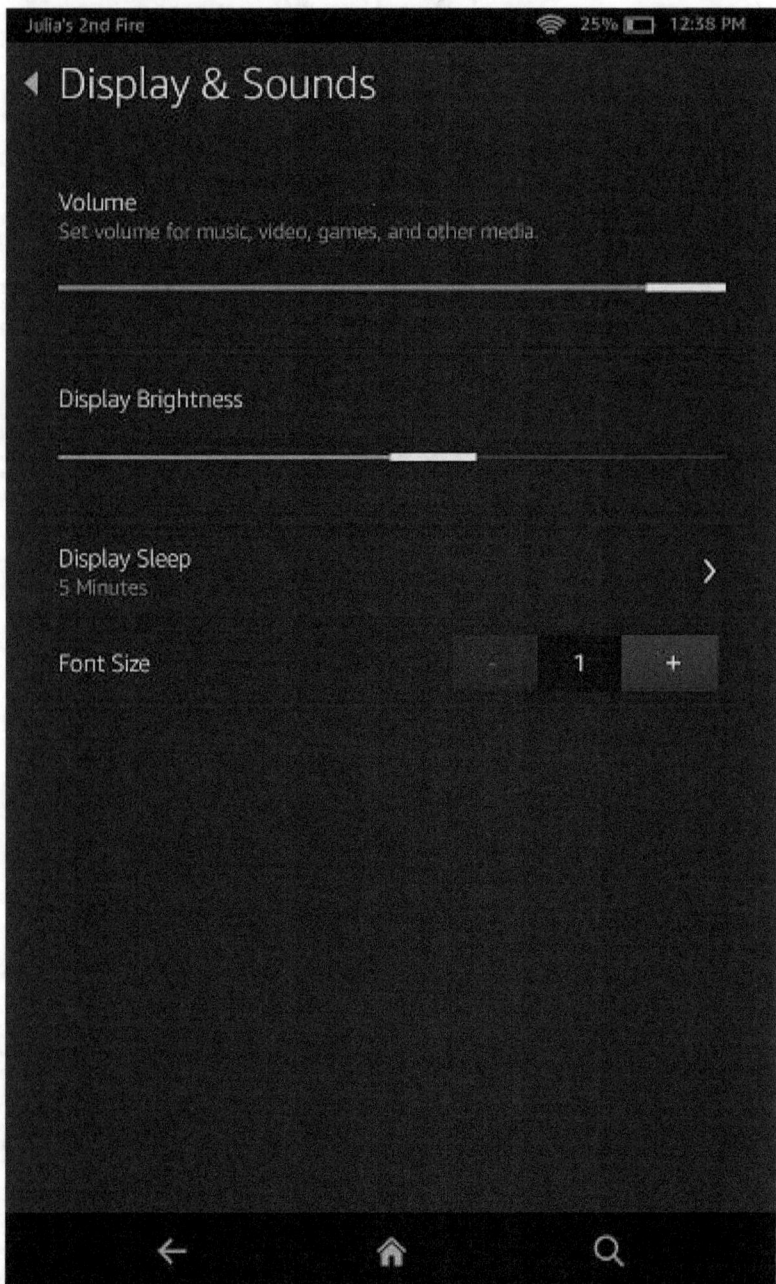

*Figure 24: Display & Sounds Settings Screen*

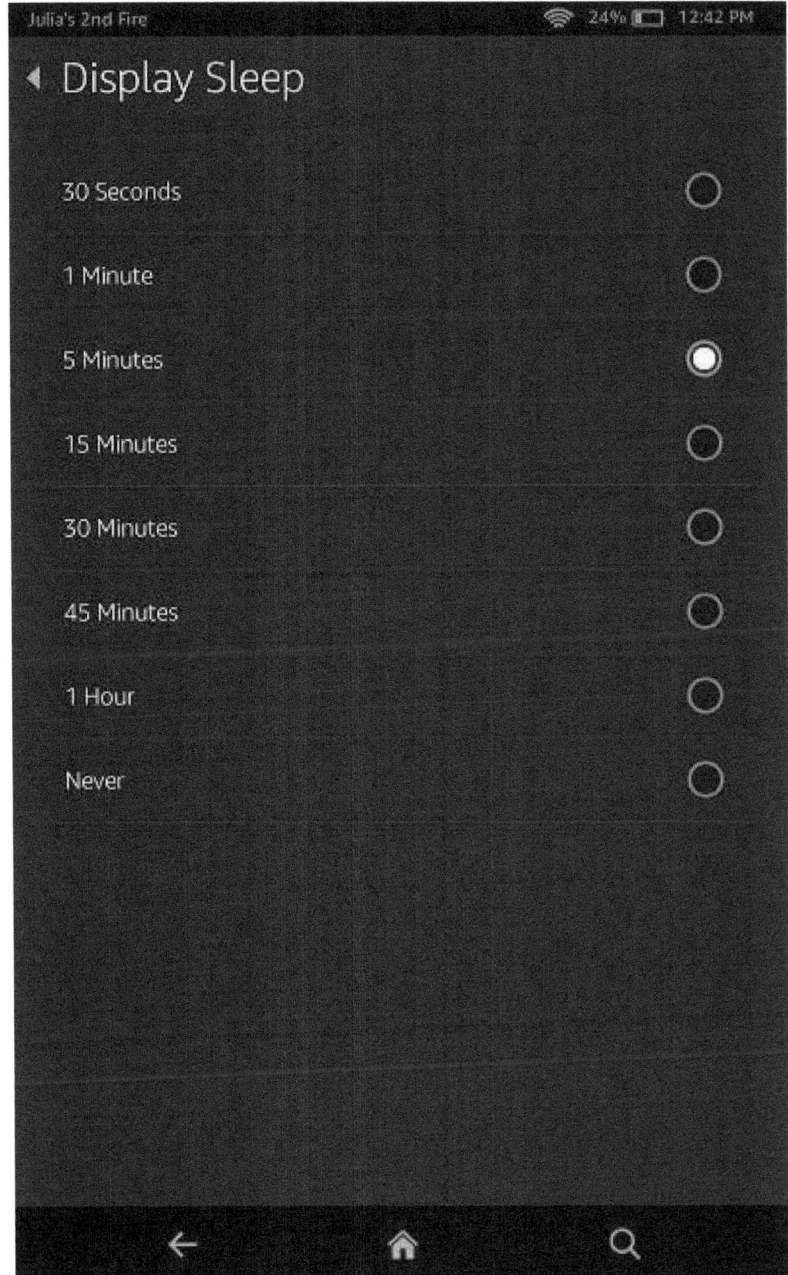

*Figure 25: List of Screen Timeout Options*

# 14. Adding International Keyboards

The Kindle Fire HD 6 allows you to input text using various international keyboards. To switch to another language while typing, touch and hold the space bar. To add an international keyboard:

1. Touch the time at the top of the screen and slide your finger down. The Quick Settings Banner appears.
2. Touch the ⚙ icon. The Settings screen appears.
3. Touch **Language & Keyboards**. The Language & Keyboard screen appears.
4. Touch **Keyboard Language**. A list of available international keyboards appears, as shown in **Figure 26**.
5. Touch a language in the list. A check mark appears next to the language and the keyboard is added. You can also touch **Download Languages** if you do not see your preferred language in the list.

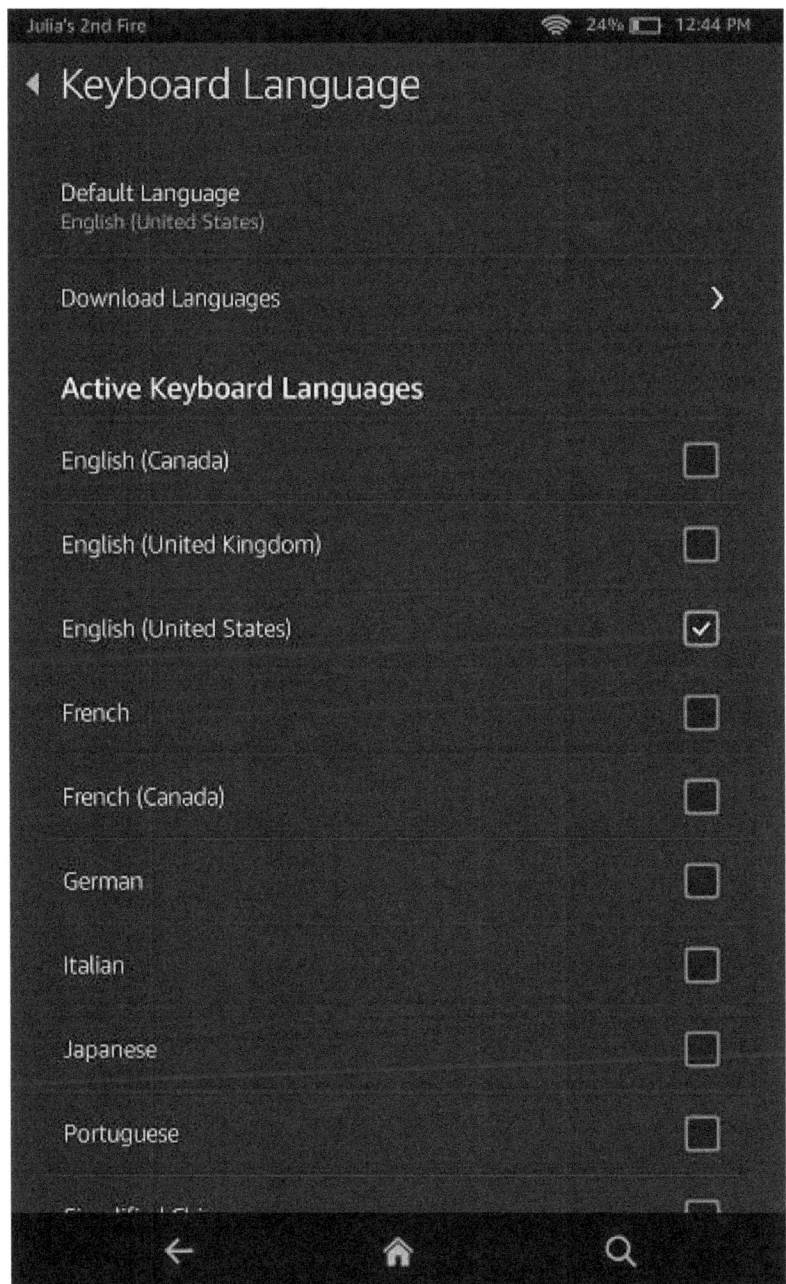

*Figure 26: List of Available International Keyboards*

# 15. Setting Up a Lockscreen Password

You may wish to set up a lockscreen password to prevent unauthorized access to your device. The device will ask you for your password every time that you try to unlock it. To set up a lockscreen password:

1. Touch the time at the top of the screen and slide your finger down. The Quick Settings Banner appears.
2. Touch the ⚙ icon. The Settings screen appears.
3. Scroll down and touch **Security & Privacy**. The Security & Privacy screen appears, as shown in **Figure 27**.
4. Touch the [OFF ON] switch next to 'Lock Screen Password'. The Lock Screen Password screen appears, as shown in **Figure 28**.
5. Enter a PIN, which must be at least four digits in length. You may also touch the [OFF ON] switch next to 'Simple Numeric PIN', if you would like to enter an alphanumeric password.
6. Touch **Finish**. The Lockscreen Password is set up, and will be required to unlock your device.

You may also touch **Require Lock Screen** on the Security Settings screen to set the amount of time that the device should wait after you have locked it before requiring the password. For instance, if you set the Require Lock Screen time to five minutes, and try to unlock it after three minutes, it will not prompt you for your password.

*Note: If you add one or more Child household profiles, the Lockscreen password is set until you turn it off from the Security & Privacy screen. Refer to* "Setting Up Parental Controls" *on page 208 to learn how to add household profiles.*

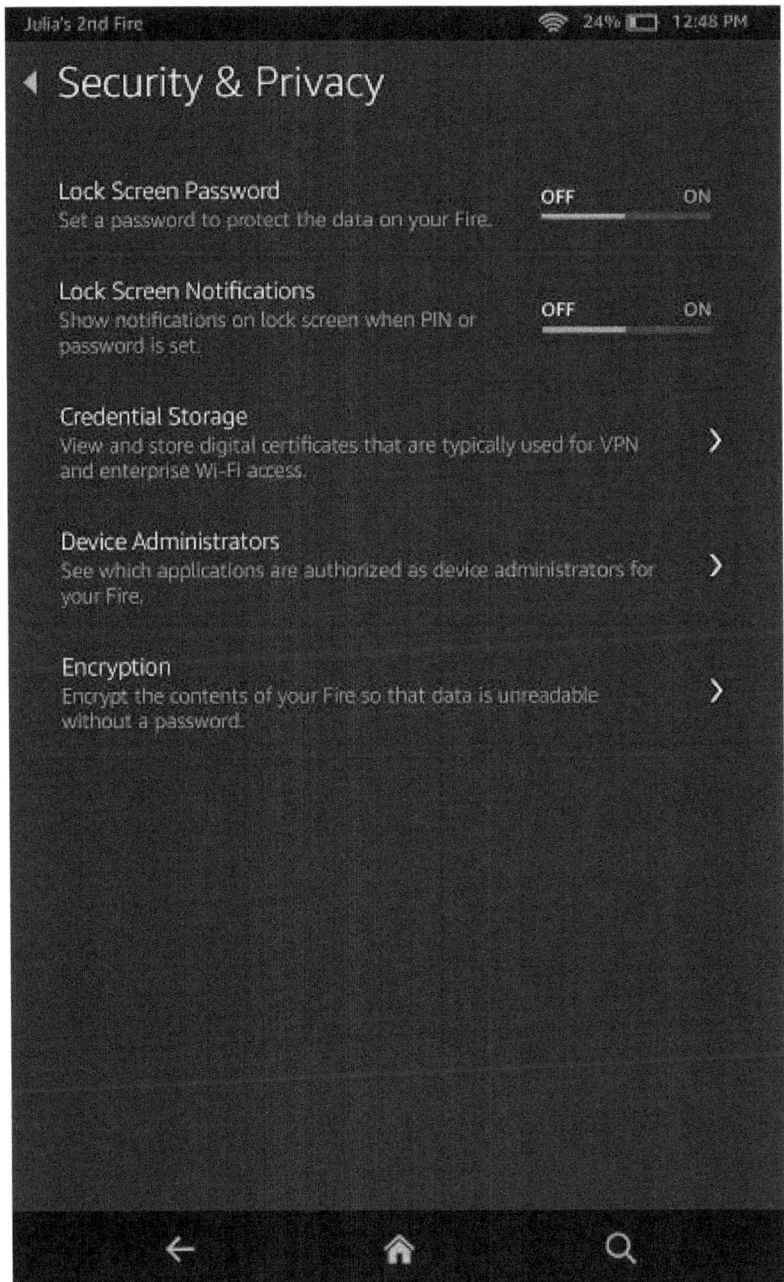

*Figure 27: Security & Privacy Screen*

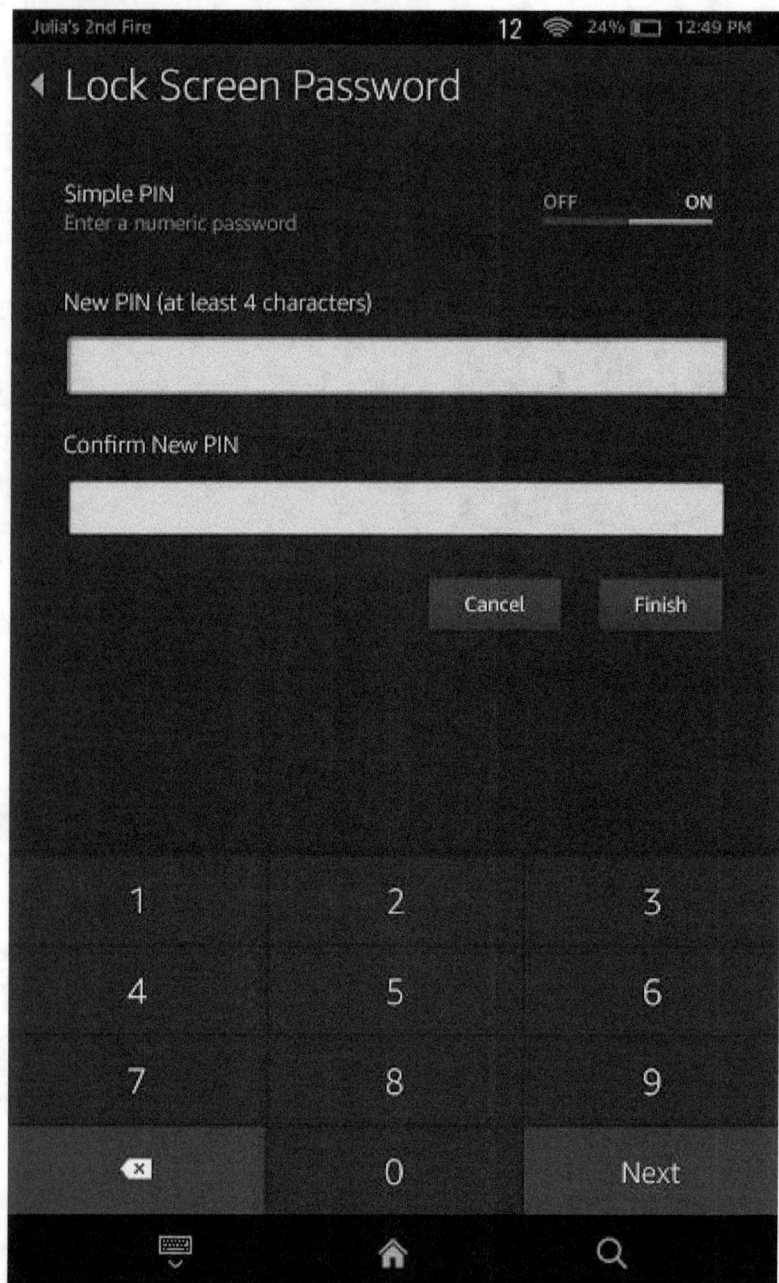

*Figure 28: Lock Screen Password Screen*

# 16. Logging In to Your Facebook and Twitter Accounts

The Fire HD 6 allows you to connect to your Facebook and Twitter accounts, which can be used to share passages while reading, as well as in many other applications. To log in to your Facebook and Twitter accounts:

1. Touch the time at the top of the screen and slide your finger down. The Quick Settings Banner appears.
2. Touch the icon. The Settings screen appears.
3. Touch **My Account**. The My Account screen appears, as shown in **Figure 29**.
4. Touch **Social Networks**. The Social Networks screen appears, as shown in **Figure 30**.
5. Touch **Facebook**, **Twitter**, or **Goodreads**. The corresponding credentials screen appears.
6. Enter the credentials associated with your social network account, and touch **Connect**. The social network account is added to your device.

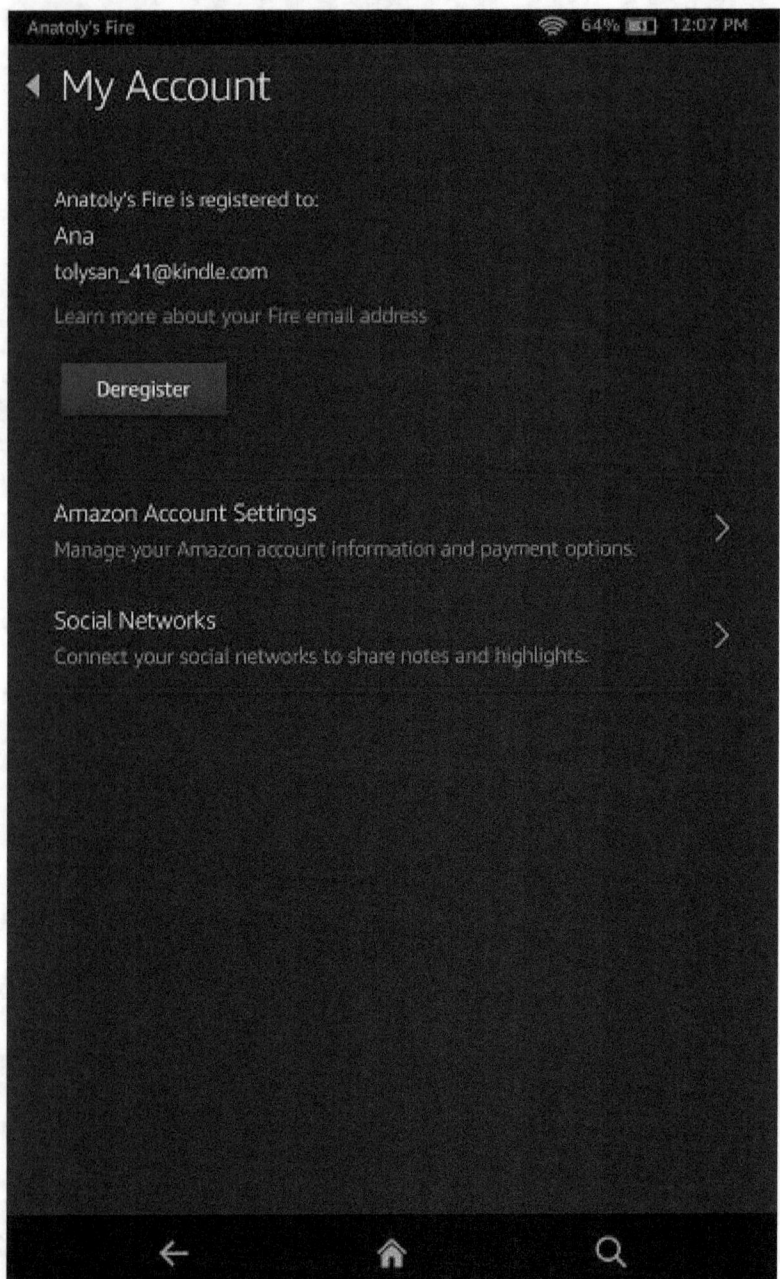

*Figure 29: My Account Screen*

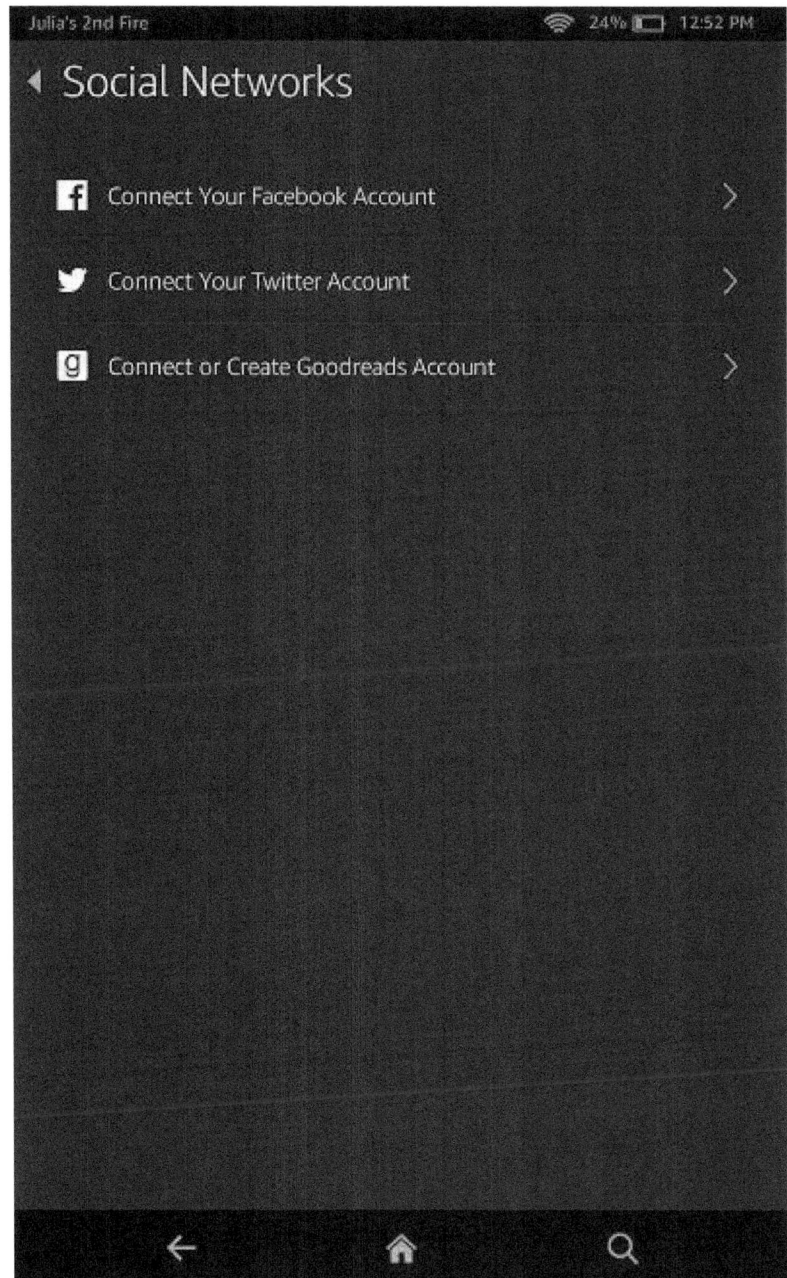

*Figure 30: Social Network Accounts Screen*

# Tips and Tricks

## Table of Contents

## 1. Maximizing Battery Life

There are several things you can do to increase the battery life of the Kindle Fire HD 6:

- Lock the Kindle Fire HD 6 whenever it is not in use. To lock the device, press the **Power** button on the back of the device once.
- Keep the screen timeout feature set to a small amount of time to dim and turn off the screen when the Kindle Fire HD 6 is idle. To learn how to change the screen timeout, click *"Setting the Screen Timeout"* on page 241.
- Turn down the brightness. To learn how to change brightness settings, click *"Adjusting the Brightness"* on page 206.
- Turn off Wi-Fi when not in use. To learn how to turn Wi-Fi off, click *"Setting Up Wi-Fi"* on page 226.

# 2. Checking the Amount of Available Memory

To check the amount of available memory at any time:

1. Touch the time at the top of the screen and slide your finger down. The Quick Settings Banner appears.
2. Touch the ⚙ icon. The Settings screen appears.
3. Touch **Device Options**. The Device Options screen appears.
4. Touch **Storage**. The Storage screen appears, and the amount of available memory is shown, as well as a breakdown of the types of media taking up the space on your device.

# 3. Freeing Up Memory

There are several actions that can free up memory on the Kindle Fire HD 6. Try one or more of the following:

- Archive applications that are no longer needed from the device. Click *"Archiving an Application"* on page 193 to learn how.
- Archive any music that you do not currently need. Refer to *"Archiving Music"* on page 117 to learn how.
- Archive any movies or TV shows that you do not currently watch. Refer to *"Archiving Movies and TV Shows"* on page 100 to learn how.
- Remove all temporary internet files. To delete these files:

1. Touch the time at the top of the screen and slide your finger down. The Quick Settings Banner appears.
2. Touch the ⚙ icon. The Settings screen appears.
3. Touch **Applications**. The Application Settings screen appears.
4. Scroll down and touch **Silk Browser**. The Silk Browser Settings screen appears.
5. Touch **Clear Browser Data**. The Clear Browser Data dialog opens.
6. Touch the types of internet files that you want to delete, and then touch **Confirm**. The corresponding files are deleted.

## 4. Searching an eBook for a Word or Phrase Quickly

You can search for a word or phrase in an eBook without typing it. Touch and hold the word in the eBook. The Word menu appears. Touch the ⋮ icon, and then touch **Search in Book**. A list of locations where the word appears is shown. You can also search for a whole phrase by touching and holding a word and dragging your finger to select the rest of the phrase.

## 5. Viewing the Trailer for a Movie

In order to make a more informed decision when purchasing or renting a movie, you can view its cinematic trailer. To view a movie trailer, touch **Watch Trailer** in the movie description. Refer to *"Browsing Movies and TV Shows in the Video Store"* on page 88 to learn how to find browse the Amazon video store.

## 6. Closing All Tabs at Once in the Silk Browser

In addition to closing one tab at a time, you can also close all tabs simultaneously in the Silk browser. To close all tabs, touch and hold a tab and then touch **Close all tabs**. Once all tabs are closed, the Most Visited screen appears.

## 7. Deleting a Bookmark in the Silk Browser

*Warning: Once a bookmark is deleted, it is gone for good.*

Clean up your Bookmarks by deleting unneeded ones. To delete a bookmark from the Bookmarks screen, touch and hold it, and then touch **Delete**. A confirmation dialog appears. Touch **OK**. The Bookmark is deleted.

# 8. Closing Applications Running in the Background

When you return to the Home screen after using an application, it is left running in the background. Some applications take up a lot of memory and may slow down your Kindle Fire HD 6. To close an application running in the background, touch the bottom edge of the screen and slide your finger up. A list of open applications appears. Touch an application icon and slide your finger up. The application is closed.

# 9. Viewing the Back Issues of a Periodical

By default, only the latest issue of a periodical is shown in your Newsstand library. To view all issues of a periodical that you have received on your device, touch and hold the cover of a periodical and touch **Show Back Issues**. All previous issues appear. Touch and hold a cover of any issue and touch **Hide Back Issues**. Only the most recent issue is shown.

# 10. Displaying the Current Battery Percentage

By default, the Fire HD 6 only shows an ambiguous battery icon, which does not tell you the exact battery percentage. To display the current battery percentage:

1. Touch the time at the top of the screen and slide your finger down. The Quick Settings Banner appears.
2. Touch the icon. The Settings screen appears.
3. Touch **Device Options**. The Device Setting screen appears.
4. Touch the switch next to 'Show Battery Percentage'. The Battery Percentage appears in the upper right-hand corner of the screen. Touch the switch next to 'Show Battery Percentage'. The Battery Percentage disappears.

# 11. Turning on the Screen Reader for the Visually Impaired

The Screen Reader feature can be used by those who are visually impaired, and will pronounce anything that you touch on the screen. To turn the Screen Reader on:

1. Touch the time at the top of the screen and slide your finger down. The Quick Settings Banner appears.

2. Touch the ⚙ icon. The Settings screen appears.
3. Touch **Accessibility**. The Accessibility Settings screen appears.
4. Touch **Screen Reader**. The Screen Reader settings appear.
5. Touch the `OFF ON` switch next to 'Screen Reader'. The `OFF ON` switch appears and the Screen Reader turns on and the Screen Reader tutorial begins to play. You will need to touch every button and item two times quickly to select it while the Screen Reader is turned on.

## 12. Turning On Closed Captioning

You may turn on Closed Captioning in order to display subtitle on supported videos, which is a feature specifically made for those who are hard of hearing. When browsing the Videos store, each video will indicate whether it is compatible with Closed Captioning. Look under 'Subtitles' in the video description. For instance, a video may have **English (cc)** written next to 'Subtitles' to indicate that it is compatible with Closed Captioning. To turn on Closed Captioning:

1. Touch the time at the top of the screen and slide your finger down. The Quick Settings Banner appears.
2. Touch the ⚙ icon. The Settings screen appears.
3. Touch **Accessibility**. The Accessibility Settings screen appears.
4. Touch the `OFF ON` switch next to 'Closed Captioning'. The `OFF ON` switch appears and Closed Captioning is turned on.

# Troubleshooting

## Table of Contents

## 1. Kindle Fire HD 6 does not turn on

If the Kindle Fire HD 6 will not power on, try one of the following:

- **Recharge the battery** - Refer to *"Charging the Kindle Fire HD 6"* on page 10 to learn how. Do NOT use the USB port on your computer to charge the Kindle Fire HD 6.
- **Replace the battery** - If you purchased the Kindle Fire HD 6 a long time ago, you may need to replace the battery. You will need to contact Amazon to do so. Refer to *"What to do if your problem is not listed here"* on page 260 to learn how.

## 2. Kindle Fire HD 6 is not responding

If the Kindle Fire HD 6 is frozen or is not responding, try one or more of the following. These steps solve most problems on the Kindle Fire HD 6:

- **Restart the Kindle Fire HD 6** - Press and hold the **Power** button for 20 seconds. The screen goes black, and then **Amazon** logo appears. Release the Power button. The Kindle Fire HD 6 restarts.

- **Remove Media** - Some downloaded applications or music may freeze up the Kindle Fire HD 6. Try deleting some of the media after restarting the device. To learn how to delete an application, refer to *"Archiving an Application"* on page 193. You may also reset and erase all data at once by doing the following:

*Warning: Any erased data is not recoverable.*

1. Touch the time at the top of the screen and slide your finger down. The Quick Settings Banner appears.
2. Touch the icon. The Settings screen appears.
3. Touch **Device Options**. The Device Settings screen appears.
4. Touch **Reset to Factory Defaults**. A confirmation dialog appears.
5. Touch **Reset**. All data is erased and the Kindle Fire HD 6 is reset to factory defaults.

## 3. Kindle Fire HD 6 battery dies too quickly

According to Amazon, the Kindle Fire HD 6 provides up to 8 hours of mixed use. If you find that the battery is dying considerably faster, turn down the brightness. Refer to *"Adjusting the Brightness"* on page 206 to learn how. The Kindle Fire HD 6 does not have an automatic brightness feature. You may also want to turn off Bluetooth. Refer to *"Setting Up Bluetooth"* on page 229 to learn how.

## 4. Cannot access the Web when connected to a Wi-Fi Network

Some Wi-Fi networks, such as those in airports, coffee shops, or hotels, may not require a network password when connecting, but do require authentication once you open the Silk browser. If authentication is required, the icon appears in the upper right-hand corner corner of the screen. Touch **Web** and then enter the authentication password to connect to the internet.

## 5. Screen does not rotate

If the screen does not turn or the full horizontal keyboard is not showing when rotating the Kindle Fire HD 6, it may be one of these issues:
- The application does not support the horizontal view.
- The Kindle Fire HD 6 is lying flat while being rotated. Hold the Kindle Fire HD 6 upright for the view to change in applications that support it.

- Screen rotation is locked. Touch the time at the top of the screen and slide your finger down. Then, touch the ⟳ icon. The ⟳ icon appears and screen rotation is unlocked.

# 6. Touchscreen does not respond as expected

If the touchscreen does not perform the desired functions, or does not work at all, try the following:

- Remove the screen protector, if you use one.
- Make sure your hands are clean and dry. Oily fingers can make the screen dirty and unresponsive.
- Restart the Kindle Fire HD 6.
- Make sure the touchscreen does not come in contact with anything but skin. Scratches on the screen are permanent and may cause malfunction.

# 7. Computer does not recognize the Kindle Fire HD 6

If your computer does not recognize the Kindle Fire HD 6 when you connect it, it may be one of these issues:

- You are using an incompatible cable. Only use the USB cable that came with your Kindle Fire HD 6 to connect the device to your computer.
- You are using a USB hub. Connect the device directly to the computer, since some USB hubs will not be able to recognize the Fire HD 6.
- You are using Windows XP or earlier. You need to install Windows Media Player 11 or later in order for your computer to recognize the Kindle Fire HD 6.

# 8. Photo or video does not display

If the Kindle Fire HD 6 cannot open a photo or video, the file type is most likely not supported. Supported file types include:

*Images*

- BMP
- GIF
- JPEG

- PNG

*Videos*
- 3GP
- MP4
- VP8

## 9. Media in the Cloud is not available for streaming

If you first registered the Fire HD 6 to a specific user, de-registered it, and then registered it to that user again, you will not be able to stream content that is not already on the device for 180 days. Register the Kindle Fire HD 6 to the user account that you will be using as your main account when you first receive the device.

## 10. What to do if your problem is not listed here

If you could not resolve your issue, contact customer service using one of the following methods:

- If you are in the U.S., call **1-866-321-8851**.
- If you are outside the U.S., call **1-206-266-0927**.
- Email Kindle at **kindle-cs-support@amazon.com**
- Visit **http://www.amazon.com/kindlesupport**.

# Index

# Other Books from the Author of the Help Me Series, Charles Hughes

*Help Me! Guide to the iPhone 5S*

*Help Me! Guide to the Nexus 7*

*Help Me! Guide to the Galaxy S4*

*Help Me! Guide to the Kindle Fire HD*

*Help Me! Guide to the HTC One*

*Help Me! Guide to the iPhone 4*

*Help Me! Guide to the iPod Touch*

*Help Me! Guide to the iPad Mini*

*Help Me! Guide to the Kindle Touch*

*Help Me! Guide to the Samsung Galaxy Note*

*Help Me! Guide to the iPad Air*

# Help Me! Guide to the Kindle Fire HD 6

Author: Charles Hughes

This book is also available in electronic format from Amazon.com